Who Killed Confederation Life?

ALSO BY ROD McQUEEN

The Moneyspinners (1983)
Risky Business (1985)
Leap of Faith (1985)
Both My Houses (with Sean O'Sullivan, 1986)
Blind Trust (1987)
The Last Best Hope (1995)

Who Killed Confederation Life?

The Inside Story

Rod McQueen

M&S

Canadian Cataloguing in Publication Data

McQueen, Rod, 1944–
    Who killed Confederation Life? : the inside story

Includes bibliographical references and index.
ISBN 0-7710-5631-1

1. Confederation Life Insurance Company. 2. Business failures – Canada – Case
studies. I. Title.

HG9010.Z9C65 1996   368.3'2'006571   C96-931372-1

The publishers acknowledge the support of the Canada Council and the Ontario Arts
Council for their publishing program.

Typesetting by M&S, Toronto
Printed and bound in Canada

McClelland & Stewart Inc.
The Canadian Publishers
481 University Avenue
Toronto, Ontario
M5G 2E9

1 2 3 4 5   00 99 98 97 96

CONTENTS

INTRODUCTION

"The world of finance is a mysterious world in which, incredible as it may appear, evaporation precedes liquidation. First, capital evaporates and then the company goes into liquidation."

— James Conrad, in his novel, *Victory*

Patrick Dennis Burns opens the front door of his ranch-style home in the Toronto suburb of Don Mills. It is a warm October day in 1995, fourteen months after the firm he headed, Confederation Life Insurance Co., went under and three years since he was driven from his downtown office by berating regulators and a baying board. At sixty-seven, he is a shadow of his former self. Once a robust and bluff hail-fellow-well-met, he now seems shrunken, even wizened. Grey hair clings to his scalp, the shoulders are rounded, and sticklike arms hang limp from a short-sleeved golf shirt as he pads about in stockinged feet.

The handshake remains firm, but all else about Burns seems to have slipped more than a few notches since his ten years at the helm of Confed. His nose, the same grog nose that employees inspected at annual meetings to see if it had grown more bulbous since the previous year, now looks like a gnarled burl on the trunk of an oak tree, all rumpled and roiling. His breath has a certain tang of liquor, or maybe Listerine.

His is not the manner of a man who raped the system and retired to royal living. The Ford Tempo parked in the driveway has seen better days. This is no fancy-pants neighbourhood; Underhill Drive begins with a scuffle of townhouses, slides past a school, then ambles up a slight incline to this "better" part, where Burns and his wife, June, live among single-family homes that sulk cheek by jowl. Grass is mowed, not manicured. Gardens are tended, not groomed. Lawn furniture is white moulded plastic, not black wrought iron.

He is worried about a lawsuit that has been launched in the state of Michigan against him and twenty-six other officers and directors for their part in the Confed debacle, but there is still some of the old bravado left. "Some of the numbers they're talking about, I just can't rationalize," he says, dismissing the work of those liquidators, litigators, and creditors who are picking over the bare bones of the business that he did so much to build.

Proof is close at hand that other government seizures may not have been necessary. In the newspaper that very morning were allegations that, in December 1992, the federal government had taken over Sovereign Life when it didn't need to. According to a lengthy peer-review process by the Canadian Institute of Actuaries, Sovereign's actuary, Bryan G. Sigurdson, had overstated Sovereign's liabilities by $31 million. Sovereign's board had called in two outside actuaries, Kenneth Clark and Paul McCrossan of Eckler Partners Ltd., of Toronto, who disagreed vehemently with Sigurdson's findings, but Finance Minister Don Mazankowski had declared that Sovereign was undercapitalized, and the government stepped in.

The announced findings on Sovereign come as no surprise to Burns. Among his industry roles, Burns served from 1990 to 1993 as the founding chairman of the Canadian Life and Health Insurance Compensation Corporation (CompCorp), the industry-financed protection plan that not only bailed out Sovereign but even now has come to the aid of Confed policyholders. "Which is a bit ironic," Burns notes with a wry smile.

Total loss as a result of Confed's insolvency could reach $2.6 billion. This amount includes losses of $1.3 billion in Canada and the United States by trade creditors, bond and commercial paper holders, and other debtholders who are unlikely to recover any of their invested funds because there simply aren't enough assets to pay off policy-holders who rank ahead of other debtholders.

Such priority treatment still means that policyholder losses in both countries could also hit $1.3 billion even if liquidators and rehabilita-tors recover 95 cents on the dollar in a drawn-out asset-sale process that is likely to last until the year 2004. The policyholder losses include $275 million that the Canadian industry expects to pump into Comp-Corp; $175 million in losses by those policyholders above the Comp-Corp limits; and $800 million in losses by American policyholders.

Not only does the $2.6-billion loss make this the largest insur-ance-company failure in North America, it catapults Confed into fourth place on the all-time global list of financial-services flops, ahead of Barings (US$1.3 billion), Banco Ambrosiano (US$1.4 bil-lion), and Franklin National (US$1.8 billion) and behind Continental Illinois (US$4.5 billion), BCCI (US$7 billion), and Credit Lyonnais (US$14 billion).

By the end of 1995, professional fees paid in the United States and Canada, mostly to lawyers and liquidators, had already reached $80 million, with a further $45 million likely to be billed by the end of 1996, for a two-year total of $125 million. The vultures feeding off the Confed carrion are no endangered species.

Burns would have preferred there to be more options to deal with the troubled company, as there are in the United States. "The problem was that there was no regulation that would allow people to come in [and do an American-style rehabilitation]. I'm sure there could have been better solutions than the one that was chosen."

Still, Burns knows he's carrying the can for both the economic times that went sour and the go-for-growth strategy that sent Confed belly up. "The business is a long-term business. So if anything went wrong, it didn't happen overnight. It happened when I was there. I was the head man, so I take responsibility for that. These are my atti-tudes. But, on the other hand, I think that there has been almost too easy an acceptance of, okay, let's sit back, if the media's giving this guy a hard time, let's let him have it. I'm obviously not thrilled about that."

Even though he's willing to be the whipping boy, Burns wouldn't mind a little loyalty from those cronies and confidantes who once soldiered beside him, did his bidding, and carried out some of their own bright ideas, too. "Hindsight's a beautiful thing. I haven't been happy with some of the people related to Confed who have made statements."

He's particularly upset about the stance taken by insurance superintendent Michael Mackenzie, who has spent much of the previous year claiming that he'd warned Confed about its financial transgressions for so long that it seems he must have been doing it ever since he was a small boy. Burns finds everything about Mackenzie, his past role and his rise to top cop, a little strange. "Mike Mackenzie was the auditor with Clarkson Gordon, [later] Ernst & Young. So he did know us." Mackenzie met with the Confed board in his capacity as Confed's auditor, then, mere days later in 1987, was appointed chief regulator. Such a distance in so little time; from the company's side to the other side. It's a move that struck Burns as somehow turncoat at the time and has him shaking his head still.

While Burns may be a husk compared to what he was in his glory days, he steadfastly refuses to see his insurance career as anything but a success. After all, he started as an eighteen-year-old in 1946 delivering the mail and made it all the way to the executive suite. "I enjoyed it. I did almost everything except be the doctor or the actuary."

Too bad. In the end, Confed could have used the professional services of both.

When Confederation Life Insurance Co. was seized by regulators on August 11, 1994, it ranked as the fourth-largest insurance company in Canada, was among the top thirty in North America, and had $19 billion in assets.* Among the politicians and bureaucrats in Washington and Ottawa, the rallying cry used to be "too big to fail," a phrase taken to mean that governments would step in to save a sick

---

*   All figures in Canadian dollars unless otherwise stated.

giant for fear a failure would send other, smaller, firms crashing down like dominoes.

In this case, "too big to fail" came to mean that nobody believed bankruptcy was possible until it was suddenly inevitable. Confed went under because there wasn't a single director, officer, regulator, auditor, politician, or industry honcho who completely fulfilled his or her job.

Directors did not hold management sufficiently accountable; officers acted irresponsibly and with reckless disregard; regulators were tardy to react, then threatened with a stick too small; auditors peered at the books but missed the big picture; weak-willed politicians had neither courage nor conviction; and, rather than help, the industry leaders were reduced to a mere dither.

Pat Burns isn't the only person who should be taking the blame for Confed going bust, he's just the most obvious. The rest can hole up in their homes in shame or hide in their offices behind obfuscation, claiming to have done all they could, but there is plenty of blame to go around. More than two-and-a-half-billion dollars' worth.

In fact, no one did nearly enough. Any individual among all of those six constituencies could have shifted the course of this corporation's history sufficiently to prevent the debacle. All of them – directors, officers, regulators, auditors, politicians, the industry – comprise the gang that couldn't think straight.

Confed didn't need to fail. But fail it did, taking 4,400 jobs with it. Thrown into financial disarray were the 300,000 individual policy or annuity holders in Canada, another 450,000 worldwide, half in the United States.

The Confed disease quickly infected other firms, because the financial-services sector is all about full faith and confidence. Without public trust, the system cannot function. There are 127 Canadian life-insurance companies employing 96,700 and doing business in twenty countries. More than five million people outside Canada – three-quarters of them in the United States – own life-insurance policies worth $730 billion issued by Canadian companies. The collapse of Confed has so damaged public confidence that the entire industry will never fully recover. This is the whodunit tale of who killed Confederation Life.

CHAPTER I

In the Beginning,
There Was the Word

"Survival for 100 years, then, is no mean feat. Ours is, in
miniature, the history of continual assessment and renewal. It is a
success story, without guarantees for the future."

– *Confederation Life Insurance Company, 1871-1971*,
a prescient corporate history, 1971

S electing the name Confederation for the new company took
less than ten minutes. The scene was late winter 1871, and the
bill to incorporate the "Dominion Life Association" had
passed the Senate of Canada and received first reading in the House
of Commons. The legislation was being studied by the banking and
commerce committee; the members rejected the name "Dominion"
by one vote. John Kay Macdonald consulted with his fellow peti-
tioners and quickly came up with a new name – "Confederation Life
Association." Who, only four years after the Confederation of
Canada, could be against that word? This new name passed muster
and, by act of Parliament, Confederation Life was created on
April 14, 1871.

Macdonald, a Scottish immigrant to Canada at eight and treasurer
of York County at twenty-nine, was the key mover in setting up the
new company by the age of thirty-four. In 1869, he had realized that,
of the twenty-four life-insurance companies operating in Canada,

only one was Canadian, the rest were all foreign. The one Canadian firm, Canada Life, had more business in force in Canada than any of the rest. Clearly there was demand for insurance from a Canadian company.

Macdonald gathered twenty-one prominent men, all of whom agreed to invest by participating in a stock subscription. They included: Sir Francis Hincks, minister of finance in the government of Sir John A. Macdonald; Sir William Howland, lieutenant-governor of Ontario; E. B. Wood, treasurer of Ontario; and William McMaster, president of the Canadian Bank of Commerce. According to founder Macdonald, the cost of getting started was just $400 – not much, even in an era when steak cost ten cents a pound and a man's suit was $12.

The Fathers of this Confederation were not without their warts and past embarrassments. As one of the founders of the Reform Party in 1841, Hincks had eventually served as leader, but his ministry, tainted by railway corruption, was defeated in 1854. He took himself to the Caribbean, where he was governor of Barbados and the Windward Islands before returning to serve in the Macdonald government. He joined Confed in 1874. Among his accomplishments as minister was changing the country's currency system from pounds, shillings, and pence to the decimal system, a step that was not universally welcomed. Hincks headed the Consolidated Bank, which went under, and he was convicted of filing false annual returns. Other founders were more upstanding. Professor J. B. Cherriman, the company's first actuary, later became the first superintendent of insurance for Canada.

For all his organizational efforts, J. K. Macdonald was not the first president. That honour went to Hincks, who was president for the company's first two years. He was succeeded by Howland, who was president for twenty-eight years. On the preliminary prospectus, Macdonald, then thirty-two, was called manager. Before the business was even launched, however, he resigned as manager to travel the country, finding backers and setting up agencies. It would be forty-one years before he became president in 1912. At the time, one of the directors said Macdonald – by then in his mid-seventies – had been appointed because "he now had sufficient experience to become president of the company." The director was probably serious.

The founders were forthright about their role in the prospectus, calling themselves "promoters," but they also claimed to be more interested in the safety of the policyholders than in their own self-interest. "The leading aim of the promoters," read the purple passage, "and the chief purpose of all interested in the organization of this Association, is to conduct it in the interest of the policy owners – giving to the stockholders only a moderate return for their invest-ment, the rate of dividends being limited by express provision in the charter."

The licence required that $50,000 be raised from subscribers and placed on deposit with the Department of Finance in Ottawa. By June, the money had been gathered, by September, it had been remit-ted to Ottawa, and so, on September 26, 1871, the company licence was issued. A month later, rates for six different policies had been calculated and one application for life insurance had been received from an individual. That first client turned out to be particularly healthy. The insured in question lived a further fifty-seven years, dying in 1928.

Confederation Life was off to an auspicious start, two years before the North-West Mounted Police – now the Royal Canadian Mounted Police – was formed. The order of events may say something about Canada, or at least what mattered to the young country's ruling classes. Money before law. Personal security before public order.

At the time, Toronto was home to 59,000 souls. Confed's first office space consisted of two rented rooms in the Masonic Hall at 18 Toronto Street, the same thoroughfare that is home today to the Canadian headquarters of Hollinger Inc., headed by Conrad Black, a Confed director for fifteen years, from 1977 to 1992. During the first decade, an aggressive Confed moved twice to larger quarters on Toronto Street, as agents sold individual policies and Confed bought blocks of business from other firms, such as the St. Louis Mutual Life Insurance Co. The middle years of the decade saw a severe depression grip Canada and the United States, but Confed managed to increase insur-ance in force by $1 million in 1875, standing second in Canada, and to hit $10 million by 1883. Tough times seemed to inspire people to buy protection.

Growth was so fast that Confed soon required its own building. Even in those days, Confed did nothing by halves. In 1889, it acquired the land in an entire block bounded by Yonge, Richmond, Victoria, and Queen streets in downtown Toronto, and held a design competition for architects, which was won by the Toronto firm of Knox, Elliot and Jarvis. The second- through fourth-place finishers received cash prizes of $500, $400, and $300 respectively. The amounts were significant. Prizes to losers alone totalled three times the $400 cost of starting the company less than twenty years earlier.

Nor did Confed scrimp on the seven-storey Romanesque structure with its towering spires. The May 23, 1891, edition of the *Daily Mail* described the new offices as a "magnificent pile of buildings now in course of construction," and later called it "a noble addition to the architectural output of Toronto and one which would grace the finest street of the greatest city of the world." Staff in the new head office prided themselves on their efficiency. In 1894, the average time for processing a claim was said to be three and a half hours.

Not all claims went uncontested. In one celebrated case, Confed had sent out notice of cancellation to a policyholder, George Miller of Markham, Ontario, who died in August 1884, before the cancellation notice arrived. Confed refused to pay the death benefit. The family took the case all the way to the Supreme Court of Canada, which in 1887 ordered Confed to pay the claim.

Competition was also heating up, and, in those free-booting days, a company would fabricate any story about another firm in order to promote its own products. Confed tried to rise above it all, at least for public consumption. An 1886 circular claims: "Gentlemen, Managers and Agents of rival companies have used all sorts of means to damage the business and reputation of the Confederation Life. No statement, however exaggerated, or lacking even the semblance of truth, has been too much for them to make, and no medium, however low and obscure, has been considered unworthy of their purchase. A discerning public will sooner or later see through and condemn such dishonorable tactics."

Confed, however, did fight back in kind. "[C]ompany officers attacked, or permitted their associates to attack, other life companies, impugning their motives, questioning their honesty and, sometimes, even their soundness and solvency," admitted V. R. Smith (who would later become president) in a 1931 speech made when he was assistant general manager and actuary. "How could we expect the public to have confidence in us, so long as we persisted in crying from the house-top that everyone in the business (except, of course, ourselves) needed careful watching?"

Neither the boisterous industry methods nor belated soul-searching stopped growth, however. By 1900, the company had $32-million worth of insurance in force, was operating in what are now all ten provinces, and began looking at expanding to other countries. From 1902 to 1914, Confed opened offices in Trinidad, Jamaica, Mexico, the United Kingdom, Cuba, the Canal Zone, Guatemala, San Salvador, and Costa Rica. Head-office size doubled in 1908 with the addition of what was called the Annex. The First World War interrupted expansion outside Canada, but growth was rekindled in 1926 when Confed opened in the United States. Over the next twenty years, the company launched operations in the Dominican Republic, British Honduras, Hong Kong, Singapore, Puerto Rico, Hawaii, Colombia, and Venezuela. In 1931, Confed's silver-jubilee sixtieth year, insurance in force was $369 million and assets were $81 million.

Nonetheless, for all the expansion, it was a conservative business. In the first one hundred years, the highest average interest rate earned by Confed on assets was 7.3 per cent between 1879 and 1883; the lowest occurred in 1948, 3.61 per cent. For the most part, changes from one year to the next were only gradual, far different from the double-digit growth of the eighties. Nor was there any lack of regulation. A 1906 royal commission investigated industry abuses, and the Insurance Act of 1910 put in place a supervisory regime said to be tougher than those in either the United States or the United Kingdom.

The Macdonald family dominated the presidency. J. K.'s son, Charles Strange Macdonald, was president from 1930 to 1944. His accession to the throne came at a younger age (fifty-seven) than his father had been when he was appointed, but he'd been with the company thirty-two years. In turn, his son, John Kenneth (known as the "young J. K.," so he would not be confused with his founder grandfather, who died in 1928 at age ninety) joined Confed in 1926 and did not become president until 1947. He was a relatively young forty-three at that point, but had twenty-one years' experience, and would not have taken over even then except for the unexpected death of Confed's seventh president, V. R. Smith, while on a business trip to Britain.

During the Roaring Twenties, Confed tried a few innovations. In 1921, it became the first company in Canada to issue life-insurance policies without requiring medical examinations. That same year, the family policy was introduced, giving protection to mother and children in proportion to the amount taken out on the father. Double indemnity (where death by accident increases the payout to twice the face amount) was added in 1922. Group life and health was begun in 1927 when Beatty Bros., of Fergus, Ontario, was issued policy G-1000.

The Depression drastically altered business. "There were some two thousand farm loans which were affected by the moratorium on mortgage loan repayments," the young J. K. recalled in an interview given in 1969 and quoted in the company history. "We tried to keep the farmers on their farms and many remained as tenants. We became the owner of farm animal stock. When a new litter of pigs was born, the farmer kept half and we were entitled to half. Also, after deducting enough grain for feed, we were entitled to one-half the money from the sale of his crop."

In those years, individual policyholders became celebrated for their dealings with the company. Typical was Dr. D. E. Foley, a medical doctor and Roman Catholic priest, who purchased an annuity in 1912 that paid him $220 annually. He'd send a letter every year from California to remind the powers-that-be what they owed him. "I will be in the Capital of Ontario this summer," he wrote in 1933, "and I must call and see you and note if your company will go into insolvency or remain in statu quo." Another year he noted that they'd better pay because he had proof of his purchase "secreted in a fire-proof cellar." When the Dionne quints were born in 1934, he wrote to say that he hoped everyone would "keep well and free from quintuplets." He died in 1938, having collected a total of $5,788 for his investment of $3,146 twenty-six years earlier. His passing was duly noted in the *Bulletin*, the company publication.

Employees received particular attention, as if they were extended family. Confed began providing life-insurance and retirement benefits to its own employees in 1924. In 1942, a staff house was built next door to the headquarters to provide employees with a cafeteria, an auditorium, a library, lounges, and a games room, as well as facilities for dramatics and other club activities.

Along with its paternalistic feelings towards staff and their happiness, the rules were positively Victorian. In the early forties, single women working for Confed who decided to marry had to quit their jobs. Having a married woman on staff was simply not appropriate. At a time when Rosie the Riveter was changing the way women were regarded in the workplace and in society, Confed remained mired somewhere in the nineteenth century. In the decades to follow, Confed modernized somewhat, of course, but the place never really caught up to the rest of the world. Some parts of Confed and some people always remained in a bit of a backwater, where the past was preserved, whether it was worth saving or not.

By 1943, Confed hit the $500-million mark in insurance in force and $161 million in assets, half of that invested in war bonds. The war did not diminish expansion; from 1939 to 1945, growth was 44 per cent. Insurance in force was $621 million, assets $188 million.

In 1947, when president V. R. Smith died and "the young J. K." was thrust into the role, J. K. pretended to be taken aback by his own appointment. Informed that the board had chosen him, he said, "I thought they would appoint Mr. Waldie," a reference to the senior board member. Macdonald was the last connection with the founding Macdonalds and would serve as president until 1969, then as chairman until 1976. In many ways, he was the bridge to the modern era.

In 1953, Confed wrote its one-millionth policy and, in June 1955, moved to a new ten-storey Georgian-style buff-limestone and red-brick building at 321 Bloor Street East, known warmly as home office. Over the entrance is a sculpted relief with an allegorical family scene and the company motto, in both Latin, SIC VITA VITALIS, and English, THUS IS LIFE LIVEABLE. The five people in the scene, two male, two female, and a baby of indeterminate gender, were soon dubbed "The Naked Family" by staff. In fact, it's only the two females, both down on bended knee, who are without clothing. The baby is well swaddled, and the two males – a father and son complete with bows, a dead animal, and a hunting dog – are wearing loincloths.

Confed acquired the first computer in the industry in 1958, an IBM 705. Installation required two years, and start-up was regarded as such a seismic event in corporate history that employees were decked out for the occasion in costumes depicting the various eras of mankind – from the Stone Age to the Space Age, with Victorian garb in between.

The newfangled contraption was not without its problems. "[I]t was soon discovered the computer imposed a discipline beyond original expectations," declares the company history. "As a pioneer user, we were breaking new ground with all the experimental trial and error runs this involved. There were periods when the possibility of backtracking and starting over was very real." The man who oversaw the installation was Pat Burns.

The computer era of the sixties paralleled other changes in society. When 321 Bloor was built, a new staff house was erected next door at 100 Huntley Street. There was an auditorium for meetings or badminton, and individual rooms for a host of pursuits, such as the camera club or the leathercraft group, the glee club or the choir. In the basement was a rifle range.

Just as the facilities opened, however, staff began to lose interest. Employees were increasingly moving to the suburbs and, with longer commutes, were less likely to want to spend time with co-workers before heading home. Moreover, flexible hours had been instituted, so people were arriving and departing at diverse times. The staff house was closed in the sixties.

Legislative changes also had an impact on the business. In 1957, the federal government passed a bill providing for the mutualization of insurance companies, and Confed became a mutual company in 1968. The change meant that ownership altered from that of a few families, so that all of the firm's tens of thousands of policyholders were the owners, a cooperative view that was seen as the best way to prevent foreign take-overs of the industry.

While the intended patriotic effect was attained, there were down-sides. The mutual culture shielded management from criticism and meant officers could do exactly what they wanted without having to answer to anyone. Policyholders had little interest in how the place was run, just so long as it was still standing when they died, so benefits could be paid. The change also meant that capital – the base on which the business is built – could be supplemented only through internally generated profits, because shares could not be sold to the public.

At the time, such constraints did not seem troublesome. There were other pursuits to keep them occupied. On February 3, 1916, fire had destroyed the centre block of the Parliament Buildings, and among the losses had been the famous 1884 painting by Robert Harris of the Fathers of Confederation. As a project for Canada's Centennial in 1967, Confederation Life commissioned Rex Woods to recreate the painting from sketches and a charcoal drawing by Harris. Much of the work was done in the company boardroom, where space and lighting conditions were best and where the directors could keep an eye on progress during the four years Woods spent completing the work. The canvas, measuring thirteen feet by seven feet, was finally unveiled in the Railway Committee Room of the centre block on Parliament Hill on February 3, 1969, fifty-three years to the day after the fire.

When Macdonald turned sixty-five in 1969, he retired as president (but remained as chairman) and was replaced by J. Craig Davidson. Insurance business in force has risen to $6 billion, up eightfold in the twenty-one years since 1947 when Macdonald took over, and assets were $737 million. Three generations of Macdonalds had been chief executives for fifty-one of Confed's first ninety-eight years.

Said Davidson of his rise when he was anointed, "I really didn't *know* I would become president. But I can tell you one rule that guided me. I tried to make sure that, if there was an opening coming up I knew about – or even didn't know about – that whoever had to make the decision could say, 'Davidson – well, he's the best prepared of all the candidates.'"

Among Davidson's first steps was to change the name of the company from Confederation Life Association to Confederation Life Insurance Company. The alteration was regarded as a final break from the past. Association had been a usage of Scottish origin, describing a group that had come together for mutual benefit. Over time, Confed management now argued, association had come to mean a more loosely knit organization, and no longer fit the modern ways.

Davidson's goal during the seventies was to expand the business by two and a half times. Anything seemed possible. Certainly, the author of the company's centennial history had high hopes. "By 1980, we may be offering trust and borrowing services, mutual funds, plus investment and planning services of various kinds in addition to life, health, pension and other insurance products."

Other more fanciful notions that might be possible by the year 2000 included: transportation from Toronto to Vancouver in forty-five minutes via a "human pipeline"; twelve-week annual vacations; and an overall "breakdown in the willingness and desire to work hard."

None of those predictions now appear likely. Perhaps Confed's grand expansion plans into so many other financial-services areas would have been better left unrealized, too.

CHAPTER 2

─◆◈◆─

Hijinks in High Places

"In life, there are things worse than death, like spending an evening with a life insurance salesman."

– Woody Allen, in the film *Love and Death*

For decades, the figureheads at the top of insurance companies were symbols of respectability to the public. Five former prime ministers became presidents of life-insurance companies. Sir John A. Macdonald was at Manulife from 1887 to 1891; Alexander Mackenzie headed North American Life from 1881 to 1892; Sir Mackenzie Bowell was at Imperial Life from 1903 to 1912; and Crown Life had two such eminent statesmen, Sir Charles Tupper from 1901 to 1904 and Sir Robert Borden from 1928 to 1937.

Insurance companies, said such names, were going to be around forever – and it was just as well there was such reassurance. Outsiders could not possibly understand the business, and the actuaries who charted the future didn't make matters easier. Manufacturers make a product at a certain cost, sell it at a higher price, subtract overhead, expenses, salaries, etc., then decide whether the year was profitable.

Insurance is far more mystical. A life-insurance policy sold today is paid for by monthly instalments – premiums – over many years. Those premium levels have to be set at the time of sale, using the best estimates available of future corporate expenses, interest rates, and mortality tables, plus some idea of how many death benefits will actually be paid and when. A second difference between the life-insurance business and the rest of the corporate world is that, during the first year a policy is in place, costs far outweigh the income from that policy. Because of the bonus arrangement, agents can actually earn more than the premiums collected that year.

Just to add to the peculiarity, if a life-insurance company has a good year and sells a record number of new policies, that puts such a strain on the system, because of all those first-year costs, that the new business is not profitable and neither is the company. By the same token, if agents did not meet targets and sales were down, profits would go up.

The result is that outsiders, even some members of the board of directors, find the business so opaque that they try to pay as little attention as possible, and management gets a clear run to do things as it wishes. Until, that is, events reach the point where even the most baffled director can figure out that something has gone badly wrong.

In the mid-seventies, Confederation Life was mired in just such a crisis. President J. Craig Davidson was not a well man. Alcohol had wreaked havoc on his health. He was in no real hurry to leave, but, when he did go, he said that he wanted to be succeeded by Pat Burns, who, like himself, had been around Confed forever and liked to take a drink or two.

Burns was born in Toronto on August 9, 1928. He attended St. Michael's College School (of hockey-team fame) and, when it was time to go to work, responded to a newspaper ad for a company that he'd never heard of, Confederation Life. He joined the premium accounting department on September 3, 1946, right out of high school. That first job turned out to be one that taught him about the company's different life-insurance policies and introduced him to the workings of some of the branches.

In the fifties, he was transferred to planning and became involved in the company's move from the Richmond Street head office to 321 Bloor in 1955. Next he joined what was then called electronic data processing when computer systems were first being installed, and headed that area from 1965 to 1968. "A major lesson I learned in dealing with the creative people who worked in the systems field is that you cannot fit everyone into a mould or expect that we all have similar career aspirations," says Burns.

His first vice-presidential appointment came in 1970, when he was named controller, replacing Ben Holmes, an actuary who had been both his tutor and mentor. When David Watts, who headed group insurance, suffered a heart attack, Watts and Burns switched roles, with Burns becoming vice-president, group, in 1971. "It was in this role that I learned that nothing happens until something is sold," says Burns. "I also learned the importance of service." It was also the first of his jobs that came with bottom-line responsibilities attached.

In 1974, he was named vice-president of Canadian operations, dealing with individual life sales, and thus became one of the senior officers of the day. At Confed, under J. K. Macdonald, everyone was pretty much in charge of their own shop. "I'm not sure he ran a very tight ship," says Burns of J. K. "We always thought it was kind of a family affair." Burns patterned his own management style on that same easygoing way.

Although Burns was Davidson's choice to succeed him, Burns did not get along well with the patriarchal Macdonald. "Maybe not a thousand per cent," Burns admits. "I was a pretty brash, I-knew-everything kind of guy." Neither did it help that Burns was Roman Catholic. In those days, religious bigotry was commonplace in the upper reaches of Toronto the Good. Macdonald was not alone in his prejudices. The wise young man looking for a promotion took his family to the church of the boss's choice on a Sunday to see and be seen. Burns, who attended mass weekly, was on his knees elsewhere.

But religion wasn't Macdonald's only problem with Burns. Macdonald was a bit of a snob, and he didn't like the way Burns handled his cutlery. "He didn't have the York Club veneer," says a director of the day. "He couldn't mix socially properly. I told Pat this several times, that he did not have enough culture to be the head man. Pat wasn't pleased to hear it, but a fact is a fact."

It didn't help matters that Burns refused to show Macdonald the kind of respect Macdonald believed was his due. When Macdonald walked into a room, for example, he expected lesser mortals to stand. Burns would not. The company was Macdonald's personal fiefdom, and, if he didn't like someone, even if that person was being backed by Davidson, no one – not even the board – had much to say about it.

The stalemate paralysed the company's upper reaches. Finally, some of the directors, led by George Mara, captain of Canada's Olympic hockey team (which won a gold in the 1948 Olympics at St. Moritz), got fed up and said, according to one who was there, " 'If Pat's not the guy, we've got to get an interim guy in.' Craig didn't want to change. He got shoved, hard."

In 1976, the board told Davidson that the job and the alcohol were killing him and he should help both the company and himself by stepping aside. Davidson finally relented and retired in July, a veteran of thirty-nine years. Now, who to appoint? With no internal candidate who passed Macdonald's muster, a search committee of directors was established to look outside Confed for a successor.

One came quickly to hand. Jack Rhind had been CEO of National Life Assurance Co. of Canada since 1966 and had decided in 1975, at fifty-five, that he wanted out, thirty years after joining the firm. He appointed a new CEO, actuary Charles Galloway, said he would stay on for a year as chairman, then took some time off that autumn and back-packed around Europe, happy to have shed his role as "Mr. President."

Rhind had cut quite a swath at National Life. It was he who had come up with the idea for the insurance industry to be a major sponsor at Expo 67 in Montreal. In the end, seventy-six companies contributed a total of $750,000 to create the Man and His Health pavilion, build a theatre, and offer stage shows.

In 1970, at fifty, Rhind had become enamoured with minibikes after his seventeen-year-old son got a Honda. Rhind bought a red 80cc Yamaha, which he rode to work and to meetings downtown. "I think it gives some people a bit of a shock at first," he said at the time. "I don't know whether it's a proper example to my staff. But it's really very practical. Businessmen of all levels should use motorbikes. It would save a lot of traffic congestion – and people's time. There could, of course, be no wintertime riding."

From 1971 to 1973, Rhind was president of what was then called the Canadian Life Insurance Association, and he modernized the trade organization by urging that the industry build bridges to key groups among its various publics. "The principles which govern our investment operations are often misunderstood," he said as he noted that he was looking for ways that the industry could explain these and other matters to the public "in simple, understandable language."

"We touch on the lives of so many, but the public is poorly informed about our products and industry," he said, calling for a major communications project. "I don't know what the price will be, but I am convinced it is less than the cost of doing nothing."

One of his ideas, a national consumer phone-in show with a panel of life-insurance CEOs, was not approved. The overall program, called Operation Bridge, was. The concept included phone banks in a call centre, manned by insurance-industry retirees, plus national advertising, consumer booklets, and outreach committees in seventy different companies. Today the centre handles tens of thousands of calls each year, including queries about failures.*

Rhind was approached by the Confed search committee and soon learned the dilemma it faced. "Macdonald had some prejudices," says Rhind, "and didn't like the idea of Pat Burns." Rhind was more to J. K.'s liking. Born in Toronto, Rhind had grown up in establishment Rosedale, on St. Andrews Gardens. As a lad, he was a member of Sunday school and the Boy Scouts at Rosedale United Church. He attended University of Toronto Schools, then graduated with his bachelor of commerce degree in 1942 and master's in business administration from the University of Toronto in 1953. In the mid-fifties, he bought a stately brick house across a small park from Rosedale United and has lived there ever since.

Rhind was well known in the small pond that was the life-insurance

---

* The Montreal office fielded 9,260 calls about the failure of Les Coopérants in a six-week period in 1992, and 8,600 calls in three months in both Toronto and Montreal about the Sovereign insolvency. By 1994, calls would soar to 80,000, with 8,000 calls relating to fears about Confed in the six weeks after seizure.

industry. Rhind and Macdonald had each been presidents of their respective companies and had therefore served together at the industry association. Rhind also knew several Confed board members such as Donald McIntosh, a partner in the Toronto law firm of Fraser & Beatty; Ray Wolfe, chairman and CEO of The Oshawa Group Ltd.; and George Mara, then chairman of Jannock Corp.

The committee looked no further. Rhind began in September 1976 as president and CEO of Confederation Life. For his part, the switch in roles was beyond belief. "It was something that I'd never dreamt would happen. If you'd told me when I started in the industry that someday I'd be the chief executive of Confederation Life, I would have said, 'That's a joke.'" Rhind was indeed entering a different league; Confed had 2,500 employees and $1.7 billion in assets; it was about four times the size of National.

The board wanted to be sure that there was smooth sailing ahead, so the directors convinced Macdonald to step down as chairman now that Confed was in the right sort of hands. In February 1977, Macdonald was replaced by Page Wadsworth, who had been a Confed director since 1961 and had just retired as chairman of the Canadian Imperial Bank of Commerce. Macdonald kept an office on the executive floor, fussed around the place dusting and adjusting paintings, travelled a bit on behalf of the company as an elder statesman, and died in September 1977.

The transition was not without bumps. "The board were concerned that, if they parachuted me in, there would be a lot of disappointment among the other senior officers who had been there so long," says Rhind. To allay concerns, directors McIntosh and Wadsworth met with senior management to tell them that Rhind would designate an heir apparent – from inside Confed – within three years, thereby assuring them that they hadn't forever been cut off from the climb to the top. The cadre who were in their mid-forties, including Burns, who was forty-eight, had another shot.

Burns was far from mollified. He'd spent his entire adult life crawling his way higher, only to be held back by the silver-spoon crowd. He, Pat Burns, was as good as they were, the WASP establishment that kept him down. When his turn came, he'd show them. Meanwhile, he'd withdraw and lick his wounds, knowing that business was like the game of curling that he so loved. Eventually he'd have last rock. Victory would be his.

With Davidson gone, some measure of tranquillity returned. "It wasn't like taking over a ship that needed to be steered off on a different course," says Rhind. "They were a strong team. They all knew their jobs. There wasn't one of them that I felt should be removed. The company was doing well. I didn't need to clean house." He did not alter the management set-up that Davidson had put in place that included a "president's advisory council" of the seven senior vice-presidents.

Rhind made only one change in senior management. A. J. Trusler, head of investments, was set to retire in January 1977 after forty-seven years with Confed. To replace him, Rhind designated John Watson as vice-president, investment. Compared with the rest, at age thirty-three, Watson – who had joined Confed's bond department as an investment-analyst trainee in 1967 – was but a whippersnapper.

The officers had every reason to kowtow to Rhind, because he had their futures in his hands. Still, there was an initial period when feathers were ruffled both by Rhind's arrival and the silken ease with which he quickly flew in formation with the board. Rhind could feel their unspoken, hostile question: "Who does he think he is, coming in here?" Further down in the company, there were questions, too. Everyone knew that National was one-quarter Confed's size; employees felt they deserved someone with more stature.

The board laid down no specific objectives for Rhind, no stretch targets it wanted him to meet. Davidson and his drinking problem were gone from the scene, replaced by a CEO of their own background and breeding. It wasn't so much that corporate governance had been served as that an embarrassing situation had been ended. They just assumed Rhind would get on with the job in a way that would satisfy them, without requiring further instruction. For them, being on the board of a mutual company was a bit of a bore. Profit that year was $5 million.

The Macdonald family tradition had created a certain tone of formality and decorum at Confed. "The atmosphere from level to level – particularly between management and the board – was some-what of an old-fashioned one," recalls Rhind. "The management team were in such awe of the board that it was stultifying. [They'd say,] 'We can't do that, the board wouldn't want that.'" Good ideas, if there were any, were rarely brought to the board, on the assumption that they would not be approved.

Management held the same attitude towards the CEO. Victorian gentlemen rarely talked about what really mattered; those one step down were expected, if not to touch the forelock, certainly to defer to their superiors, who must know better because they *were* superi-ors, after all. At Confed, it was a culture of contentment, a place where the status quo was revered, even worshipped. If you had a new idea, you kept it to yourself, and it was safe to do so because the other life-insurance companies weren't very innovative either. There was no need to be progressive. "Pioneering don't pay," phil-anthropist Andrew Carnegie had said, and, if it worked for Carnegie, by gum it would work for Confed. For a long time, Burns himself operated that way. "There isn't much reward for innova-tion," he said in 1984. "If a company comes out with a new product today, we can copy it tomorrow."

At first, Rhind was frustrated by the lackadaisical approach. "It wasn't extreme, but it wasn't a healthy thing. It annoyed me because I like to operate the opposite way. That's something I learned from Harold Lawson." Lawson, his mentor and former boss at National Life, had told him, "'You draw out the best in people when they're not trying to think about what you [as boss] want them to say.' You destroy creativity. I made a very strong effort to free up the role of the CEO and the role of the board. Not that there was any less respect for the board, but the inhibitions that existed were removed."

But Rhind's style could also be confrontational, something that Confed managers weren't used to. He attacked everything like the ban-tam rooster he was – with gusto – whether it was tennis or teamwork, and he didn't mind dressing down an officer in ways that could embar-rass the alleged transgressor in front of his peers. There were benefits that came with his arrogance. "Jack brought a sophistication and class to the company that, despite J. K.'s money and Craig's brilliance, the company never had," says John Heard, who had joined Confed in 1947, just like Burns had done a year earlier, fresh out of high school, and was vice-president, personnel, under Rhind. "Jack was quite a different fellow than we'd ever had before. He had social standing."

Throughout his time in office, Rhind made few major changes to Confed's strategy. He had a particular interest in the investment business and wanted to take Confed into the mutual-fund and the trust-company fields in a big way, but he was never quite able to pull it off. The lack of success was frustrating for Rhind. At one point, when he was told that another firm had purchased a trust company that Confed had also been trying to acquire, Rhind said, "I'm going to be the only kid on the block without an electric train. Get me an electric train."

Rhind did, however, follow through with the commitment to pick a successor from within. There were really only two candidates: Peter Lloyd, who was vice-president, United States and Caribbean, and Pat Burns. Rhind picked Burns, and a popular choice he was among the rank and file. He was one of *them*, and had been patient as Rhind played peacemaker and bridge to the next generation. He'd paid his dues.

For Rhind, Burns was also the obvious successor. "He had a very, very quick mind and an extensive knowledge of the business in both a micro and macro way. He knew the company; he'd been there so long. He understood so much about the industry. He was a very easy person to work with in that he didn't have a strong ego. He put forward his view in a reasonable way. I could depend on him to be insightful and get at the heart of things very quickly. I couldn't have had a better person to bounce things off. He was a liberal kind of a guy, in the small-l sense of the word. There are different styles of management from the autocratic, non-liberal. His style was the more liberal style."

Rhind also admired Burns's ability to get done what Rhind regarded as an enormous amount of work in a short time. And while Rhind had had the good fortune to attend prep school and collect his MBA, he did not look down his nose at Burns's high-school education. Rhind was not above sending back a memo because someone had employed poor grammar or mangled syntax. But, although Burns had no university degree, Rhind approved of him and thought he could write well and speak convincingly.

The culture shift that Rhind's choice embodied did not sit well with everyone. When Rhind informed directors at the December 19, 1979, board meeting that he wanted Burns to succeed him, some of the directors who remembered Macdonald's dislike for Burns were dubious. There was, however, little choice; they could not admit defeat and go outside again. And, anyway, there would be a transition period as Burns, over time, slowly picked up the titles of president and CEO from Rhind. Once Burns had those two, it was understood that Rhind would continue as chairman. So directors agreed, and Burns was named executive vice-president and a member of the board, effective February 1980.

With that sign of approbation, Burns became Confed's chief operating officer, despite the fact that directors knew his professional profile included both strengths and weaknesses. "Burns was steeped in hard work, rising to the top over many years in a staid, structured life insurance company," says a director. "He was no Conrad Black."

Burns now set out to show the board, the company, and the world what a mistake had been made in slowing his arrival. From its founding in 1871 to that point, more than a century later, Confed had managed to accumulate assets of $2.7 billion. Burns would preside over a sevenfold increase. He'd make them wish they'd picked him years ago.

In fact, competition was already heating up in the United States, where Confed was represented by general agents who acted for several companies at a time. In Canada, the system was different: career agents worked solely for Confed. From 1968 to 1978, the number of general agents in the United States who were handling Confed products increased from 26 to 165, and, as the number of general agents selling Confed products in the United States grew, so did demand for new products. If Confed did not offer a full range of choices, general agents simply turned to another firm they also represented. Confed's annual sales growth during the 1968-to-1978 period in the United States was 16.3 per cent, well above the industry average. By 1981, there were almost 300 agents in the United States.

In 1979, a new sales office for group life and health insurance was
opened in Atlanta, Georgia, and a claims office was added the next
year. In 1981, Rhind and Burns decided to relocate the head office for
United States and Caribbean operations from Bloor Street to the
United States, and Atlanta was selected over the other two cities on
the short list: Houston and Tampa. In 1982, fifty-five staffers were
transferred to Atlanta and about 250 people were hired locally to work
in a new $9-million building in the northwest suburbs. The location
in the deep South meant a few pleasant perks, such as "golf twelve
months of the year," as Mike Regester, vice-president, United States
individual insurance, put it.

Meanwhile, interest rates went on wild swings in Canada and the
United States – prime reached 22.75 per cent in 1981 and fell to 12 per
cent in 1982. Group life and health lost money, but individual insurance sales continued to increase by double digits annually, fuelled by
good times and the changing demographics, as baby boomers looked
for protection and investment. New products had to be quickly
stitched together and trotted out to keep abreast. In early 1983,
Confed began offering something called the Life Builder series, an
insurance policy in which cash values were adjusted regularly according to interest rates at the time. Not only were they new, but actuaries were flummoxed about how to price them. They could only make
a stab in what was becoming a superheated market. Within a year, the
new policies proved so popular that they amounted to half of all sales.
In the United States, a concept was taking off called universal life,
with coverage and investment possibilities that could be altered at the
whim of the policyholder. "Hot money" had arrived.

Confed was still attempting to proceed with some caution. Future
cash flow from premiums was suddenly unpredictable; after a century
of doing business a certain way, upheaval had become the order of the
day. For a time, Confed stuck with its core business. Many Canadian
companies were not only talking about one-stop financial-services
shopping, they were actively establishing the corporate relationships
that would allow them to be all things to every customer.

At the same time, the industry was in a flap in 1983, trying to sort
out the differences in views about the future. Stock companies

seemed to have an advantage over mutuals in this brave new world. London Life looked like the way to go. They'd hired Earl Orser from Eaton's to run the insurance company and were bringing the various forms of financial services under the Trilon umbrella – Wellington Insurance for property and casualty, London for life insurance, and Royal Trust for investments. Crown Life was taking a similar one-stop approach under another outsider CEO, Robert Bandeen, the former chairman of Canadian National.

It was Bandeen who led the stock companies in the fight against the more stolid mutuals. Consensus between the two groups within the Canadian Life and Health Insurance Association seemed impossible. At this rate, a common viewpoint would never be presented to government; legislation would stay as it was, and stock companies would keep their advantage. Bandeen felt so confident that Crown and the other stock companies would run roughshod over the more constrained mutual companies that he said, "We've got them by the balls." When the quote was published in 1983, Bandeen's standing at the association skidded, and he stopped attending meetings.

Many in the industry had been waiting for Bandeen to fall on his face. Rhind liked to be entertaining at annual policyholder meetings. One year he went on at great and humorous length about how "The Naked Family" over the front door should be clothed. In 1984, he decided to take on Bandeen, who had been on the insurance-industry committee chaired by Rhind, which was trying to find common ground. "The committee worked out some recommendations which provided a reasonably level playing field for the stock and mutual companies," Rhind told about three hundred Confed policyholders and others who had gathered at the February annual meeting. "You can imagine my reaction when I read the following in an article on Mr. Bandeen in *Toronto Life*, entitled 'Crown's Prince.'

"Before I read this, I warn the more fastidious among you that this contains an expression that I would not normally use at an annual meeting. In referring to the association committee discussions and the mutual companies, he said, 'We've got them by the ———'" Rhind suddenly stopped, a smile playing across his face, as the audience roared with laughter. As quiet returned, Rhind continued, "I cannot bring myself to say this word at an annual meeting of Confederation Life. The Fathers of Confederation would rise from their graves." Of course, there was more appreciative laughter.

But Rhind was just getting nicely under way. He plucked a newspaper clipping from the podium that turned out to be a recent column by *Globe and Mail* society writer Zena Cherry, in which she had mistakenly identified Bandeen as the head of Confed. "Not only does Mr. Bandeen feel he holds us in an uncomfortable fashion," quipped Rhind, "but he appears to have taken over my job."

While the speech said a lot about Rhind and his capacity to laugh at himself in public, the incident also offered some insight into Burns. Rhind had sent Burns an advance draft of the speech. Burns could not believe that Rhind was actually going to deliver the words as written. "This is a special copy," Burns said hopefully when he next saw Rhind. "You've written this just for me." Where Rhind was deft, Burns was flat-footed and had little flair.

Through 1984, Rhind remained very much in charge. While there were continuing attempts to acquire businesses outside the insurance world, the year passed with no such progressive step taken. "To date, it has seemed wise to invest in opportunities within our existing fields of activity: in distribution systems, agent training and compensation, new products, EDP systems, policyholder services, and other new developments," explained the message to policyholders signed by Rhind and Burns in the 1984 annual report. "Directing funds to such approaches appears to be a good way to keep Confederation Life in front."

Behind the scenes, however, Burns was beginning to position himself for his much-postponed time at the top. He was appointed president in 1982, and two retirements in 1983 had given him an opportunity to pick his own spear carriers. David Watts, vice-president, corporate, retired after thirty-five years; Paul Wortman stepped down as vice-president and general manager for the United Kingdom after thirty-four years with Confed. To replace them, Burns elevated four vice-presidents and gave each the new title of senior vice-president. Included were John Heard, Canadian operations; John

Watson, investments; Ken Hilton, United Kingdom; and Peter Lloyd, United States and Caribbean. While there was some tidy-up to other divisions and reporting relationships, Burns showed his hand with only one other appointment. He made William Douglas vice-president, corporate development.

Vice-president, corporate development, is one of those wonderful roles that can mean either everything – or nothing. For some, the title might mean they are simply marking time, with no particular responsibilities, waiting for retirement. Douglas did not fall into that do-nothing category. For him, the designation meant a free hand to do just about anything he wanted.

With Watts so inactive in the role because of poor health, Douglas had slipped into the vacuum and taken charge of all planning-and-research activities. To most people, Douglas was a bit of a mystery. In the seventies, he always wore the same blue-grey suit and seemed to do little other than sit in his office, drinking coffee, smoking his pipe, and reading the newspapers. Once in a while, he'd be seized by a coughing fit. Douglas wrote few memos, but, every two or three months, he'd go into a flurry of activity, during which he'd produce a thick sheaf of papers that looked at current business plans and set out an agenda of action for the future.

Born in Toronto in 1940, Douglas had graduated from the University of Toronto in 1965 with a bachelor of commerce degree. While at school, he worked in research at Canadian Business Services, then joined Confed's investment department as an analyst in 1966 and was made a vice-president of planning and accounting in 1979. Unlike the rest, he never actually worked in the insurance operations, preferring the more cerebral world of analysis, where people didn't matter, thoughts did.

But Douglas was much more than just some egghead churning out ideas unconnected to reality. As Burns moved up the ladder, Douglas had always been pulled along with him, continuing to report to Burns as Burns took on each new role. Douglas was like the pilot fish that swims with the shark, always protected against attack by the larger species, yet needful of the symbiotic relationship for life itself.

Douglas had become Burns's alter ego, the other half of the marketing mentality, the place where the ideas came from. Burns was the doer, but he needed some help with what to do; Douglas supplied the fuel. If Burns was the style, Douglas was the substance. Burns, who didn't have enough ideas of his own, was propelled by what appeared to be winning strategies and could take the credit. Bill Douglas made Pat Burns look good.

Without the need to worry about outcomes, Douglas was dismissive of fools who didn't catch on to what he was up to at first blush. Once he'd come up with whatever the Big Idea happened to be in the particular circumstances, he just assumed someone else would carry it out. His attitude was "We'll worry about how it works later. We've got an organization that's big enough to pick up on the details."

Separately, neither of them were enough. Together, they could be too much. Douglas could be positively off-putting, attending entire meetings without saying a word, just looking professorial. Burns was okay in small groups of two or three, but he wasn't at ease with larger groups and didn't shine socially. Says a director of Burns, "He never would've won a charm contest."

When Burns finally got the top job as CEO in 1985, he made his move. He'd been waiting for this moment since 1976; in his mind, it was long overdue. Each year, the highest-ranking eighteen officers attended a weekend retreat to hear business reports from the various divisions, including the United States and the United Kingdom, and to plan strategy. The meetings were usually held away from the office, outside Toronto at inns such as Millcroft in Alton or Deerhurst in Muskoka.

The 1985 retreat at the Delta Meadowvale in Mississauga marked the beginning of the new era. Aided by advisers from a group called Western Consultants, Burns and Douglas presented their new vision for Confed. "We were all challenged to become entrepreneurs rather than just manage passively," recalls Heard, who had replaced Burns as senior vice-president, Canadian operations. If Confed were to have a future, the officers were told, the company must become a well-rounded financial-services empire, not just continue to be a provider of insurance. Legislative changes in the offing provided more freedom.

"We were challenged to go away and become involved in other types of businesses," says Heard.

At the time, Burns liked to cite the occasion in the late sixties when he had signed up for a management-training course at the University of Western Ontario and found that his fellow "classmates" were surprised that he would even bother to attend. "After all," Burns quoted them as saying, "life-insurance companies are guaranteed success regardless of the quality of management."

When his classmates heard that he worked for a *mutual* insurance company, they were even more bemused by his presence among them. "Since mutual life companies have no ownership or shareholder group demanding profits, dividends, or performance excellence, they lack the marketplace discipline to maximize profitability or return on investment," Burns quoted them as saying.

Burns, of course, disagreed. Noting the "cooperative" approach of a mutual company, he argued that the primary consideration of a mutual company is to "meet our obligations." He was so concerned about this duty to pay off death and other benefits that he claimed that not only did Confed keep sufficient reserves for future liabilities, but the company also "maintains an additional voluntary reserve of capital surplus . . . [that] gives us the flexibility to meet extraordinary claims or cushion the effect of adverse market conditions and provides capital for growth opportunities."

The second consideration was to obtain the best possible return on investment for clients and policyholders so as to ensure "the existence of the company in perpetuity." This is a grand phrase, and one that captures the attitude of many mutual-company chief executives who wrap themselves in a cloak of religious fervour about their position in the corporate firmament.

According to Burns, mutual firms had an advantage over stock companies, because mutuals could take the long-term view. "The investment decision is uncluttered by the need to show short-term results to satisfy shareholder demands or free up cash flow for shareholder dividends," he said. Profit didn't matter, because no one was looking for the immediate return on investment. It was this misguided view of himself and his company – growth rather than profit – that was at the core of the growth-in-any-direction strategy Burns proposed to his colleagues at the Delta weekend, the strategy that would eventually be his undoing.

In 1985, Burns and Douglas decided that Confed had the resources to grow, increase market share, and become more than simply a life- and health-insurance firm. With such an ambition, "[W]e should spread our wings, take advantage of the many new opportunities now available to us, and embrace a new goal of being a broadly based financial-services company. In future we would measure our success against the performance of other members of the financial-services sector, rather than against the insurance industry alone."

Burns recognized that success using this strategy was not guaran- teed. "This commitment to deliver the best return is a two-edged sword." That's because growth requires capital, and mutual companies have few sources for increased capital.

In the industry, observers were beginning to take notice of an awakening Confed. "It was a conservative, musty company. For years they were akin to Canada Life – they stuck to their knitting," says Bruce Powe, former vice-president of the Canadian Life and Health Insurance Association (CLHIA). "The industry was changing from an insurance business to a money-management business. Confed was laden with career types – people who had been there thirty to forty years. When Burns took over, a different climate was emerging. They said, 'Let's go join the pack.'"

In that regard, Burns was an unusual product of the Confed culture. "Pat Burns was a self-made, non-establishment type," says Powe. "He came up through the group-marketing system. You have to be quick on your feet and nail down big clients. Your business is constantly under attack from other companies. So he came out of a wheel-and-deal business that is fast-moving, tricky stuff, with million of dollars in premium income at stake."

The sea change being demanded by Burns was massive, yet those being ordered to make the leap were given neither guidance nor support. Without any injection of outside expertise in their ranks or helpful training of any type, Confed officers were being told to reinvent themselves and become something they had never been. Moreover, there wasn't much breadth; each man was pretty much the same as the other. "There was no professional discipline, there was a Confed discipline," says Mike Regester, who would later become Burns's protégé. "There wasn't a lawyer, actuary, or investment person among them."

Rather than merely manage cautious money, Confed officers were suddenly to be aggressive in fields about which they knew nothing. "Pat decided that the status quo wasn't satisfactory. It wasn't for self-aggrandizement. He felt he really had to do something," says a director.

While Douglas and Burns both presented the empowering message at the Delta that weekend, there was no doubt from whence the bold direction sprang. "Bill was the idea generator. He was the brains behind it all," says John Heard. "He thought we should be a bank. We'd start with a trust company, turn it into a bank, and then fold the insurance operation into it."

However, some of the attendees at the 1985 retreat were reluctant to take off towards these uncharted heights, and said so. In particular, Ken Hilton, senior vice-president and general manager for the United Kingdom, protested that such thinking was wrong-headed. The opposing view was acknowledged, but dismissed by Burns and Douglas as unnecessarily cautious. When aggressive growth targets set by Burns were easily reached that year and the year after that, everyone learned to keep quiet. From 1986 to 1989, Confed was the fastest-growing firm among the major Canadian life-insurance companies, achieving annual growth rates of 25 per cent.

Douglas became as pervasive as he was persuasive. Burns gave him free rein and seemed to enjoy having him as front man. For his part, Douglas revelled in the role. In the United States and the United Kingdom, away from head office, Douglas deployed particular power as he represented or interpreted Burns's view, sometimes causing resentment in the ranks.

For example, Douglas would travel to Atlanta every three or four months and say something to the troops that went like this: "You made

$30 million last year, we'd like you to make $60 million this year." But doubling profit requires more than just doubling the marketing effort. Companies can't simply order general agents to double sales targets and expect results. Doubling the number of sales reps isn't a much better approach, after taking into account the costs of recruiting, training, office space, and getting people up to selling speed.

Douglas, who had the declared goal of making Confed the largest insurance company in Canada within five years, would respond to their concerns by switching strategies and telling them to increase volume by lowering premiums and thus undercut the competition. In turn, they'd remind him that lower premiums would only produce lower profits. "We used to have battles at those meetings," says Frank di Paolo, financial vice-president for the United States. "He would give us hell for not selling enough and making enough money. We would spend hours trying to let him know that's not the way you do business." Atlanta would try to get Douglas to agree to a more reasonable increase in business, perhaps something like 20 per cent. At least in Atlanta they knew what they were talking about and could muffle Douglas's excesses in one area among the many businesses Confed got into. "He found a fair amount of discipline on the insurance side," says di Paolo. "That was not the case at the trust company."

Such motivational speeches and glory goals were more likely to come from Douglas than Burns. Burns had his close friends in the company, people like secretary Mark Edwards and vice-president, human resources, Roger Cunningham, but he wasn't always successful at drawing the best from people. Sometimes he could barely carry on a conversation. People learned that there were occasions when the only way to deal with Burns was to sit very still and say not a word.

At an off-site sales meeting, for example, anyone who found himself during a break sitting beside Burns in the hotel lobby might get nothing but dead silence, an unnerving message from a boss that most underlings take to mean disapproval. Burns wouldn't seize the opportunity at such moments to put a colleague at ease or seek to discover what was going on in that person's professional life.

After hours, Burns liked to play, and when he played, he enjoyed drinking, just like the stereotypical Irishman that he was. At dinner, after everyone had downed a couple of highballs, Burns would come alive. If he were entertaining the executives, as he did every Christmas at his Toronto club, the Donalda, he'd get his kicks by ribbing certain people. He always had his favourite targets, and some of the comments could be cutting. If conversation lagged, he would stir things up, playing devil's advocate just for the sheer fun of setting people against each other. On one occasion, Tom Pitts, the head of Canadian insurance, struck back by dumping a beer on Burns's head.

On the golf links, Burns was also a lively animal, laughing, obviously having fun, and setting up bets for complicated combinations of holes, shots, and scores. He was a good golfer, who played a round in the mid-to-high eighties, rarely taking chances, most of the time keeping out of trouble by staying in the middle of the fairway.

Like a lot of sales-based organizations, Confed rewarded top agents with trips. The international convention, held every two years, was the ultimate reward. There was another meeting, an annual session for the fifty leading producers, usually held in either Arizona or Florida. Burns was always on hand for both. The annual gathering was meant to be businesslike, with presentations on topics such as estate planning. Fun and games would be limited to one afternoon of golf.

The international meeting, however, was all fun and frivolity. Mostly, the event is just a junket, a time to swap gossip, recharge the batteries, and let off a little steam in swank surroundings. In 1987, the blowout was in San Francisco; in 1989, Monaco; even in 1993, after the hard times arrived, they managed to squeeze in some festivities in Hawaii. More than half the high-flyers who qualified came from the United States individual market, and, in May 1991, about 350 agents plus spouses descended upon the Desert Springs Marriott in Palm Desert, Arizona. The three-day program was frothy and contained little substance beyond a few motivational speakers and congratulations all round.

The entertainment at dinner one night that year in Palm Desert included a Marilyn Monroe impersonator/singer. Part of her performance included selecting someone from the audience at random and bringing that lucky person onstage with her. The mark that evening, apparently arranged in advance, was none other than Pat Burns. As the buxom blonde sang to Burns in front of the seven hundred Confed sales reps and guests, she began coaxing him to strip. Rather than just dance a little, laugh it off, or try to make a gracious exit, Burns began to comply with her breathy solicitations. First he took off his tie, followed by his jacket, and then he removed his shirt as well.

The audience was aghast at his hijinks. "People were quite scandalized that such a conservative and button-down life-insurance company would have a CEO do something like that," says Bill Bowden, director of agencies in the Atlanta office and the man who dealt regularly with the cream-of-the-crop winners who watched, agog, that night. "Mr. Burns wasn't the person we thought he was. I was kind of embarrassed."

Executives from Toronto head office were equally chagrined with his performance. As the evening wound down, John Heard ran into Roger Cunningham and accused him of being the one who set up the whole thing. Cunningham vehemently denied the charge. No one would admit to any involvement in the skit that turned sour.

That evening provides evidence that Burns's judgement could be poor, perhaps because it was clouded by alcohol. "He's a self-admitted heavy drinker," says Bill Douglas. "It's hard to imagine that it doesn't impact one way or another on your work. He seemed to enjoy the booze on occasion. He did drink to excess at some company functions, so I assume he did elsewhere, too."

Burns's behaviour could also take a bizarre turn in other venues. When Burns visited the Atlanta headquarters, as he did two or three times a year, his wife, June, usually went along. Rather than stay at the Marriott, a handy five minutes from the company's office in the northwest suburbs, they'd check into the Ritz-Carlton Buckhead, the city's finest hotel, in the best residential section. The reason must have been that the location put June close to the nearby shopping malls. It certainly wasn't so Burns – a meat-and-potatoes-man – could enjoy the offerings of chef Guenter Seeger in what ranks as one of the best dining rooms in America.

One evening, when Burns invited colleagues from the Atlanta office to eat with him at the Ritz, he looked at the menu a long while, then demanded of the waiter, "Where's the beef?" Others at the table urged the hapless server to try and find some beef. This *was* their president, after all. The waiter retreated to the kitchen and within seconds came flying through the swinging door as if he'd been shot from a gun to say that the chef had informed him in no uncertain terms that the reason that there was no beef on the menu was because there was no beef on hand. Burns ordered rabbit and picked at his food all night.

Burns decided to buy a holiday home in the area so he could combine the regular business trips to Atlanta in winter with a few rounds of golf. He chose the Sea Islands, which lie in the Atlantic Ocean off the coast of Georgia and stretch from the southern border of South Carolina to the northern tip of Florida. They are called "The Golden Isles" because, in the gilded age of the nineteenth century, this is where the tycoons came – the Morgans, the Astors, and the Vanderbilts.

Carnegies and Rockefellers built on Cumberland Island. The Cloister, a Spanish-style hotel in stucco and terracotta erected on Sea Island in 1928, still draws the rich and powerful. Playwright Eugene O'Neill wrote at his place on Nineteenth Street. Today the area is populated by industrialists from the northern states who own second homes here for holidays and their eventual retirement. Values run to as much as $3 million, and lots average a minimum of three-quarters of an acre. Houses to rent, if available, can cost up to $25,000 a month. CBS journalist Bob Schieffer, who divides his time between Washington, D.C., and Sea Island, is among the resident local celebrities.

The attraction, in addition to the lack of riff-raff, are the golf courses. And so it was to St. Simons, one of the Golden Isles, that Pat Burns came. He bought a villa on Linkside Drive, a chip shot away from Sea Palms Golf Club, where he could hob with the nobs. Of all the houses on all the streets on the Golden Isles, Burns's place is just average.

But St. Simons had the advantage of being handy to Atlanta, just a one-hour flight to the nearby town of Brunswick, with an airport so down-home that bags are sent to the curb outside for easy transfer to the car, rather than dumped on some endless carousel to bounce about. He and June could be on the golf course thirty minutes after touchdown, far from the madding crowd.

In Palm Desert, Burns thought he could woo a crowd; instead, he made his colleagues cringe. On St. Simons, Burns would have liked to wheedle his way into the Establishment; but he possessed neither the cash nor the caché. Try as he might, he just didn't seem to fit anywhere.

CHAPTER 3

The Delta Strategy

"If you're going to sup with the devil, bring a long spoon."

– Anonymous

I f there is someone who almost universally gets the blame for what happened next at Confed, it is Bill Douglas. A modicum of loyalty to Pat Burns remains among employees, even some residual sympathy for his plight, but there is no such fond feeling for Douglas. Yet it was Burns who gave Douglas his head, his power. And the worst sort of power it was: power without responsibility. There is someone like Douglas in almost every organization, a figure who is just out of sight offstage, always at the ready to set events in motion like some master puppeteer, but rarely around if there is the slightest whiff of a problem.

The appointment of Burns as CEO, with Douglas, as usual, in tow, coincided with an industry-wide awakening in the mist of a go-go era. Douglas's operating style seemed as far from careful as possible – it was cavalier. People couldn't decide if he were very bright and had thought everything through or if he literally had no idea of the implications. Ideas and answers offered by Douglas often appeared to be nothing more than back-of-the-envelope solutions. "There was a certain amount of resistance," says vice-president, investments, Barry Graham, "but there was also admiration. His power came from Pat Burns."

"Pat encouraged him. He paid a lot of attention to Bill's theories," says a director who also admits that, despite the fact he believed Douglas had too much influence, too much leeway, no one even tried to stop his headlong rush. "He was at the right place at the right time. His creativity was infectious."

In the eighties, interest rates turned volatile and launched a whole new form of business with future implications that the old guard didn't understand. Rather than sell basic insurance with a specific death benefit and slow-to-build cash value, Confed was catapulted into the business of policies such as universal life, which allowed consumers to switch among products, have cash side funds, and take more chances.

Consumers demanded high interest rates, and, in order to pay returns of, say, 12 per cent, Confed had to find investments that returned 15 per cent or more, so there was enough difference to pay overhead, as well as produce a profit on new products with very slim margins. Unlike traditional life insurance, which required one payment upon death, these new products involved several different sorts of obligations at scattered dates far out into the future. Assets had to be found that matched those liabilities – but who knew when the money would be needed? Or how much? With traditional life insurance, there was a fairly predictable payout stream. With these new products, there was no past experience upon which the company could plan ahead.

Choices for long-term assets to match such liabilities were slim. Government bonds were solid and secure, but didn't pay nearly enough. The stock market was too unstable. Only commercial and residential real estate, as well as mortgages backed by property, appeared to offer a predictable opportunity for high returns over the long haul. A company that had been all but asleep was suddenly plunged into a competitive race, creating a wide range of financial services, spending money on modern technology, and trying valiantly to keep up with a new world gone mad with change. The trouble was that no one knew exactly how to act.

Even a canny man like William Bradford, who had been a bank president under Bill Mulholland – the Bank of Montreal chairman and CEO who single-handedly revolutionized banking in Canada – admitted incapacity. Bradford joined North American Life in 1988 as CEO and soon saw the insurance sector's dilemma. "We were wrestling with the fact that – perhaps belatedly – we had come to understand that we were going to have to change, and with the realization that we really weren't very sure how to go about doing it. Our customers had become more demanding and sophisticated, and, frankly, as an industry we hadn't done a very good job of keeping up with them. By and large we were slow to learn."

The problem wasn't just at the top with the floundering executives. There was a corporate culture that existed throughout the entire insurance sector, a culture that was stuck in a time warp. "If you went out into the field forces twenty years ago and asked them what an actuary did, they probably didn't even know what an actuary was," says John Thompson, deputy superintendent, Office of the Superintendent of Financial Institutions (OSFI). "Nor were they too concerned with the expense side of the books. There was very little appreciation for what level of earnings within a company was a reasonable level of earnings to expect. Within a mutual company, the field force may even have wondered why the company had to make money! People were allowed to operate in their own little vacuums."

Thompson's description of the seventies applied to the first half of the eighties as well. Suddenly, however, the business was changing drastically beneath their very feet. By 1985, 75 per cent of life-insurance sales were in products that were adjustable in some way to interest-rate swings, new products that hadn't even existed two years earlier. The number of Confed general agencies in the United States had reached 370 – more than twice as many as there had been just seven years earlier. By 1989, almost 60 per cent of Confed's net premium business in the United States was in the helter-skelter annuity area.

While Confed was moving into new arenas, Burns gave only the slightest hint in public of what else he had in mind. "[W]e will develop," he said in the 1986 annual report, "a branch-based financial services network." More competition was coming; he would meet and match the action using "new expansion opportunities which we will exploit vigorously." To accomplish that change, Burns would have to alter the very nature of the assets held. In 1985, 49 per cent of assets worth $4.7 billion were invested in mortgages and real estate.* That level was already 25 per cent above the industry average; Burns decided on the risky strategy of pushing it higher.

To achieve the rate of growth they sought, Burns and Douglas decided that they would take Confed into three areas about which neither man knew very much: real estate, leasing, and the trust business. Douglas's company-wide influence was extraordinary. With a word or the lack of a word, he could encourage people to reach for the commanding heights of performance or send them plummeting into the depths of paranoia as they tried to carry out ideas that had combusted in his fertile mind.

Corporate development was all about coming up with ideas outside current areas of business, but someone else had to say yes or no and Burns never said no to Douglas. "He was really the president de facto," says long-time officer Frank di Paolo. "To get anything done, you had to go to him." Di Paolo found Douglas "pretty shallow [and] inconsistent with his decisions. He would set an objective today and change it within a week. You never knew where he was going."

Federal legislation was trying to keep pace with the marketplace, allowing insurers to set up subsidiaries and get into lending, trust operations, and other fiduciary services. Douglas was rubbing his hands with glee at the prospects bubbling around him and said, in

---

* Segregated funds, those funds given to Confed for investment management, often by corporations or pension funds, are not included in this calculation, because they are run like mutual funds with their own portfolio of investments separate from the core assets that have been entrusted to Confed by policyholders.

1987, "The additional freedom will mean that the mutuals will do an awful lot that will be higher profile than in the past."

But Douglas and Burns weren't the only ones at Confed who were interested in the high-stakes games that executives play. Chairman Jack Rhind was rooting for them, because he could see that the pair might achieve the expansionist growth that he had longed to carry out. Beyond Rhind, the board of directors were co-conspirators, approving the go-for-broke strategy every step of the way.

During the early eighties, Confed had lunged and lost, bidding on trust companies that were for sale. They concluded that most of the good companies were unlikely to come on the market, so they decided to get on with the desired strategy by building one from scratch. Douglas and Mark Edwards, vice-president, general counsel, and secretary, travelled across Canada early in 1987, looking for a suitable trust-company charter. Getting into the trust business was far simpler if an already-existing but dormant charter could be purchased, rather than having to convince legislators to approve a start-up company.

They finally found what they were looking for in Halifax, Nova Scotia. Halifax Trust Co. was a provincially chartered company that had been established in 1985. Confed bought the corporate shell for $200,000 and changed the name to Confederation Trust Co. in July 1987. The vehicle was in place; now to find a driver.

During their talks with people in the trust business, Douglas had stumbled upon G. Barry Walsh, who was then in Vancouver running Discovery Trust. Discovery was a tiny company with about $150 million in assets. Douglas did not want Confed to buy Discovery (it was acquired by Winnipeg businessman Izzy Asper and became Canwest Trust Co.), but he liked Walsh and recommended that he be hired to run Confed's new electric train.

Burns designated one of his pals, John Heard, senior vice-president, Canadian operations, to be chairman and CEO of Confed Trust. Heard's role was more titular than anything else. "It was like putting me in charge of a fashion show," says a colleague with little clothes-consciousness. "He would have been outweighed by his adversaries." Nor did the four outside directors have an intimate knowledge of real-estate development or running a trust business; they were all lawyers at the Halifax law firm of Stewart, MacKeen & Covert, who, if nothing else, were close at hand. Every quarter, the board of directors met in Halifax, because that was where head office was located, although the company was run in Toronto.

Among Douglas's financial forays were some deals on Confed's behalf with a leasing company, and he liked the entrepreneurial environment he saw in places like that, where employees could own shares. That owner-employee was just the sort of model he had suggested at the Delta strategy session. Unlike the leasing company, the trust company would be a subsidiary of Confed, however, so it could not be structured to offer share ownership to employees. Instead, the annual compensation was altered to reward officers in a different way. No straight salary for them; they would receive bonuses based on the return on equity. Targets exceeded would mean higher compensation. Explains Douglas, "What was to accrue to the leasing-company shareholders as long-run benefits as a result of their shareholdings, in effect was paid to the trust-company employees as short-term cash."

Walsh was hired as executive vice-president and chief operating officer, then he recruited the rest of the crew: James Meldrum, who had worked with a general insurance company for twenty-five years, became vice-president, financial intermediary services, and Charles F. "Chuck" McIlravey, an eighteen-year veteran of the industry, was hired as vice-president, mortgages.

Confederation Trust offered a full range of financial-product services: term deposits, guaranteed investment certificates (GICs), commercial and residential mortgages, Registered Retirement Savings Plans (RRSPs), Registered Retirement Income Funds (RRIFs), and savings accounts. Burns was beginning to make noises about getting into home and auto insurance, too.* By year-end, only six months after opening its doors, Confed Trust had $132 million in mortgages on its books.

---

*   Fortunately, he never did.

As the trust company grew in 1988 to assets of $609 million, more executives were added. Derek Piddlesden was named vice-president, finance and administration, then was promoted to senior vice-president. Confederation Life approved of what Walsh was building. In January 1989, he was elevated to president and named to the board of directors, but others called the shots. "We did everything we were asked to do. We went in the direction they asked us to go with new business, to grow," says McIlravey. "They knew the real-estate exposure they had and they wanted more business. We went out and got it; it was as simple as that."

In this new world there were few rules. When mortgages were put on the books of the trust company, the upfront fees paid by the mortgagee to the company were counted as income; that showed quick profits in the early years. More-conservative accounting, the kind that had been carried out at Confed for a century, would not have been so aggressive. All those fees and high rates generated fabulous returns. By pushing the boundaries in this way, return on equity (ROE) at the trust company kept beating targets. By 1989, only two years after start-up, Confed Trust had $1.1 billion in assets and an ROE of 18.76 per cent, a figure that was better than just about any other financial institution in the county. Of that $1.1 billion, $906 million was in mortgage loans. In 1990, assets jumped another 36 per cent, to $1.5 billion (with 80 per cent, or $1.2 billion, in mortgages). ROE was a healthy 16.4 per cent.

Walsh's annual salary was $150,000, but that's not where the real money was. The riches flowed from the performance bonuses. In 1988, 1989, and 1990, the top four officers at the trust company each made more than $1 million a year – twice as much as Pat Burns himself, who, in his peak earning years, received $500,000, plus a bonus of up to $150,000, depending on Confed's overall performance. In 1991, the top twenty officers at Confed earned a total of $5.7 million, making their average compensation about $285,000 – healthy incomes, to be sure, but a long way from the high-flyers in the trust company. "We allowed them to benefit from short-term activities," admits John Heard. "Their growth generated short-term profit that couldn't be sustained over the long term."

Initially, Walsh moved his family to Toronto, but they didn't like the city, so he moved them back to Vancouver. With head office in Halifax and operations in Toronto, Walsh decided to spend half his time in Vancouver. That was why Vancouver was one of the first Confederation Trust branches to be opened – so he'd have a place from which to operate.

The company paid his airfare as he shuttled between the coast and Toronto, as well as for a $1,000-a-month *pied-à-terre* twenty minutes from the Toronto office. He drove a not-so-new Volvo he'd brought with him from Vancouver. Management meetings were held at Ontario resorts like the Briars or Nottawasaga Inn. Christmas parties were at the middle-of-the-road Board of Trade.

While there may have been little apparent extravagance, however, the allure of high incomes must have been blinding. Right from the beginning, the quantity of mortgages and the return were carefully measured, but little attention was paid to the quality of those loans. The quality issue infected the entire life-insurance company, not just because Confed Trust was a wholly owned subsidiary, but because in many cases a 30-per-cent share of a mortgage loan accepted by Confed Trust would be placed into the life-company portfolio. "Corporate synergy" they called it.

In 1989, the first three retail branches were opened in Halifax, Montreal, and Vancouver as the trust company tried to move away from its reliance on wholesale operations (buying deposits from brokers, or what Meldrum called "second-storey" deposit-taking, because most brokers were in walk-up offices) to a retail operation where customers supplied the low-cost funds that could in turn be loaned out in the form of higher-interest mortgages. By then, fully 84 per cent of deposits were coming from two thousand independent financial agents across Canada, and each of those deposits attracted commission payments. To help make the switch to retail and attract more consumer money, Confed was forced to introduce new daily-interest savings accounts, personal lines of credit, and other lending products.

The firm also tried to build market share by paying higher interest rates than its competitors. On March 29, 1990, for example, when Canada Trust was paying 11.5 per cent and the Royal Bank 11.25 per cent for five-year GICs, Confed Trust was offering a fat 12.25 per cent. Such rates meant that the mortgage portfolio, where those deposits were eventually reinvested, had to be ever more aggressive. The high-cost branch deposit-taking strategy never did pay off. By December 31, 1992, agents were still generating $3 of deposits for every $1 gathered in the branches. Worse, half of all that money from both sources was "hot," sitting in term deposits due in less than one year, ready to move elsewhere for a one-quarter-of-a-percentage-point gain.

Even if the retail strategy had been sound, some of the expansion made little sense. A branch was opened in downtown Toronto, even though the market was elsewhere. The clients sought by the trust company lived in the suburbs, where there was new housing construction and lots of condo towers. But there was a view among the higher-ups that there should be a "flagship" branch, so a 7,500-square-foot street-level branch was opened on the northwest corner of Yonge and Wellington streets, with fine wood panelling and shiny brass fittings. A branch was also opened in conjunction with Confed Life head office at 321 Bloor, and another one in Calgary. Even through the teeth of the recession in 1991, additional branches were established in British Columbia and Ontario, bringing the total to nine.

Because the life company wanted the trust company to grow quickly, Walsh knew he wasn't going to comply by marketing just to individuals or going out knocking on doors looking for business. Right from 1987, the action was in large part driven by a connection with one Toronto-based firm, Reemark Group, which built condominiums and then sold the individual units to investors such as dentists looking for tax-sheltered deals. If Confed Trust had been a car, a turbocharger had just been added to the engine.

Other Reemark buyers had fewer resources behind them than did the dentists. The condo market got so crazy in the late eighties that office clerks were using their credit cards to make down payments, in the full expectation that they'd never have to put up the rest of the money. Someone else would come along to take the condo off their hands, and they'd reap a quick reward. Others loaded up the units with first and second mortgages, fully intending to sell the units as the resale market went higher and take a golden parachute to safety.

For Confed Trust, the potential for trouble lay everywhere, like landmines buried by warring factions who'd long ago departed, leaving behind no maps of the deadly deeds. The individuals involved were often in over their heads. Any market turbulence would mean trouble. Loans were often made for as much as 95 per cent of a unit's appraised value. It didn't take much of a market downturn to drop the actual value below the appraised value. In fact, the appraised value was probably inflated to begin with. The joke in the industry is that the professional accreditation designation, AACI, used by an appraiser, actually stands for "appraisal according to client's instructions." The trust company would lend buyers the money after doing the most modest of credit checks, secure in the knowledge that the condo property was collateral. This was a self-perpetuating soap bubble, where foolish investors who get in early hope they will be reimbursed by the even bigger fools who arrive later.

Reemark was run by Sheldon Fenton, his younger twin brothers, Barry and Brian, and Ottawa lawyer René Gareau. Shelly Fenton was a lawyer who had been called to the bar in 1977, but never practised, then worked for three years at the Canadian Imperial Bank of Commerce (CIBC) before establishing Reemark. In all, the firm was involved in about sixty-five different projects, including subdivisions of single-family homes and tax-sheltered condominium deals in Ontario, British Columbia, and Florida. The Fentons were so smart that they claimed they even knew what not to do. The mistake, according to Barry Fenton in 1990, is "over-leveraging, spreading yourself too thin like Trump or Campeau, or putting all your eggs into one big basket." Confed was doing just that.

Here's how the deals between the Confederation group and Reemark worked. Under Ontario rules covering trust companies, Confed Trust itself couldn't lend funds for construction and development, so that portion of the deal was placed in an affiliated company, Confederation Financial Services. If the going interest rate was 8 per cent, because these were high-ratio loans, the rate was hiked to 10 per cent, plus a 2 per cent fee, so the rate was really 12 per cent, with the resulting profits higher than conventional lending. Says Dwaine Knight, who joined Confed Trust in November 1987 from

Family Trust and saw all the deals in his position as controller, "The higher the rate, the higher the fee, the higher the risk. That's just a rule of thumb."

Once the building was ready to be marketed, Reemark would "splinter" or "fracture out" the individual units for sale. Financing for this step would be done using what's known as "take-out mortgages," which replace the money supplied by the original lender. The law allowed Confed Trust to hold the take-out mortgages. If the going rate for three-year mortgages was 8.75 per cent, Reemark would ask the trust company how much it would cost to drop the rate down to, say, 7.5 per cent, in order to make the unit more attractive to buyers. This is called "buying down the rate." Of course, all Reemark does is hike up the price of the unit enough to cover the buy-down cost. Reemark would also manage the property, find tenants, and guarantee rental income to owners for as long as three years.

As a result, Confed Trust not only gets the mortgage business on its books, but also collects the set-up fees from buyers, and the buy-down payments from Reemark, all of which can be classified as income. "Those were great days to be in the real-estate business," says Shelly Fenton. "They were pursuing business like the other major financial institutions."

Inside Confed Trust, a new corporate culture was fuelled by the excessive profits. At Confederation Life, there was no investment for personal reward, even though there were no hard-and-fast rules, no ethics commissioner to monitor activity. At the trust company, however, officers like Walsh, McIlravey, and Knight thought nothing of buying units in Reemark buildings for personal gain.

John Heard claims he sent a memo to the officers asking them to dispose of any investments they held personally in projects in which the Confederation group was a participant. At the bottom of the memo, he added a handwritten postscript, saying that he wanted the company to be "squeaky clean." Heard didn't like the idea that he had to send such a memo. "Most of us growing up in a Scottish Presbyterian atmosphere just assumed everything would all be above board," he says.

Walsh says he received no such memo. Heard says Walsh assured him that condo ownership ended. In fact, the differing versions about the memo are irrelevant. McIlravey asked for a legal ruling from the secretary and counsel of Confed Trust, Helene Yaremko-Jarvis. She studied the matter and concluded, in December 1988, that there was nothing stoping them from personal investments in development projects.

As a result, McIlravey and his wife, Dorothy, as well as Walsh and Knight, bought condos in Reemark buildings in both Ontario and British Columbia. Like everyone else in that era, they made money for a while, then lost. McIlravey says his biggest benefit from buying the units came from the deductions those investments meant against his income tax.

Beyond the deals, a few favours were doled out, too, like boxes of cheese and wine at Christmas or all-expenses-paid trips. For example, each year Reemark invited forty people – including lawyers, appraisers, and financiers with whom they worked – for three days of golf and tennis in the Bahamas.

But the perks were only one symptom of the disease known as real-estate greed sweeping through Confederation Trust. "They were caught up in the frenzy," says Knight. "They never should have gone that heavily into it, but they did."

Confederation Life might have been able to handle a trust company gone wild, but not in combination with the bloated real-estate investment portfolios elsewhere in the corporate structure. At first blush, real estate seems like just the right kind of investment for an insurance company. After all, policyholders entrust money to such firms on the grounds that they'll be around to pay the death benefit owing decades hence. So companies adopt investment strategies that are similar to the products they sell in terms of duration and return.

Now comes the hard part, matching those liabilities (what's owed to policyholders) to assets (what's owned by the company). The Dickens character Micawber expressed the dilemma precisely when he said, "Annual income twenty pounds, annual expenditure nineteen nineteen

[and] six, result happiness. Annual income twenty pounds, annual expenditure twenty pounds ought and six, result misery." Now, how to achieve that happiness where income exceeds expenditure, not just this year and next, but whenever the liabilities taken on today come due.

The best way to proceed is with a balanced portfolio of investments, diversified across a spectrum of equities, government and provincial bonds, mortgages, and real estate. Said investments should also be spread among the many sectors of the economy, regions of the country, even the different continents.

But everything can't be tied up long term. There are constant demands for cash – right from staff payroll to capital equipment. When creditors get a whiff that a company's hurting, confidence ebbs, and a run can develop, whereby the nimble institutional investor gets out, leaving the little folks holding a bag too small.

When Confed sold a large block of business, like a multimillion-dollar life-insurance policy covering dozens of top executives, Confed needed to match that long-term liability with a long-term asset. There are two basic choices: a bond or a mortgage. If the liability is costing the company, say, 7 per cent annually, and bonds are paying 8 per cent, then that spread of 1 per cent, or 100 basis points, is what pays for overheads, salaries, and profits. Mortgages usually have higher returns than bonds, as much as 150 basis points higher, which means 250 basis points to play with – so there is more money available to cover expenses and return a profit. Of course, the reason mortgages pay higher rates is because the risk is greater. A developer is more likely to default than is a country.

Throughout the sixties and seventies, long before Confederation Trust was even a bad idea in the fertile brain of Bill Douglas, real-estate investment at Confed consisted of a tiny operation located in Vancouver that reported to the mortgage department in Toronto. The West Coast subsidiary, called Denham Place Investments, provided a cautionary tale. In the sixties, Confed had entered into a joint-venture partnership with a Vancouver developer who was building the Denham Place Hotel. When the local real-estate market collapsed, Confed ended up with 100-per-cent ownership. Thus stung, Confed ventured no further into real estate for the next ten years.

By the early eighties, however, institutional memory being as bad as it is, real estate was back in favour. A whole new crop of people thought they were smarter than the previous bunch and couldn't possibly suffer the same sorry consequences. In addition, other life-insurance companies, such as Sun and Canada, were getting into real estate, usually to offer pension-fund clients another vehicle for investment. So, in 1981, Confed established its own real-estate investment department under John Watson, who had joined the company immediately after obtaining his MBA from the University of Toronto in 1967.

The new entity was aimed at the pension-fund business. Corporations and institutions did not want to manage their own employees' pension money, so they were turning to professionals. Life-insurance companies seemed like an obvious place, since they were already investing money for the long haul and, if there's anything a pension manager desires, it's a guarantee that the funds will be there when the pensioner retires.

But that's not the only item on the wish list. What companies really want is a high rate of return on the money handed over for care. That's where the competition comes in. Confed had to offer double-digit returns to pension funds, or it wouldn't even be able to bid for business, let alone beat out someone else. Ownership of real estate provided a route to higher returns, because not only was there the flow of income from the tenants in the properties and the mortgage payments from the developer, but there was also a capital gain as property appreciated in value.

And so the Confederation Life Real Estate Fund (known by the ugly acronym CREF) was born on January 1, 1982, to handle pooled funds for pension clients. By 1984, the fund had grown to $48 million and provided an annual rate of return of 14.28 per cent, sufficient for first-place ranking in the Johnson & Higgins Willis Faber survey of pooled real-estate funds that year.

Confed acquired a variety of holdings, including such properties as the Thomson Corp. tower in Toronto and Place Longueuil, a shopping centre outside Montreal. Real-estate activity also increased in the United States, where a record level of US$58.6 million in mortgage loans was approved and a 50-per-cent interest acquired in a San Francisco office tower. New mortgage correspondents were appointed to nab business in Georgia, Colorado, and California.

In 1985, Confed took a 50-per-cent share in six office buildings in Calgary and Vancouver, including the Guinness Tower in Vancouver. In 1986, CREF added White Oaks Mall in London, Ontario, and the Richmond–Adelaide Complex, a group of four downtown Toronto office buildings. New mortgage-loan approvals were up sharply to $362 million from $172 million in 1985. Foreclosures and mortgages in arrears, however, also increased, to $50 million.

When Confederation Trust was launched in 1987, the appetite for properties and mortgages both for CREF and the trust company became insatiable. Place Longueuil was expanded by 60,000 square feet, and other malls were renovated at great expense. Even the normal British reserve was abandoned. By the end of 1988, after just four years in the business, Confed had amassed a £404-million portfolio of residential mortgages in the United Kingdom.

In May 1989, the Confed group announced its largest real-estate project ever, a 50-per-cent interest in The Portals, a four-phase, $650-million colossus for the east end of Washington, D.C. Plans included 2 million square feet of office space, 125,000 square feet of retail, and the 568-suite luxury Fairmont Hotel. The money was to come out of the corporate surplus account, funds that were supposedly the excess of the company's assets over its liabilities to policyholders. Those funds were meant to be an extra cushion against extraordinary losses. But if a downturn came, real estate was hardly a liquid asset that could be converted into cash for policyholders.

The assets of CREF peaked at $380 million in 1990. Performance of the segregated portfolio from 1983 to 1989 had been excellent, with total annual returns averaging 15.2 per cent. No small feat. The growth strategy appeared to be working.

———•◦•◦•———

As Confed bought up real estate wherever it could, and expanded its staff exponentially, the company's own office space became too limited. By 1985, staff in Atlanta had doubled to 625 and was quickly outgrowing the building erected only three years earlier. A new twelve-storey edifice was planned, with a completion date of 1987.* In the United Kingdom, offices in Chancery Lane in London also were becoming too small for the 300 employees. A new building was erected in Stevenage, thirty miles north of London, and was officially opened in 1988 by Roy McMurtry, Canadian high commissioner to the United Kingdom. So spiffy were the digs that the popular TV mystery series, featuring Colin Dexter's Inspector Morse and starring John Thaw, used it for a filming location. In all, 3,000 employees now worked at the various Confed operations in the three countries, about two-thirds of them in Canada.

Confed had outgrown 321 Bloor, even though the building had been expanded in 1973 and had spilled into three more office towers nearby, as well as a new location in Willowdale, north of Toronto. After all that clambering to the top, Pat Burns wanted to carve something into the corporate totem pole. Even better, why not build an entirely new totem pole, a new building, that would assure his place in corporate history. It was as if he had succumbed to the edifice complex.

For a time, a dozen suburban locations were considered, but word came down from the board of directors to build adjacent to 321 Bloor, since the company already owned land, a pie-shaped piece of property on which was located the staff house and a parking lot.

There was just one problem. Confed intended to raze the staff house for the project, but the building was occupied by a tenant. Not just any tenant, either. The evangelical television program "100 Huntley Street" had been saving souls five times a week from that location since 1977.

Rev. David Mainse had begun singing the praises of the Lord in 1962 via television in Pembroke, Ontario, when he was a Pentecostal pastor at Atomic Energy of Canada Ltd. He moved to Sudbury,

---

* Confed later held a mortgage on the original building, had to foreclose on the property, and ended up owning it again.

Ontario, in 1964, then to Hamilton, Ontario, in 1968, and by 1971, he was devoting his full attention to the electronic ministry on the Global television network. He moved to Toronto and, in March 1977, signed a twenty-year lease on the staff house and began broadcasting in June using the street address as the name of the show.

Within a year, the live show, which features members of the audience and callers-in, was bringing families back together and getting teenagers off drugs right across Canada. The studio was the very room in which Confed annual policyholder meetings had been conducted. The viewing audience regularly topped one million each week.

Confed was delighted to have such an exemplary tenant, especially since the other contender was said to be someone who wanted to turn the staff house into a disco. Mainse was told that he was an easy choice as a tenant, because there was a provision in the Confed charter that prohibited alcohol on company premises. Rent started at $160,000 a year for the 53,000 square feet, but was later cut in half when special laws were passed in the Ontario legislature exempting "100 Huntley Street" from paying property tax.

Despite the long-standing relationship, there was a provision in the twenty-year lease that Confed could terminate the arrangement after fifteen years. So, in 1987, Burns – who parked his car beside the former staff house – invited Mainse around to his office, told him about Confed's building plans, and gave the TV host five years' notice; he was to vacate in 1992. Mainse decided to build, too, and erected a $20-million studio in Burlington, Ontario, although the name of the show was not changed after more than four thousand shows from the previous location.

In the end, staff house was not torn down. Says Mainse, a bit wistfully, "In hindsight, with what happened to real estate, if we'd had the full twenty-year period, we would have just stayed there." But Mainse remains stoic. "I have to believe there is a purpose for us building this new building." Burns could make no such claim. It was as if Confed's guardian angel had been asked to leave so the devil could move in.

Burns invited four local architects to submit designs, and put crony John Heard in charge of the building project. Pat Burns may have been the boss, Bill Douglas the ideas man, but Heard was Mr. Confed.

He'd been around almost as long as Burns; he joined in 1947, and in the fifties had been an outgoing young employee, playing on Confed baseball and basketball teams and participating in staff bowling.

In 1955, when the company moved to Bloor Street, he was the tour leader, the person responsible for acquainting staff with their new home. According to the July 2, 1955, issue of *Clan*, the chatty company publication of the day, during one of those tours "while they were in the security vault, the power failed, and there he was, in the pitch dark, with umpteen lovely ladies!" *Clan* did not report the outcome.

Heard was so rah-rah that, on the occasion of his fortieth anniversary with Confed in 1987, staff in Canadian operations gave him a thirty-foot flagpole for the front lawn of his home. They also tried to find a flag-maker to create a pennant showing a general on a horse holding a standard with Confed colours. When they had no success, they gave him a company flag, light blue with the corporate logo in gold. Heard, who eventually retired in 1992, earned $300,000 a year and was, at the time, probably the highest-paid officer at the life-insurance company after Burns.

There was never any question that the new structure would be grand. After all, it seemed that growth would go on forever. In 1955, when the firm had moved to 321 Bloor from the castellated Romanesque structure on Yonge Street, there were 700 on staff. In 1973, 321 Bloor was extended; by 1984, it housed 1,325. Why, at this rate, there'd eventually only be two classes of people in Canada: those who worked at Confed and those who were Confed policyholders. Better get a-building.

Within four weeks of the initial call for designs, the four architectural firms had submitted their preliminary work. At his first meeting with Burns and Heard, Eberhard Zeidler, of Zeidler Roberts Partnership, showed off his proposal, using what's known as a "massing model," a twelve-inch-high, three-dimensional representation of the buildings, done in white. The design featured four octagonal towers, ranging in height from twelve to seventeen storeys, the tallest topped with a turret. There was even provision for another tower to be added later, a concept that appealed to Burns's sense that unbridled growth would continue well into the next century. The only questions Burns and Heard asked focused on the location of the cafeteria. Zeidler was awarded the contract. The bake-off was over almost before it had begun.

Groundbreaking was on December 4, 1989. Construction would take three years. By the time of the official opening of One Mount Pleasant Place in October 1992, Burns would be on his way out.

Zeidler's firm worked around the world: the Eaton Centre and Ontario Place in Toronto, Walter C. Mackenzie Health Sciences Centre in Edmonton, Place Montreal Trust in Montreal, Canada Place in Vancouver, MediaPark, an urban community on fifty acres in Cologne, Germany, as well as towers and atriums in Philadelphia, Baltimore, Mexico City, Jakarta, Indonesia, and London, England.

Confed was not as sophisticated as the firm's usual clients. "The people we dealt with at all levels were naive about development," says Robert Eley, the Zeidler associate who was project manager in charge of design. The first year was spent in the usual wrangle with the City of Toronto about density and heights. Nothing was left to chance. Drawings were produced, showing how the structure's shadows would fall on the surrounding neighbourhood at three times during the day and at different seasons of the year. The officers played a major part in the eventual look and feel of the edifice. "They were intimately involved in designing the building," says Eley.

The building Burns approved was huge – 456,616 square feet above grade – plus four levels of underground parking, enough for 296 cars. In the glowing words of the design description, the building is "a uniquely Canadian architectural expression firmly rooted in the history of Canada. It evokes memories of our Parliament Buildings and the original CPR châteaux built shortly after Confederation and in essence the very symbol of Confederation. The apex of the site is crowned with a turret, in scale with and reminiscent of the traditional mansions in nearby Rosedale to the north. The base of the office component on the west façade has a grand scale, although still human; the sixty-feet-high base creates a grandeur appropriate to the entrance and 'front door' of this major Canadian head office."

A bridge over Mount Pleasant Road linked the new building with 321 Bloor, using a steel framework ninety-five-feet long and weighing twenty-four tons. In a nod to decorum, the glass in the lower windows was partially obscured, so drivers in vehicles passing underneath would not be distracted trying to peer up the skirts of women tripping along in the passageway.

The cafeteria that Burns had worried about could seat 260. The eight-thousand-square-foot fitness centre featured ten exercise stations, free weights, and an aerobics studio with a sprung-wood floor. The exterior would be clad in three varieties of granite – Carmen Red quarried in Finland, Atlantic Blue from Quebec, and Barre Grey from Vermont. Marble in the lobby was Statuario Venato, white with a grey vein, from Italy. All the marble – exterior and interior – was shipped to be cut and polished in Montignosso, Massa, Italy. The pale-green roof was made of enamelled steel, produced in Hamilton, Ontario.

Elevator interiors were decorated with Swiss pear wood and mirror strips. The reception area on the seventeenth floor boasted a domed ceiling and polished oak floor. Walls and pillars were finished in gold, bronze, and purple. Door fixtures were art-deco stainless steel. The floor housed a conference centre with six meeting rooms to accommodate groups ranging in size from eight to thirty-two people. Dining service was available, as was sophisticated audio-visual equipment.

Even the office furniture and fittings were far from humdrum. The chairs were pomegranate red and foxglove purple; screens were deep-sea green-grey, the carpet a heather blend, carefully selected so that it wouldn't go out of style like the despised orange-and-brown carpet at 321 Bloor. The lobby featured a grand sweeping staircase. Outside, on the street, was installed a thirty-five-foot-high stainless-steel sculpture by Michael Snow, weighing 16.5 tons. It was called "Red Orange and Green," but, in fact, had no colour at all and looked like different trees when viewed from various angles because the piece consisted of three vertical planes.*

---

* Snow had an historic connection with Confed. His great-grandfather, William H. Beatty, was a director when the company was founded in 1871 and was president from 1902 to 1912.

Along a walkway, there was also a commissioned mural, called "Headed Your Way," created by Joanne Tod, that depicted Canada's multicultural society. It was done in two sections, like an open book, and each panel measured sixteen feet wide by eight feet at the outer edge, tapering to six feet in the middle. The mural showed heads of various ages, sizes, and ethnic origins interspersed with Confed logos on a salmon-pink background with a border of fluorescent lighting meant to illuminate the nearby pathway. Sixteen trees were removed to make room for the walkway and were donated to the Metro Toronto Zoo. Pat Burns was building himself the eighth wonder of the world.

As if all that weren't pretentious enough, a time capsule had been installed a year and a day after Burns and Toronto Mayor Art Eggleton had turned the first sod in 1989. The nine-inch-square stainless-steel plaque,* located at the base of a stainless-steel support column rising eighteen feet to the lobby ceiling, reads:

Confederation Life

A time capsule, representing our lifestyles,
interests and concerns was placed here
on December 5, 1990, by

Patrick D. Burns
Chairman
President and Chief Executive Officer

Among the contents of the capsule were predictions by employees of what the world would be like in 2090. Visions included: pollution will be eliminated; one government will rule the planet; computers and robots will run the word; love, peace, concern, and respect will

---

* Heard participated in the ceremony with Burns, but did not get his name on the plaque, so he left his mark elsewhere. He placed a shiny new coin in the wet cement of a curb in the parking garage.

flourish; life expectancy will exceed 120 years. No one, it is safe to say, guessed that at this point Confed's own life expectancy was less than four years. The other items deposited in the time capsule were as banal as they were predictable: the 1989 Annual Report, product literature, a company history and phone directory, a piece of the orange-and-brown floor covering from 321 Bloor, known as "the carpet that everyone loved to hate," photographs of the other new head offices in Atlanta and Stevenage, England, a booklet on AIDS, that day's *Globe and Mail*, Canadian stamps and coins in daily use, a grocery-store flyer showing prices, a ride guide to the Toronto Transportation Commission system, a solar calculator, a few fashion magazines, and, in a nod to Burns's favourite pastime, a Blue Jays program.

Construction cost was $150 per square foot, or about $90 million, including furnishings. "I can't imagine why they built that building," says Adam Zimmerman, former chairman of Noranda Forest Inc., who joined Confed's board in 1990 after construction had begun. He calls it the last gasp of "flying high." In fact, that tower was a mere blink among many blunders. In 1989, as construction was just getting under way, real-estate values were beginning to slide in the United States and Canada. Confed had built its house on sand, and the foundation was beginning to blow away. Worse, from the standpoint of Confed's future, the excessive corporate growth and dumb-headed strategy had finally caught the attention of the regulators. Despite every opportunity to get back on a more conservative course, Confed would undertake even crazier activities in the days to come. The head office, meant to be the capstone of Pat Burns's career, would become, instead, his corporate tombstone.

CHAPTER 4

On Borrowed Wings

"Even a turkey can fly in the wind."

– Anonymous

All these zany goings-on in the trust business, real estate, leasing, and head-office expansion occurred under the very nose of the financial police. In 1987, Michael Mackenzie was named to take over from William Kennett as the chief federal regulator overseeing financial institutions.

Mackenzie seemed like the ideal appointment. "[A]n auditor with long and distinguished experience in the auditing of banks," Judge Willard Z. Estey called him. Indeed, Mackenzie knew all about how loan-portfolio concentration, an expansionist program, and large loans to a few corporate borrowers caused two banks, Canadian Commercial Bank (CCB) and Northland Bank, to fail in 1985. Mackenzie's firm, Clarkson Gordon, was the auditor for both. He also knew the seismic shock those failures sent through the system, even though they "were two small banks which had reached a state of development that had not carried them to national stature by the time of their liquidation." They were so small that they amounted in total to only 1 per cent of the entire banking sector's assets. By contrast, Confed was a major player with a 10-per-cent share of the insurance market.

At Clarkson Gordon, Mackenzie had been auditing financial-services companies like Scotiabank and Citibank. His only direct contact with Confed came in the December before his appointment as regulator. His partner on the Confed audit suffered a heart attack, so Mackenzie filled in for a few weeks. At that point, Confed was in good shape.

Mackenzie was sixty, retirement age at his firm, so the timing of the seven-year term as superintendent was perfect. Mind you, there was a bit of a drop in salary, plus he had to catch up on some tax that had been deferred as a result of being a partner in an accounting practice. Mackenzie's salary in the public sector was $150,000 a year, about one-third what it had been as an accountant. In 1988, he paid more income tax than he earned as a regulator.*

The initial title of the post was Inspector-General of Banks, but with new legislation later that year, his job was widened to make him superintendent with authority over insurance companies, banks, and trust firms. Parliament combined the two previous departments, the Department of Insurance and the Inspector-General of Banks, into the Office of the Superintendent of Financial Institutions (OSFI) and gave OSFI broadened powers. About one-third of the staff worked in Toronto, the rest were in Ottawa.

Mackenzie was given a sweeping mandate for change, because all participants agreed that the previous system had not worked in the case of Northland and CCB. "Everyone fumbled in that situation,"

---

* Mackenzie had to undergo a security clearance, so gave, as requested, the names of three friends for officials to interview. The investigators finally got around to the job in the summer of 1987. One of Mackenzie's friends received a telephone call at 10:30 P.M. on a Sunday and was asked if now was a good time for the interview. He agreed, and an RCMP officer was at his door within minutes. Most of the inquiries were straightforward, such as was Mackenzie a family man, but, as the officer was leaving, he asked one final penetrating question. "Is there anything really odd about Mackenzie's personal habits?" "Yeah," the friend replied, "he eats porridge for breakfast."

said Mackenzie, "from the inspector to auditors to the company officials." As the Clarkson Gordon senior partner in charge of bank audits, Mackenzie himself had signed Northland's financial statements in December 1984, statements that showed a profit when they should have a shown a loss – if conventional accounting practices had been used.

The difference was $5 million, and Mackenzie had tried to persuade Northland to use conventional methods, failed, and got no help from then-inspector-general of banks, William Kennett. Said Judge Estey in his findings, "Kennett left it to management and the auditors for resolution and showed unquestioning relief when this was achieved. In the end, a bargain was struck between management and the auditors which resulted in a reversal [a reduction in income agreed to by management] of $550,000 instead of about $5 million as originally proposed. This left the bank's income statement in a profit position."

"There is nothing to indicate any penetrating inquiry by the [inspector-general of banks] to determine the extent of the differences between management and the auditors," said Estey. "There is not even much evidence of curiosity to determine how such a material issue (profit or loss for the year) could arise so late and be settled so quickly." As for Mackenzie's role, Estey was not much impressed either, saying that his "assistance was illusory."

Mackenzie himself later admitted that he wished he'd done more. "I should have said to [Kennett] to get his ass out to Calgary. I blame myself. My real regret is, I should have told him I wouldn't sign the financial statements until he came out and had a look at the problem. I have a lot of respect for Bill Kennett, but he should have gotten on a plane to Calgary, gone into the bank, closed the door, and said to management, 'Now, what the hell is happening?'"

Mackenzie looked forward to his new role and claimed he wanted to become involved in a public-service role. "It may sound corny," he said shortly after his appointment, "but I really care about this country and look forward to doing whatever I can." In the end, it wasn't enough.

Mackenzie was born in Toronto and raised in London, Ontario. He graduated in 1948 with a BA in honours history from the University of Toronto, and received his Harvard MBA in 1955 and his accounting accreditation in Ontario in 1953 and Quebec in 1969. He joined Clarkson Gordon, the most WASPish of Toronto accounting firms, and ended up staying more than thirty years. Mackenzie also served for years as the chairman of the Palliative Care Foundation, which specializes in care for the dying. He and his first wife divorced. Cancer claimed both his second wife and his father. He is now married to his third wife.

As one of the conditions of taking on the role as superintendent, Mackenzie insisted he work out of Toronto, not Ottawa, where the job had traditionally been headquartered. That meant he was close to the action, since about 75 per cent of the institutions he regulated were within a thirty-minute drive. The location also meant he could continue living near Lake Ontario, outside Cobourg, an hour east of Toronto.

The superintendent has an almost impossible job. The agency regulates 61 banks, 163 insurance companies and fraternal societies, 231 property-and-casualty-insurance companies, and 1,100 pension plans. All this is to be done with a staff of four hundred, only forty of whom are actually on-site life-insurance examiners. The annual budget of $40 million is paid by the financial-services sector through an assessment based on each company's asset size.

In the early going, Mackenzie was gung-ho and knew he needed to cast a wide net for information. "While one can glean some knowledge of financial institutions from the forms they file, you need meetings and street gossip to identify flash points." As a result, he planned close monitoring. "Some auditors of trust companies are going to get a real shock when I ask them to give me a report proving that their trust companies are clean," he said.

In private, Mackenzie was more revealing. In his first round of meetings with the life-insurance board audit committees, he admitted that there were too many companies for him to be able to spot all the problems. He told directors that he was counting on them to be his eyes and ears and tell him when things went wrong.

In public, he constantly preached prudence – and some of his comments were prescient. "Safety lies in a solid capital base to enable a financial institution to take inevitable risks, manage its growth, and withstand shock. Adequate capital combined with good earnings is also essential to raise new capital in the market," he said in a November 1988 speech at the annual-report awards sponsored by the *Financial Post*.

"Safety also lies in good risk management, the holding of a portfolio of assets diversified as to risks and appropriately matched with funding sources. It also involves carrying adequate liquid resources to meet obligations and fund opportunities on an ongoing basis. Banks, trust companies, and life-insurance companies all operate with liability-to-capital ratios of fifteen or twenty to one. This means that even relatively small accounting and valuation errors can have a major impact on the measurement of the capital base.

"It is characteristic of institutions with high leverage that there is a very great reluctance to face and book losses in a timely way. The management of such institutions operates in a pressure-cooker when facing difficulties in the market. There is great pressure to show that earnings stability is very high over time and to avoid sharp fluctuations that can threaten confidence; sometimes there is a temptation to use creative accounting to achieve this." Mackenzie knew what to look for. The question was, would he act when he found it?

Mackenzie's predecessor, William Kennett, had begun to use retired bank credit officers to buttress full-time staff, and when Mackenzie took over the role in 1987, he expanded their use, but he admits now he didn't employ that approach enough. No such similar help was hired for the life-insurance side. In December 1991, when Donald Macpherson, deputy superintendent in charge of deposit-taking institutions, retired at age sixty, Mackenzie's stamina to fight for staff seemed to have diminished. Macpherson was not replaced. The department reduced the number of deputies to two from three.

Kennett had also begun to establish advisory committees of audit partners, and Mackenzie built on that, too, but the committees felt constrained from discussing individual companies for competitive reasons and did not, for example, pass much along about who

Mackenzie should investigate, because that would mean they would be treading on clients or revealing information they regarded as confidential. "They were a little shy on the gossip," he says.

The industry was uncooperative and did not trust government bodies. "The insurance industry doesn't like being regulated. I mean, nobody likes being regulated, but they like it less than the people in the banks, because they felt that they had all these actuarial disciplines." Moreover, a life-insurance company had never failed in Canada, as Mackenzie kept being reminded by the insurance crowd. Mackenzie needed help that he was not getting. "The industry was changing quite dramatically," he says. "We were looking at a moving target."

To make matters worse, Mackenzie found it almost impossible to get a "clean read" on specific companies, based on what they were telling him. "One of the big problems of the actuarial profession is that they hate giving opinions. Accountants come to a point where they have to fish or cut bait and give an opinion. Tell that to an actuary," says Mackenzie.

During the late eighties, high interest rates attracted vast amounts of money into the financial system. There was spectacular growth in deferred annuities sold by life insurers. For life-insurance companies such as Confed, real estate was an easy place to invest that inflow of money, with low administrative costs, fat fees, and low risk, because appraisals tended to balloon value, and high inflation would continue to drive values higher. "It became fashionable – the thing to do – and there was an element of irrationality about it," Mackenzie told the Empire Club in 1993. "Many did not know where else to put the money.

"I do not believe that there were many well-articulated strategies that reflected a real understanding of the risks involved in real-estate lending. Boards may, in many cases, have been inundated with documentation on these loans, but little of this dealt with what could happen if the inflationary assumptions about resale prices and rental rates did not pan out. Construction delays and cost overruns were common, but all too often did not appear to have been factored into loan financial analysis," said Mackenzie.

In 1989, OSFI audited Confed, the first such inspection since 1987,[*] and the regulators began to be concerned about Confed, working with 1988 figures. "We did a risk-based assessment of the company at that time, and there were a number of issues. The most critical one on our agenda was the real-estate exposure, and the process and management controls in place for realistically appraising that real estate. We were somewhat dismayed with what we saw," said John Thompson, deputy superintendent, insurance and pensions sector, a twenty-seven-year veteran of the industry and former vice-president at Canada Life.

Dismayed was hardly the right word. Real-estate exposure in 1988 had reached 71.6 per cent of assets, but they had been high the previous year, too, at 65.2 per cent. OSFI staff relayed their worries about this to Confed, and OSFI pushed Confed up what the regulator calls the "ladder of compliance." That means reporting requirements by the company are increased, examinations are more frequent, directors are informed, and the regulators work with management to make sure there's a business plan that's being followed.

Mackenzie met with the directors of Confederation Life in the fall of 1989. There were two meetings, first a session with the full board, auditors from Ernst & Young (formerly Mackenzie's old firm of Clarkson Gordon), and senior management. A second meeting followed immediately, with only the outside directors attending. The two-step approach was geared to allow outside directors to ask specific questions without management listening, and it was becoming typical of the sessions Mackenzie held with all major financial institutions. "We were starting to get concerned about the investment controls [in both the life and trust companies]. They weren't very good."

The directors, who had spent years playing lap dog to management, did not seem concerned. About the only immediate result of the whole process was to arouse the ire of Pat Burns. "[That's when]

---

[*]   When Mackenzie became superintendent in 1987, life-insurance-company examinations were done only every three years; he changed that to every two years.

Mackenzie and Burns started to dislike each other," says Mackenzie. Mackenzie, however, now admits that he may not have sent as tough a message as he should have. "In hindsight, we should have been a bit stronger than we were. I've discovered that a word to the wise isn't enough. I guess I was a bit naive."

Mackenzie also had an internal problem at OSFI. He worried that he was not getting all the information he needed from his staff. "I walked into a whole tradition in the predecessor offices of the Department of Insurance and IGB [Inspector-General of Banks], where stuff that came up from the field would be muted by the time it got to Ottawa," he says. "It took me a long time to realize the extent to which this was embedded in tradition."

Not that it mattered. No one at Confed was paying much attention, anyway. Burns was flying high in the late eighties. Everything he'd set out do, he accomplished, and OSFI's concerns were dismissed as just so much bureaucratic whining. Assets had tripled during his first four years as CEO. Operating profit had risen to $103 million, a 65-per-cent jump. Since 1983, assets under investment management and revenue each grew at average annual rates approaching 25 per cent. The board of directors had given him his head and weren't about to listen to Mike Mackenzie, especially since he seemed so easy to dismiss. "The board accepted whatever Burns said," said Frank di Paolo, vice-president, financial, who, like other senior officers, had taken turns attending board meetings throughout the eighties. "Pat dominated the board, and the members of the board – except for one or two members who would ask questions – were just passive." Attendance by outside directors was poor; when they were present, most of them said very little.

If there is a moment of hubris when pride cometh before a fall, this was it. History is replete with stories of emperors who become intoxicated with power. Yet, who could stop him? He could fly higher yet. Growth in 1989 was up 30.3 per cent over 1988, compared with Sun's growth of 11.9 per cent and Great-West at 9.4 per cent. Traditional business had never been stronger. The pension division alone in the United Kingdom brought in the equivalent of $1 billion in new business, a record for Confed in any division.

In the United States, there seemed to be no ceiling to the possibilities. There, Confed was into four main areas: individual life insurance; corporate-owned life insurance (COLI) and bank-owned life insurance (BOLI); guaranteed investment certificates; and annuities. New-mortgage approvals that year hit $900 million. Annuity sales in 1989 reached $242 million, up 50 per cent from the previous year. Additional staff were moved from Toronto to Atlanta. Structured settlements (annuities set up to pay court awards or employment-severance deals) were headed for sales of US$1.3 billion and guaranteed investment certificates (GICs) for US$1.9 billion at their respective peaks. Individuals signed up for $800 million worth of policies that year, some of them with sizeable death benefits. Typical was Leonard Davis of Dade County, Florida, who, between 1989 and 1991, bought US$14 million worth of life insurance for himself, his wife, and his family. Annual premiums for Davis ran to US$260,000. All the hot money was headed Burns's way. As for Mackenzie, "Shoo fly, don't bother me."

Burns told employees in a 1990 company publication that Confed had "adopted the goal of being not only the most rapidly growing company in the life-insurance industry, but also that of gaining in size in comparison to other financial institutions." Bill Douglas was right there, too, spurring Burns ever higher. "Moving towards the chartered banks in terms of size is a reasonable ambition," said Douglas. "We're doing it now, and we'll continue to do it in the future. As a company we're doing all kinds of new, different, and exotic things." When he compared Confed to the banks, Douglas liked what he saw, and he was quick to cite figures to prove it. From 1984 to 1989, assets at each of the big five banks had grown as little as 3 per cent, to as much as 47 per cent. During the same period, Confed's assets had ballooned 243 per cent, more than five times the expansion rate of the fastest-growing bank.

"We simply are not who you think we are," Burns crowed in a speech to the Canadian Club of Toronto in January 1990, mere weeks after Mackenzie's so-called warning shot across the boardroom table. "We are not afraid of competition. We are ready to take on the world – which, by the way, includes the big banks."

Then his comments switched from boastful (about his own talents) to derisive (about his predecessors). He noted that, when he joined Confed, the company was active in fifteen different countries, including Cuba, Trinidad, Jamaica, Venezuela, Colombia, Mexico, San Salvador, and Guatemala. "I've never really been able to find out why," said Burns, disdain dripping from his lips. "The more cynical of us believe it was because the then-executives wanted a six-month trip, every year. Others believe that the company's founders were genuinely missionary minded and decided to take the product of life insurance to the unconverted . . . on warm beaches."

This was Burns at his irrational peak. Public presentations by him were rare, and the fact that he mocked those who had gone before him in his own company showed that he lacked both judgement and class. He seemed to be thumbing his nose at those who had kept him down. Now he felt all-powerful. This, after all, was the same man who, in 1984, had worried about Jack Rhind's speech that mildly twitted an industry rival. Six years later, Burns was prepared to call into question the business ethics of his predecessors. Equally important, there was no one around Burns who was prepared to question his views and dampen his excesses.

Burns's biggest blunder was to assume that any success achieved by Confed during the crazy eighties was all his doing and that contrary views were beneath consideration. In the speech, he went so far as to ridicule action he and others in the industry had recently taken to protect people just like those to whom he was speaking at that luncheon. A consumer-protection plan had been developed by the insurance industry, Burns said, "in the very unlikely event their company becomes insolvent." He rattled off a list of real-estate developments that Confed had backed, and pointed with particular pride at Confederation Trust, "which is engaged in a program of opening offices across the country. Its assets now approach $1 billion. Plans call for continued expansion, to provide a full range of trust services, including administration of our mutual funds."

Burns concluded by beating his chest again and declaring, "We are international experts." He cited growth in Britain, saying, "My company's growth is unusual. In fact, I think it's almost unheard of in terms of financial services in the U.K. And I'm proud of this. I'm also proud to admit that our growth and success seem to be quite a surprise to the British, who don't quite know what to make of us."

Although the insurance companies had a long way to go to match the banks, Burns was determined to do just that. At the time, Canada's 169 insurance companies had assets totalling $85 billion. By comparison, the biggest bank, the Royal, had assets of $67 billion. But in the insurance industry, there was brave talk of street-level branches, joint ventures with all and sundry in the financial-services field, and entry into the estate-management business.

That same winter, Burns had been responsible for convincing the members of the Canadian Life and Health Insurance Association (CLHIA) to oppose ownership by banks of life-insurance companies. On another topic, demutualization of mutual companies like Confed, Burns was less democratic. He had decided to follow his own views rather than take account of other association members who believed that demutualization need not be a part of the legislative update planned by the government for 1992. Instead, said a majority of members, the question of demutualization should be postponed until the 1997 review. Burns, representing his views as the industry's, took it upon himself to tell Ottawa that the industry needed demutualization. Burns seemed to think that all that Confed had to do was issue sixty million shares to policyholders and then go out and raise money in the market.

His peers were angered by his misrepresentations. Sun Life's John McNeil was particularly upset and said to Burns, "'Once you've sent out your sixty million certificates, what have you got left to sell?' He really was naive." In retrospect, McNeil has concluded that, "At that point, he knew he was in trouble. That's why he broke ranks and went for demutualization."

Whatever Burns's inner state of mind, his public posture continued to be combative. In his 1990 farewell speech to the annual meeting of the CLHIA in May, when he stepped down as chairman, Burns took some time to denounce the consumer-protection plan that had just been created to mirror the deposit-insurance program at the banks and trust companies that was backed by the Canada

Deposit Insurance Corporation (CDIC). The industry, filled with free-market thinkers, wanted no help from Ottawa. They had argued that any federal plan along the lines of the CDIC, which had been set up in 1967 to protect depositors, would be costly, bureaucratic, and – ahem – unnecessary. In 1989, the provincial ministers responsible for financial institutions ended all the debate and gave the insurance industry an ultimatum. They said that, unless an insurance-protection system were established by the industry, ministers would set one up and the industry would pay.

The Canadian Life and Health Insurance Compensation Corporation (CompCorp) was born three months later, in January 1990, to administer the compensation fund should a company become insolvent. Coverage – for Canadian policyholders only – was up to $200,000 on insurance policies, $60,000 for annuities, and disability payments up to $2,000 a month. The money to do all this would be raised from the industry – but only after someone had gone under.

Allan Morson, former president of Crown Life, was named CompCorp president, and the industry thought that would be the end of it. "A man and his dog," Morson's operation was jokingly called, a reference to the fact that he had no office, no staff, and no likelihood of having anything to do. "It was just to keep the minister of finance quiet and in a corner," says Raymond Garneau, president and CEO of Industrial-Alliance Insurance Co. of Quebec City. The founding chairman for this outfit for which no one saw a need was none other than Pat Burns.

Burns believed insolvency of any insurance company was unlikely. "I call the consumer-protection plan a 'cruel irony,'" said Burns in his CLHIA speech. "With the plan, we are indirectly encouraging the buyer to consider price and return over quality of product. We are flagging a $200,000 limit and creating unease in the mind of the consumer who may now be afraid to buy insurance for more than $200,000 with one carrier. We are also placing the weak financial organization on an equal footing, in a marketing sense, with those companies that have acted prudently and conservatively."

Burns admitted that CompCorp was "a concept whose time had

come," but he didn't cotton to the whole notion of regulators telling them what to do. New rules were coming soon to restrict capital. OSFI was talking about changes in the ratio known as minimum continuing capital and surplus requirements (MCCSR). "There has to be a balance between the safeguards – the MCCSRs – and corporate growth," he said. "OSFI's plans for stricter MCCSRs, higher than those imposed by Comp-Corp, will strangle many companies."

When Burns was named chairman of Confed in May 1990, Jack Rhind stayed on as chairman of the executive committee. Burns now held all three titles: chairman, president, and CEO. The appointment was a sharp rebuff to the regulators for daring to suggest the previous year that there were any problems at Confed under Burns. No weak financial organization this, no need for a CompCorp. Talk about cruel irony.

The only hint of personal concern that Burns gave about the fast pace of growth would come when he discussed business plans for the coming year. He would visit Atlanta every few months and, starting in 1989, his tune changed slightly. "He'd tell us that there was the potential there that we could find ourselves running out of capital," says George Powell, financial vice-president in the United States. "If we continued to grow at the pace we were going, he might have to start putting some constraints on the growth of the United States operation."

But Burns never saw any need to invoke such constraints. When he first mentioned the constraint possibility in 1989, the step was "three years away." When he returned in 1990 and 1991, the message was the same, "Constraints are three years away." The organization continued to meet sales targets. In the three years 1990, 1991, and 1992, as Confed was sailing perilously closer to the edge, the United States continued to sell GICs to unsuspecting clients at the rate of about US$600 million annually.

Burns was so confident of his growth-at-any-cost strategy that he publicly tore a strip off Sun Life's John McNeil at a CEOs conference in Niagara-on-the-Lake, Ontario, in November 1990. As far as Burns was concerned, McNeil had too much capital, wasn't working it hard enough, and was not producing adequate returns. McNeil just shook his head, knowing that an insurance company cannot generate 25-per-cent annual growth forever.

For all Confed's expansion right through the eighties, the company added very few senior people with strengths to handle the new circumstances. Those changes that were made in the senior ranks seemed to be a step in the wrong direction. John Watson, the knowledgeable investments specialist, who'd been elevated by Jack Rhind fifteen years earlier, suddenly executed a lateral arabesque in 1990. His position as senior vice-president, investments, was left vacant, and Watson was put in charge of a new subsidiary as president and CEO of Confed Investment Counselling Ltd.

There, he oversaw research, provided investment management for pension-fund clients, and ran the equity portfolio, as well as those portions of corporate surplus not invested in real estate. His first assignment was to sell off equities, because they required more reserves backing them than some other investments. During the next three years, Confed unloaded about $400 million worth of stock holdings.

With Watson gone, no one was looking at all the elements of investment to see how the strategy was playing across the company. The position remained vacant for a year. One person who was interviewed by Burns for the job said he would only be interested if he could get rid of two people in the department that he didn't want. Burns asked, "Do you know who hired them?"

"No sir, I don't," replied the candidate.

"I did," said Burns, as if that were sufficient explanation why they could not possibly be let go. The prospective candidate was not taken on.

Finally, Barry Graham, who had worked at Confed in the late sixties and left in 1971, was rehired from MONY Life Insurance Co. of Canada as vice-president, investments. "I was struck by how much the culture was the same. I knew most of the senior guys. It was like old-home week," says Graham.

Nor did Confed retain much outside help in the form of consultants to bring other views to bear. "Confed was the most insular of all the companies," says Henry Essert, managing director, William M. Mercer Ltd., Toronto-based advisers to the insurance sector.

The only person who appeared to have any real say about investments was none other than the ubiquitous Bill Douglas, who was rewarded in 1990 with a new title, senior vice-president, corporate development. His tough-guy style remained the same. "Chatting with Douglas was a bit like going into a meat grinder," says Graham. Douglas's preferred management technique was to arrive unannounced at someone's office, then proceed to tell them about the grandiose scheme he'd cooked up.

His conversational gambit often seemed intended to knock the other person off balance. He'd say something such as, "Guess what you're going to do now?" He'd achieve his goals through a combination of the force of his personality, plus the widely held presumption that he spoke for Burns. Even if the recipient thought Douglas had a bad idea, it was usually no contest. There was no time to muster arguments or offer alternative solutions. Douglas would win easily.

"Bill was close to Pat," says Graham. "People sort of accepted Bill acting on behalf of Pat." Even when someone like Tom Pitts – who was himself close to Burns – would say to the boss, "Isn't Bill being outrageous?" Burns would back Douglas. It wasn't always clear whether Burns had previously been aware of whatever cockamamie plan Douglas was promoting or if he were just automatically giving Douglas his blessing after the fact. The timing of Burns's approval didn't really matter, however; throughout the organization, Douglas was always deemed to be acting with authority from the top, as if he were a cardinal carrying out the latest papal encyclical.

"In the mid- to late eighties, the company, and Burns in particular, was influenced by the aspirations for the company as proposed by Bill Douglas," says Roger Cunningham, who as vice-president, human resources, reported to Burns throughout the decade and was a member of the president's advisory council after 1983. "Expansion into financial services was the goal. It was not handled well."

By 1989, 73.8 per cent of Confed's assets were invested in real estate or mortgages, the peak level reached by the company. Douglas, who had force-fed Confed, was now seeing the bloated results. The real-estate market was beginning to sour with Confed's portfolio at a dangerously high level. According to a survey by rating agency Duff & Phelps, holdings in real estate and mortgages at firms of comparable size were 28.5 per cent of total assets at Manulife, 32.1 per cent at Sun, 35.9 per cent at Canada Life, and 42.2 per cent at Great-West. (Great-West had already begun to decrease its portfolio.) No other major firm grew as fast, no other firm relied so heavily on leverage from real estate. The strategy was a mistake: The firm had relied on growth projects, not profitability projects.

All the while he was revelling in such hare-brained schemes, Burns was preaching the importance of frugality and savings. The seventy-six-page booklet given to all new employees opened with a welcome from Burns, then moved to the main message on the next page: "Money is of interest to everyone. For the company, of course, it is a significant consideration. Our business is financial planning. It is important as well that it operates on a profitable basis." Burns would have done better had he followed his own wise words.

Duff & Phelps also supplied another ominous comparison in the 1989 report: debt financing as a percentage of surplus. Again, Confed was way out of whack at 141.3 per cent, compared with the more-conservative Sun Life at 3.5 per cent. The warnings went unheeded. No one was paying attention inside Confed or outside in a world gone crazy. Even in 1991, when Jeff Rubin, deputy chief economist of CIBC Wood Gundy, said that real-estate values would soon fall by 25 per cent, his prediction was met with disbelief and scorn.*

Sometimes, other companies in the same sector can see failures on the horizon, but such clarity is not all that common in the insurance industry. That's because, unlike other sectors, they do very few business deals together, so they don't hear about what's really going on. After Ed Clark, now CEO of Canada Trust, had negotiated the 1988

---

*   In fact, Rubin was too optimistic. By 1994, the capital value of all commercial real estate in Canada had fallen by at least 40 per cent from its peak in 1989. Anecdotal evidence is even harsher. The former Montreal Trust building on King Street West in downtown Toronto was sold in 1995 for $5.8 million. In 1988, the then-owners rejected an offer of $55 million.

sale of Financial Trustco to Central Guaranty Trust, he ran into Senator Leo Kolber and told him, "Central Guaranty will be bankrupt in two years" and listed five reasons, based on what he'd seen up close during the negotiations. Central Guaranty's demise took slightly longer than Clark predicted, but fail it did, four years later.

Even Burns was beginning to question – without changing his mind – how long the good times would roll. "[W]e needed to pause and ask ourselves seriously whether we could continue to finance that growth at the same rapid pace . . . we were caught in the logical but ironic trap of our own success," he wrote in an article published in the fall of 1989 in the University of Western Ontario *Business Quarterly*.

He realized that growth in previous lines of business and new ones meant "we had gradually been consuming our available capital . . . the funds that we deem to be over and above those necessary to meet our obligations and therefore free for developmental investing." The cushion, in other words, had grown thin.

What were the alternatives? Here are the five he looked at, with his responses, which, in many cases, seem flawed.

1. Raise additional capital – but, Burns concluded, Confed's status as a mutual company limited the possibilities. (That's why he had lobbied for demutualization.)

2. Slow the growth – possible but, he said, "unattractive . . . since we felt there was a solution . . . growth is inherently profitable." (A misconception if ever there was one.)

3. Change the direction and move towards more labour-intensive business lines – a non-starter, he decided, because there were too few opportunities, too high a cost, too much potential for staff turnover. (Exactly what there was, he did not specify, but it is hard to imagine there were many real labour-intensive choices in the insurance area.)

4. Less-aggressive investment positions – this looked "like an easy and simple fix," Burns wrote, but Confed's studies showed that taking the same position twenty years earlier would have meant that "the company's capital and surplus position would be substantially weaker than it is." (A less-aggressive posture should not have weakened surplus; other life-insurance companies had successfully followed such a strategy with better outcomes than Confed.)

5. Improve profitability — "the most fertile source of capital improvement would be to wage a concerted effort to improve profitability, not just in the absolute sense, but also by demanding that over time each of our strategic business units produce an adequate return on the capital it employs."

And so, this last possibility became Burns's strategic solution — be more profitable. In other words, do what he'd been doing, only better. Now, how to carry it out?

Burns noted that Confed had been run for twenty-five years using "management by objectives," a buzzword from the sixties that had a grand ring but often simply meant that management divided the company into various "profit centres," set goals, and told underlings to achieve them.

He recognized that the system had a handful of weaknesses. The first: "We almost, but not quite, told them to assume that next year would simply be an extension of what had gone before."

Second, people were getting fed up trying to meet top-down objectives. In some cases, Burns admitted, "managers tried to negotiate the lowest possible objectives so as to appear to be an 'overachiever.'" Third, there wasn't much thought given to outside-the-box thinking. "Managers were locked into growing only within the confines of their business area." Fourth, top management gave little consideration to the views of the troops, and fifth, return on capital in each profit centre received insufficient attention.

Burns also recognized that there were changes in the marketplace. Group plans were growing in importance, baby boomers would want to provide for their own financial needs as well as their aging parents, people were retiring earlier, and those employees in entry-level jobs at insurance companies were straining a system that was struggling with language and training issues. "The greatest challenge for the large employer is to create appropriate reward systems, not the least of which is empowering the individual to have as much input as possible into his or her working environment," said Burns. Finally, government regulations and taxation — the bugbear of all free-enterprisers — stood in the way and meant that "there is too much money chasing too few high-quality investments."

Deregulation of financial services offered solutions or, in Burns's words, "new vistas of opportunity," by building or acquiring "other financial institutions . . . engaging in networking and joint ventures . . . and offering products far different from the traditional." And so the plan became, in addition to better profitability, further expansion into other related financial services, to beat back the banks and to make employees even more entrepreneurial. Burns called his approach a "return on equity philosophy."

So, at the end of the eighties, just when Burns should have been consolidating his position – better yet, retrenching – he decided to ride off in several new directions at once. In Canada, Confed got into leasing. In Britain, Confederation Bank was launched and, in its first year, took in deposits of £62.3 million and created a mortgage portfolio of £410 million. In total, employees now numbered four thousand worldwide, with a further fifteen hundred career and general agents in the field. There were more than fifty subsidiaries.

To climb to the next plateau, Burns needed oxygen bottles, and the Canadian Institute of Actuaries helped him out. The institute had drawn up a set of guidelines to help actuaries navigate through the various assumptions used to set important measurements, such as surplus. Companies could continue to follow the old rules, and many, such as Sun Life, did. That route was more conservative, created less profit, and therefore meant lower taxes payable.

But within the guidelines, actuaries can fudge the numbers. If the company's total liability is $1 billion (the amount of insurance payable if everyone died and all benefits were paid) and the assets available (investments and cash on hand to offset the liability) are $1.2 billion, then the surplus is the difference, or $200 million.

Under the former, more conservative, rules, the $1-billion figure was the result of calculations by an actuary who followed the guidelines and then received approval for that stated amount from the superintendent. Under the new rules, the actuary not only did not require that approval but could also use the most aggressive end of the guideline and arrive at a new liability figure of, say, $900 million. With that same $1.2 billion in assets, the firm now has $300 million in surplus. The "extra" $100 million could be used to fund a leasing company or a bank. This arcane mathematics, understood by too few, would be at the heart of Confed's disaster.

In 1989, weaker companies such as Crown, North American, and Confed "made the best of it," says Frank di Paolo. "They went to the edge of the guidelines provided by the Canadian Institute of Actuaries. They weakened reserves, and that created a fair amount of surplus, which was added to the capital." That "found" money came in handy to fuel more growth. By pushing the actuarial calculations, Burns had a whole new source of capital.

Confed was, in effect, printing its own money. Now, where else to put it?

CHAPTER 5

———◦•◦———

Recession and the
Reemark Connection

"There's not all that much new in the world why financial
institutions fail: bad management, accidents, the world changes."

– Grant Reuber, chairman, Canada Deposit Insurance Corp.

I n the late eighties, while Bill Douglas was pushing Confed into
real-estate investments and the trust business, he concluded that
those initiatives weren't enough. He wanted to add leasing to the
financial services in which Confed was involved. If Confed were
going to become a bank, figured Douglas, it needed to be all things to
all people.

Douglas wanted Pat Burns to be an entrepreneur, ready to embrace
new ideas as soon as they were offered. At times, Burns frustrated
Douglas; he wasn't always willing to move as quickly as Douglas
thought he should. By 1986, Douglas had spotted just the kind of go-
getter he wished Burns had been: Steven Hudson. Hudson had
started his professional career as an articling student at Clarkson
Gordon in the mid-seventies working on his CA. Hudson and several
colleagues would gather over a couple of beers, talk about the financial-services companies they were seeing, and try to predict where the
sector was going. Firms in the United States were beginning to carry

more-diversified assets on their books, but most Canadian companies were conservative and hadn't sought out new areas in which to earn investment income.

The young bucks could see that Canadian firms were way behind in seeking replacement investments for the more usual three-to-five-year mortgages or fifteen-to-twenty-year mortgages. Commercial and industrial loans held out possibilities. Aircraft and locomotives, for example, with their long and useful lives, made them particularly suited to twenty-year term loans.

Hudson did not want to spend the rest of his life as a CA. He failed the exam twice before passing and saw the professional accreditation only as a stepping-stone. Before he finally made the grade, he'd taken a year off from the firm to work, earn money, and study for the exams. His role during that 1980-to-1981 period was assistant treasurer at Toronto General Hospital. There, he saw firsthand the financing needs of such institutions and matched that with his knowledge of the life-insurance business. His bright idea was to be the investment broker who found long-term money for hospitals.

In 1984, Hudson put a $180,000 mortgage on his home, gathered some more seed money from friends, and launched Healthcare Group to act as just such an investment broker. He paid himself a salary that totalled only $32,000 during the first two years. The first deal he did was to find the funds for magnetic-imaging-resonance equipment and the structure to house it, worth a total of $15 million, for Toronto General Hospital.

Hudson had worked with the team of auditors who did the Manulife books, so he knew the business. He had sold the idea of that first loan to Canada Life in 1983 by talking to them, finding out what sort of long-term deal they'd be interested in, then going out to find it, acting like a broker.

But there's more than just commission involved. The leasing company finds a client like Toronto General willing to pay, say, 10-per-cent interest for a loan, sells it at 8.8 per cent (this is known as securitization) to institutional investors, then the leasing company pockets the difference, 1.2 per cent. As brokers, they also charge an annual management fee. On a $10-million loan, the upfront fees are

$200,000 (minus overhead costs to do the deal), plus a $38,000 annual management fee.

"He had a vision beyond any of the rest of us," says Colin Grant, a Glasgow-born CA who was Hudson's chief financial officer from 1991 to 1994. "Whereas the rest of us might see a year down the road, he could see five years, ten years. He was driven to be successful, to impress people, as he does."

In the early years, Hudson handled financings for Aerospatiale, CSX Transportation Inc., Burlington Northern Railroad Co., and Hydro-Quebec. Beginning in 1986, Confederation Life became Hudson's main source of funds for the Healthcare Group. Hudson's first contact at Confed was Bill Alexander, who worked in the investment department under John Watson. Hudson soon came to Douglas's attention, and Douglas decided that he liked Hudson and the business so much that he wanted to extricate himself from Confederation Life and climb aboard the leasing express. "I thought it was a step forward to move into the leasing company, where I could have more influence," says Douglas. "That was a plan that was agreed on a long, long time before it was implemented." Meanwhile, he turned on the money taps, so Hudson was sure to succeed.

As part of that strategy, Douglas convinced Pat Burns to buy into the leasing company and, in 1989, approached Hudson seeking "preferred access to the Company's financings." Confed bought a 51-per-cent interest but agreed "to leave control over the Company's allocation of capital, sourcing of additional funds from third parties and day-to-day operations with the founding employee shareholders. Furthermore, certain fundamental matters, including the payment of dividends, the raising of capital, and changing the nature of the business and of the Company, could not be made without the consent of the employee shareholders." Confed directors appointed to watch over proceedings were the usual, Bill Douglas and John Heard.

Hudson couldn't have been treated better. He got an assured source of funds and stayed in charge. The arrangement was unusual; few entrepreneurs can bring in a majority owner without giving up control. Moreover, Hudson was allowed to deal with Confed's competitors. In 1989, when the deal was consummated, the leasing company assets were a relatively modest $101 million. By 1991, with Confed money flowing in, Hudson had six offices across Canada and total assets of $613 million.

Leasing had now become part of Burns's second-stage-growth lift-off. The name of Hudson's company was changed to Confederation Leasing Ltd., then Douglas further hiked the life-insurance company's involvement to 71 per cent by acquiring treasury shares and buying out some of the original venture-capital backers. Hudson retained a 12-per-cent ownership stake, and Douglas was dealt into the game with a 5-per-cent interest, even while he retained his day-to-day role at Confederation Life.

To Hudson, Douglas was fair but tough. "Every time I looked to him for capital, I got diluted down. At least with Bill, I knew what the box was up front. I knew the cost of going back and asking for it. I knew that every time you walked in and asked for something, there was always a cost to it. He was dispassionate. [He'd say,] 'There's the deal, if you don't like it, then don't grow.' He's not long in personal skills."

The leasing company moved to 321 Bloor, on the eighth floor with the trust company, as if they were both high-flying birds of a feather that should be housed together. Although Hudson had little to do with the trust company, it did strike him as odd that such a growth-oriented place was structured as it was, with no ownership and a fat bonus system. "They had a compensation scheme that appeared to 'incent' volume. Without money at risk and without a compensation agreement scheme that claws back for bad things or unexpected things – that was unusual," says Hudson.

If Hudson was mystified by the trust company, the corporate culture of Confed Leasing really confounded the old-line Confed crowd. The leasing company employees not only had their own kitchen and coffeemaker, there were free cookies and a microwave. Hudson not only headed a hot shop, he had a hot plate, too. In the rest of corporate Canada, such facilities might be commonplace, but at Confed, every-one was expected to use the cafeteria. Not the new crowd.

With Confed's vault at its disposal, the Hudson empire grew apace. Half a dozen subsidiaries were launched, all domiciled in Barbados, where international businesses that did not trade locally were exempt from paying certain taxes. The Barbados leasing office put a lot of business on the books quickly. By 1991, deals with Ontario Express Ltd., Continental Airlines, and Federal Express included twenty-seven aircraft worth $197,249,000.

Another Confed subsidiary was Confederation Client Services Inc. (CCSI), set up in the offshore Barbados location to handle dental and health claims for its clients. It grew to look after 30 per cent of the group life- and health-insurance business, about 1.2 million claims a year. Cost savings over running a similar clerical operation in Canada were an estimated 50 per cent, but there was another attraction – Highlands House on Sandy Lane – a luxurious former six-bedroom inn purchased for $2 million for "R&R." Officials could combine visits to check on CCSI and the leasing operations with a holiday.

Heard, the life-insurance man who served as chairman of Confederation Trust, claims he never did understand the Barbados operations. When the talk turned to these subsidiaries, he was the first to admit that this wasn't a world in which he was knowledgeable. Heard twice asked Burns to replace him on the board, but Burns refused, saying, "Who am I going to put in your place?" "We were not blessed with a lot of talented, broad-knowledge business people," says Heard.

In fact, the leasing business was amazingly simple. With Confederation Life as a sugar daddy, there was a conveyor belt of funds coming in the back door. The leasing company marked up the money, then shipped it out the front door to be used by clients wanting to acquire trucks, hydro stations, locomotives, airplanes, and other hard assets. As the leasing business grew, so did Douglas's favouritism. "The call for funds was coming from a variety of different sources. Bill Douglas was the arbiter of who got what. He was in an awkward position. One always assumed at Confed that people would do the right thing and not take advantage of any situation. The opportunity for conflict certainly existed," says Heard.

By 1993, Confed had ploughed $699 million into the leasing company, more than one-third of the total $2.1 billion raised from twenty financial institutions, corporations, and pension funds.

Employees were hard-pressed to keep up with Hudson's exhausting pace. He was particularly attached to his son, Cameron, from his first marriage. That relationship became important to his employees. Colleagues used to look forward to what they called "Cameron weekends," when Hudson had custody of his son and would disappear from the office to pick him up about 4 P.M. While he was thus occupied, staff would be less likely – although it still happened – to field telephone calls from the workaholic Hudson and be urged into action.

Hudson had left his wife to marry his secretary, who, conveniently, bore the same name, Sharon. Sharon II quit her job in 1991, and they were married in 1992. He ensconced her a Toronto dwelling that cost him $2.3 million, plus more than $1 million for renovations. The stag party before the wedding was a roast held at SkyDome Hotel to raise money for charity. Senior officers who were expected to speak at the event worried in advance about how far they should go with their remarks.

They needn't have bothered. For Hudson, it was a no-holds-barred occasion. Craig Dobbin, founding chairman of CHC Helicopter Corp., of St. John's, Newfoundland, and a Confed Leasing client, sent word via telegram that he would donate $1,000, but would double the ante to $2,000 if Hudson would drop his trousers. Hudson gleefully mooned the assembled throng.

<hr />

No amount of hijinks could mask the impending problems in Confed's burgeoning interests, however. While Pat Burns was building his financial-services empire block by bigger block, the economic environment was changing from cruise control to crash landing. By 1990, the recession had arrived in Canada and the United Kingdom. The downturn had a severe impact on an overloaded Confed. The U.S. economy fared better; individual insurance sales there in 1990, for example, were up 54 per cent over 1989. Overall, however, premiums and deposits in 1990 were up only 4 per cent – a sizeable fall-off from the 22-per-cent to 25-per-cent increases during each of the previous five years.

When recession arrives, life-insurance companies are among the first businesses to feel the hurt. Sales of policies collapse; few new employee-benefit plans are purchased and existing business shrinks as companies cut back; long-term-disability claims increase as unemployment rises; competition for investment dollars results in less-predictable margins; profits suffer because of falling real-estate prices; non-performing loans skyrocket as mortgage holders miss payments or walk away from properties; rental income drops as vacancy rates rise.

Confed was feeling every one of these symptoms. The real-estate market began turning for Confed Trust in the last half of 1990, when new business volumes dropped compared to the final six months of 1989. A pause was long overdue. The company's commercial and residential mortgage business had doubled every year since the founding of the firm three years earlier. Half of that lending was concentrated in Ontario; another 30 per cent was in British Columbia. Now that the end was in sight, the regulators had begun to take notice of the trust company. At last.

Where had the watchdogs been? The Canada Deposit Insurance Corporation (CDIC) has a vested interest in all deposit-taking institutions, but only from the point of view of backup insurance. The CDIC was created in 1967 after the failure of British Mortgage Corp. and provided $20,000 coverage per depositor. The amount was increased to $60,000 in 1981 and has remained unchanged since.*

The CDIC thought every trust company should have separate operations and not rely on a parent company. "Every tub on its own bottom" is the way Grant Reuber, CDIC chairman, likes to describe his preferred structure. And the CDIC was watching Confed Trust. "[A]s far back as 1988, this institution was embarked on policies and practices that, generally speaking, were doubtful," says Reuber. The

---

* In fact, taking inflation into account, $60,000 today is worth about $10,000 in 1967 dollars, so the protection is now about half the original coverage.

important thing is to deal with matters early, "before you get a load of these loans on the books that no one then knows what to do with. There is quite a bit of bias in the system, it seems to me, for everyone to give the benefit of the doubt, to hope that tomorrow things will be better."

But things don't always get better. The CDIC does have early intervention powers and the capacity to aid struggling companies. Companies in the deposit business, like Confed Trust, can still be solvent but not be meeting the standards required, and, in such a case, the CDIC can make a loan, or guarantee a loan, that provides liquidity support. The CDIC chose to make no such loans to Confederation Trust. No help there.

The CDIC has no powers of examination, and that's where OSFI comes in. Except for that one meeting with the board, OSFI hadn't been very active, either. Instead, it was the Ontario Ministry of Financial Institutions (OMFI) that first caught wind of Confed Trust and didn't like the odour. Confed Trust was chartered in Nova Scotia, but that province had no regulators, so ceded the role to OSFI. OSFI, however, seemed to be paying little attention, and it was Ontario superintendent Brian Cass who first got on Confed Trust's case, beginning in 1990.

Cass is a lawyer, and was called to the bar in 1972. He worked in the Attorney General's Office on lending, industrial development, and insolvency until June 1988, when he was named superintendent of OMFI. At the time, Ontario was supervising about seventy-five financial institutions, including Confederation Trust. The Nova Scotia charter was irrelevant to the Ontario regulator; any deposit-taking institution doing business in Ontario came under OMFI scrutiny. That meant Confed Trust, but not Confed Life.

Cass first became concerned in 1989, when he heard that development mortgages for building construction were being placed into an affiliated company, Confederation Financial Services (CFS), run by Chuck McIlravey, who had left the trust company in 1988 and signed a contract with the life company as senior vice-president, lending, at the affiliate. Many of the projects being funded by CFS involved Reemark. In those cases, once the condo building was completed, the take-out mortgages, the ones held by the individual unit owners, were put onto the trust company's books. Cass saw the arrangement as one set up simply to feed deals into the trust company at favourable terms. "They took the aggressive position that it was okay and didn't bend any rules. I took the opposite view," says Cass. "I didn't want an affiliate to market some real-estate properties and potentially dump take-out mortgages on these buildings into a trust company. I thought that that verged on self-dealing, that they were using their depositors' money to aggressively develop real estate."

Cass assigned his most experienced examiner, Bill Vasiliou, to the case. On January 25, 1990, Cass and Vasiliou met with Heard, Douglas, and Walsh to express their concern. The Confed attitude was confrontational, a posture that Cass found unusual. "The whole thing took me very much by surprise, because constantly the company would remind me that Confed Life was a world-class life-insurance company which had operated in this country for [more than one hundred years], and they knew what they were doing," he says. "It was quite surprising to me, not having dealt with life companies before, that they were so aggressive. Douglas and Heard were saying, 'We're responsible for these people. We're managing it, and you shouldn't doubt our ability to do this properly.'"

Cass had seen aggressive behaviour in his dealings with Financial Trust, the troubled company that had been acquired by Central Guaranty in 1988, and now here was staid old Confed Life coming on just as hard. Douglas wrote to Cass in a letter dated March 14, 1990, putting Confed Life's side in writing: the strength of the company, the history of Confed Life, his refusal of OMFI's request to examine Confederation Financial Services, and the need to run the business the way they did because of competitive pressures. (In fact, no other life company was organized like this.)

The debate continued through the spring. At a meeting in June with the regulators, Confed Life presented legal opinions it had received, stating that the activities of Confederation Financial Services and its relationship with Confederation Trust were all aboveboard. "It was difficult to grasp how a big life-insurance company that was getting into another pillar of the financial services could be so far off base," says Cass. "It was hard to believe a big life company was conducting itself in this way. I was questioning my own thoughts and concerns."

Confed suggested a corporate restructuring, but Cass refused, saying he wouldn't even look at a reorganization until loans to the affiliate were halted. "We were absolutely adamant that we were going to enforce our related-party rules," says Cass. The practice was finally stopped in January 1991, effective the end of December 1990. Confed agreed that, if CFS had supplied development financing on a building, then Confed Trust could not give mortgages to individual owners in the same building. "Big deal," says McIlravey. "By that time the market had crashed. We stopped lending in the spring of 1990."

But the more serious problem with Confed Trust was not yet visible to the regulators: concentration of assets in Reemark proper-ties. Ontario loans and trust legislation says that no one company can account for more than 1 per cent of a trust company's assets. Confed Trust was way over the line. By 1991, it had a total of $959 million in residential and commercial loans; more than half of that was with Reemark. The exact total was invisible to regulators, because the loans were in so many places, including mortgages to individual condo unit owners.

In addition to the concentration issue, Reemark was teetering. Buyers suddenly weren't quite so committed. "The real-estate market reflected the impact of the recession in 1991," says Reemark's Sheldon Fenton. "Prices were dropping, and people were trying to get out of deals."

Bill Douglas rolled up his sleeves and tried to do workouts on forty-six projects worth $500 million that were, in the parlance of the trade, under water. "My objective was to get the greatest asset value in Confed's hands as we could," says Douglas. "Where we had a mort-gage on a property, to get that property transferred into Confed's hands without a legal dispute and – also where there was value being contributed by the Reemark folk in terms of management – to have the benefits of that management continue."

"All you can do at that time is make sure that you have legal title to everything – which is a challenge in itself – and then that each property is managed as well as it can possibly be managed in the circumstances that you now face," says Douglas. "But you can't cause an economic or property recovery when there isn't one there. In many cases, you might be willing to sell at a giant loss, but if there's no buyer . . . by 1990, 1991, the commercial real-estate market in Canada was so bad."

The Ontario regulator knew nothing about the Reemark work-outs. Non-performing loans weren't showing up yet on the monthly statements that Confed Trust was required to submit to the Ontario regulators. Such bad loans can take up to eighteen months to appear. In this case, many of the deals were done using limited-partnership arrangements. A purchaser would buy a unit, take out a mortgage, then rent the unit to a tenant, using Reemark's property managers. In order to get the sale, Reemark would guarantee income from the unit for a certain period. As a result, the loan wouldn't be in arrears.

Other trust companies were beginning to blow up. Standard Trust collapsed in April 1991, the first of a string of trust companies to go bankrupt, and regulators began to worry about the rest.*

Finally, in June 1991, Confed agreed that OMFI could examine the books of Confederation Financial Services, and Vasiliou was sent in. "When he saw Reemark and Fenton and those guys, he understood what these deals were," says Cass. Non-performing loans were now beginning to appear on the books. In January 1991, the total mortgage portfolio was $874 million, with 5.85 per cent of loans non-performing (no payments for more than sixty days). The figure rose all year. By December, non-performing loans reached 26 per cent of the total mortgage portfolio of $945 million. About one-quarter of the company's mortgage assets were not only generating no income, but there was little likelihood they would produce any income for the foreseeable future. The situation could only get worse. Non-performing loans over thirty days were 37.27 per cent of the portfolio – or about $350 million – and more than half of the problem loans were with Reemark.

---

* The CDIC paid $1.2 billion to Standard's insured depositors.

Non-performing loans bite two ways. There is lost income, but there is also drag on future earnings; the company is still paying interest to policyholders or GIC holders or whoever gave the firm the money that's been invested in the bad loan. Confed Trust couldn't even bail out. No one was buying empty condo buildings; no saviour was likely to come down from the heavens. "Confederation Life invested more heavily in real estate at a time that unfortunately turned out to be the top of the market," says Sheldon Fenton.

The image of Confed Trust had long since plummeted in the industry, besmirching the life-insurance company along the way. They were a laughing stock, notorious as the lender of last resort, the place that would agree to loans – even risky construction loans to developers at floating rates – that other lenders would shun. Confed Life investment vice-president Barry Graham received a call in early 1991 from a friend who'd had dealings with Confed Trust. "I want to ask a question," the friend said. "I wondered if they're dishonest or stupid."

"None of us had enough experience to know what would happen in a downturn. When the downturn came, we got caught," says Heard, who was by then cruising towards retirement. A bout with prostate cancer kept him away from the office three months that year.

Douglas blames the trust-company officers for the mess, claiming that he was too busy at the leasing company to pay daily attention to Confederation Trust. "Even today, I couldn't tell you whether they were improperly motivated or just over-ambitious." says Douglas. "There was enough incentive in those dumb contracts that you don't need a kickback to do stupid things if you're motivated by them. In other words, the contracts in the trust company were themselves sufficient incentive to do risky transactions."

OMFI met monthly with the CDIC and briefed officials about its concerns regarding Confed Trust. The CDIC, in turn, kept OSFI posted. At OSFI, Michael Mackenzie used different tactics than Cass. Whereas Cass liked dealing with management, Mackenzie preferred appearing before the board. "I didn't disagree, he's much more senior than I," says Cass. "I sort of worked backwards on this. The depositors are at risk; fix it up. The directors have to be involved in that, but here's the problem and you've got to fix it. We would specifically identify a problem and say [to management,] 'It's got to be fixed.'"

By 1990, OSFI realized that there had been further deterioration. It applied a system called CARAMEL, an acronym for the seven areas examined: capital, asset quality, reinsurance, actuarial reserves, management, earnings, and liquidity. There were problems in most of the seven areas. OSFI despaired of a turnaround short of a market upswing. "It was too late to find a resolution to the specific issues the company was facing," says OSFI's John Thompson.

The industry was also beginning to twig to Confed's overall problems. The April 1990 issue of the *Insurance Forum*, an American trade publication, ran a list of ratios of delinquent and foreclosed mortgages compared with net worth. The magazine measured fifty-four American and Canadian companies, using 1988 financial filings with regulators in the United States. Only six companies were cited as having poor ratios; Confed was among them.

Mike Rosenfelder, vice-president, corporate actuarial and finance, had an explanation: the publication had misunderstood Confed's filings. In a memo dated March 27 to W. T. Knechtel, marketing vice-president in Atlanta, Rosenfelder wrote that *Insurance Forum* had devised the net-worth denominator of the ratio by figuring out "the difference between United States assets over United States liabilities, a figure which has no meaning and is not stable." He did not mention that all the other companies' net-worth denominators were also decided in the same manner.

A bond-portfolio analysis giving poor marks to Confed was also done in an erroneous manner, claimed Rosenfelder, because the filing on which the analysis was based does not differentiate between investment-grade and junk bonds. "The *Insurance Forum* analysis assumed that they were all non-investment grade, or 'junk,'" wrote Rosenfelder. "This is frequently a reasonable assumption, but because of an investment system problem in coding or compiling this data, we included a mixture of investment and non-investment grade." Oops. Done properly, argued Rosenfelder, Confed would have been in line with the best. As arguments go, citing sloppy filings with regulators doesn't seem like the best place to turn. Any port in a storm.

The trust company wasn't the only place where real-estate values were causing trouble for Confed. Until 1990, the Confederation Life Real Estate Fund (CREF) was healthy and paid excellent returns to both the parent company and its pension-fund clients. But, from 1990 to 1993, the equity value of the CREF portfolio of thirty-nine buildings fell by one-third; the average appraised value of the properties went from $208 per square foot at December 31, 1989, to $129 per square foot on December 31, 1993.*

CREF dealt with clients in a manner that was different than most of its life-insurance rivals.† Most life-insurance companies would buy a property, maintain full ownership of the property, and designate the cash flow and increasing value to one pension-fund client. Instead, Confed gathered all of its buildings together in one fund, then sold pieces of that fund. As a result, CREF would buy, say, three apartment buildings in Saskatoon, share some of the income and asset value with the parent company, then place the other half of the ownership in the pooled fund to be shared by all pension-fund clients. The theory was that even a small-potatoes client could share in a collection of Class A investments.

The strategy worked in good times, but only as long as there was new money coming in. In that regard, the system functioned rather like a mutual fund. A lot of little people give their savings to a mutual-fund manager, who in turn buys stocks in the market. As clients change their strategies, some want out. In a good market, that's no problem, because new money coming in usually provides more than enough cash to cover redemptions.

But when the economy turns sour and market values fall, the

---

* The portfolio included such Ontario buildings as Airway Centre, Mississauga; Consilium Complex, Scarborough; York Mills Centre, North York; the four-building Richmond–Adelaide Complex, Toronto; the forty-six-storey Canterra Tower, Calgary; the three-tower British Pacific Buildings, Vancouver; and shopping centres, including Toronto's Hazelton Lanes, Edmonton's Eaton Centre, Lime Ridge Mall in Hamilton, Ontario, and Place Longueuil, Montreal.
† Typical clients included such firms as Rio Algom Ltd., Syncrude Canada Ltd., Hoechst Canada Ltd., and Digital Equipment of Canada Ltd.

strength of cooperative ownership disappears. There is no new money, and there is only the declining value of the holdings. Clients panic; they want their money out. For the first part of the slide, Confed was able to meet requests by CREF clients for redemptions, but as requests for redemptions increased, the dilemma grew. A 100-per-cent interest in a lot of little properties would have allowed Confed to sell those properties into a declining market, take its lumps, and move on, at least having raised some cash to satisfy departures. But, if a property is worth $20 million or $50 million (as many of Confed's were), there are few buyers.

Worse, most of the ownership arrangements were so complex, no sale was possible even if there were a buyer to be found. For example, a half-interest in the Richmond–Adelaide Complex had been sold to a group of investors led by Royal Trust. Royal Trust in turn sold off half its 50-per-cent interest to other investors, including Confed. Confed thus had a 12.5-per-cent interest in the four buildings, then made matters worse by splitting that interest so that the parent company had half and CREF had half. The net result was that CREF's 160 pension-fund clients all had a piece of a 6.75-per-cent interest in the Richmond–Adelaide Complex.

Because Confed had aggressively climbed into real estate through-out the eighties, the firm dealt with just about every developer in Canada.* Developers are imaginative beasts, with vision and property (or maybe just an option), and usually lack only one thing: money. The good news was that Confed was looking for long-term invest-ments, so there were lots from which to choose. The bad news was that doing business with anybody and everybody meant that Confed got into bed with a few losers.

The aggressive approach was urged by two sources. First, there was the marketing group at Confed that was selling pension-fund management services and wanted high returns, so they could show how much better Confed was than the competition. Second, the

---

* Except for a few firms, such as Olympia & York and Bramalea, that didn't need to go to the broad market because of bank ties.

clients would also complain if they saw that there was too much CREF money sitting in cash. They wanted it at work in the market.

Confed's frenzied activity was bound to cause trouble. Beginning in 1986, Confed took an interest in four Toronto buildings known as York Mills Centre. Costs were $190 million; in 1993, their appraised value was only $86 million. Confed went from being a lender with secure mortgages to an owner with little income and no prospects. Says developer Martti Paloheimo, "They had a reverse Midas touch. That's when everything you touch turns to . . . not to gold, put it that way."

Other investments were also coming home to haunt Confed. In December 1993, after investing US$70 million of its share in the early phases, Confed became sole owner of The Portals in the Washington, D. C., market that was supersaturated with such space.

Another of the many mistakes was Hazelton Lanes in Toronto, meant to be Canada's answer to Bond Street or Rodeo Drive, a collection of shops with no major department-store anchor to draw traffic, just *haute couture* names. The original concept was created in the seventies by a trio consisting of architect Boris Zerafa, developer Richard Wookey, and Gerard Louis Dreyfus, the great-grandson of Leopold Louis Dreyfus, the Alsatian farmer who sold grain in Switzerland and founded an international trading empire. By 1977, Dreyfus became the sole owner of Hazelton Lanes. He had the clout to muscle in such tenants as Davidoff, Turnbull & Asser, and Courrèges.

The eighties, the decade that celebrated conspicuous consumption, made this development look even glitzier. So, in 1986, Confed went in with York-Hannover Developments Ltd. to buy Hazelton Lanes, with its fifty-five upscale stores and fifty condos, for about $40 million from Dreyfus. The new partners immediately set out to spend another $60 million and expand the retail space by one hundred shops in order to attract more drawing-card names like Yves St. Laurent and Valentino. Construction of seventy-one luxury condos was also launched, to be ready for occupancy in 1989.

York-Hannover's driving force was Karsten von Wersebe. Born in Germany, he had studied at McGill University in the sixties and joined Metropolitan Trust in 1968, where he saw firsthand the flow of funds coming to Canada from Europe, looking for long-term, stable returns that were taxed at rates as low as possible.

In 1973, he set up Polaris Realty so he could handle that furtive money himself. He managed people's affairs with a combination of Old World charm and a manipulative business technique that involved a series of self-financing development projects. Each compartmentalized company was allowed maximum financial leverage and mystery. "Canadians have never understood how it worked," von Wersebe once said. Confed never had a chance.

By 1989, retail rents at Hazelton Lanes were an astronomical $60 per square foot. Luxury condos, set to open the following year, had already doubled in price from the first offering in 1987. Speculators, not interested in the completion date nor in actually occupying the units, were making money, flipping the residences before construction was even finished.

York-Hannover was also busy elsewhere, sinking $150 million into the two-hundred-store Eaton Centre in downtown Montreal. In 1989, von Wersebe bought Winston's, the élite Toronto watering hole where the correct table mattered as much as the cuisine. There were also plans for a twin-tower World Trade Centre with 1.5 million square feet of space near Toronto's waterfront.

But the end was nigh. York-Hannover was stretched even more than most developers. To satisfy the greed of German and Swiss investors, von Wersebe invested their money in high-yielding second and third mortgages. When the crunch came and the Canadian property market fell, cash flow from properties shrank and returns to investors evaporated. By 1992, York-Hannover had no cash flow to make mortgage payments, and Confed became the proud owner of 100 per cent of Hazelton Lanes, which was then worth less than Confed's initial investment.

In March 1992, a banking group led by the Bank of Montreal seized the Montreal Eaton Centre and, soon after, York-Hannover was bankrupt. The bankruptcy trustees in Germany claimed that von Wersebe had funnelled more than $200 million out of his German companies to North America through a series of shadow companies in order to keep operations alive. Chrysler Canada's pension fund lost $80 million in an associated entity; the Alberta Teachers' Retirement Fund blew $16 million. Confed was in good company.

Or was it bad company? By 1995, von Wersebe would be in jail, facing criminal charges filed in Hamburg, Germany, into the bankruptcy of York-Hannover, a collapse that cost banks, pension funds, and individual investors on four continents an estimated $3 billion.

But if von Wersebe were a high-flyer, the Ghermezians were astronauts. Confed had signed on to the space shuttle with them, too. The four brothers, Raphael, Eskander, Bahman, and Nader, had arrived in Montreal from Iran in the fifties and begun selling rugs door-to-door. Soon the business expanded to hotel-room auctions, then retail stores. They moved to Edmonton and, with their father, Jacob, established Triple Five Corp. Some quick-flip land deals gave them a taste for developing and the belief they were good at it, so the family set out to build the biggest shopping mall on the face of the earth.

West Edmonton Mall was begun in 1981, expanded in 1983 to 396 stores, and was enlarged again in 1985, so it sprawled over five million square feet. The place became the destination of choice for shoppers flying in by charter jet to stare in awe not just at the stores but at the Oilers' practice ice surface and a hotel with various theme rooms, including one with a pick-up truck for a bed.

In order to receive municipal approvals for the third phase of West Edmonton Mall, in 1984 the Ghermezians proposed a development for the downtown that had been devastated by their suburban construction. They foresaw a $600-million complex, with apartment towers, office space, and retail anchored by Eaton's. The partner in this undertaking that made little commercial sense was none other than Confed.

Did Edmonton need more malls? Hardly, but the downtown megacentre went ahead anyway. Talk about overbuilt and undernourished! Even though the Eaton Centre never quite reached the original announced size (in the end perhaps $130 million was spent), the city nevertheless had seventeen major malls, with a total retail space of fourteen million square feet. To put the numbers in perspective, that was twice as much space per capita as either Vancouver or Toronto, and almost three times what existed in Montreal.

By 1991, however, the Ghermezians were running on empty. Consumers weren't spending; shops were closing. Companies were beginning to downsize, so commercial space was no longer needed in the same quantity. There was no need for another shopping mall or office tower. Bankers had suddenly come to the conclusion that they should turn off the lending taps.

By then, the Ghermezians had also built in Bloomington, Minnesota, and displayed their charms in Niagara Falls, the United Kingdom, and Germany – just about anywhere the local burgermeisters would listen to their tantalizing spiel of grand plans, development, jobs, and regional economic spin-offs. As long as there was another deal, often involving tax concessions, the operations pyramid could continue to grow.

Suddenly, there was nowhere else to go. Developers, who tend to keep past projects alive with the money they get to build the next one, hit the wall. The Ghermezians transferred their 50-per-cent interest in the Edmonton Eaton Centre to Confed, already proud owners of the other half. Confed paid $1. That was probably more than the place was worth.

Specific problems such as Hazelton Lanes or downtown Edmonton or Airway Centre with developer Inducon were only the high-profile end of a disastrous situation. In 1991, in addition to CREF's $450 million in real estate, the parent firm held a further $550 million as its share of those properties purchased since 1981. There was also Confed Trust, about $4 billion worth of real estate and mortgages in the Canadian insurance operations, plus US$4 billion in mortgages in the United States, some in the United Kingdom subsidiary – not to mention the fact that Confed had built itself three new head offices in three countries within a five-year period.

All of these investment activities – including Hazelton Lanes, the Ghermezians, Inducon – were each specifically approved by the executive committee of the board. And who was that? Any change in the investment portfolio over $20 million required the signature of three directors. Rhind and Burns were easy; they were always around. George Mara often made the third. Bond purchases or sales had a similar approval ceiling; private placements needed approval above $10 million.

Directors had given their assent to every project of size on the way up, and their concurrence would be needed all the way down, but no special meeting was required; a phone call was sufficient. Once, Ray Wolfe, chairman and CEO of the Oshawa Group Ltd., advised against investing in a Montreal retail complex, and Confed did not do the deal, but no other major real-estate deal put to the executive committee was ever rejected. Burns and Rhind rubber-stamped everything that crossed their desks. "Sometimes we'd go back for more information, but I can't ever recall getting the raspberry," says Barry Graham.

Not only does such a laid-back atmosphere mean that bad eggs are bought along with the good, but that kind of lackadaisical leadership sent a signal down the ranks all through the last half of the eighties that the guys at the top of Confed are easy marks. Put on a decent show and the deal will go. Any deal. Any day.

As the recession began in 1990, there was less money coming in the door from all sources. There was also a concurrent and horrific drop in the values of assets already on the books. At the same time, however, policyholders wanted cash-surrender value – or they died, and claims had to be paid. Confed desperately needed cash flow to keep the company afloat, an interim source of funds to sustain itself. One existed right next door in Michigan.

CHAPTER 6

In God We Trust: Michigan Pays Cash

"To borrow from one is stealing. To borrow
from many is sweet thievery."

– singer Tony Bennett

Confederation Life never seemed to choose the direct route. If there were a complicated approach, that was the path to follow. Case in point: A company was incorporated on May 2, 1983, in Toronto as one of those quickie numbered companies, 1236000 Canada Ltd. That August, the name was changed to ProGames Inc., and it commenced business developing educational games.

Confederation Financial Services Ltd. (100 per cent owned by Confederation Life) acquired ProGames on March 13, 1989, changing its activities to provide treasury services for the Confederation Group of companies, of which there were sixty various corporate entities, affiliates, and subsidiaries.

Not only was the game changed, the stakes were increased. ProGames became Confederation Financial Ltd. on April 26, 1989, then Confederation Treasury Services Ltd. (CTSL) on April 4, 1991, when the games people played were also changing. A 1991 memo from CTSL president Bill Alexander discussed the history of derivatives and proposed that Confed go into that business. CTSL would offer products such as interest-rate swaps to governments, financial institutions, and larger companies. Such institutions might, for example, have an obligation coming due in a foreign currency in six months. Someone else might be expecting a payment of a similar amount in the same currency in six months. Neither firm wants to risk losing money because of changes in exchange rate, so entities like CTSL bring them together to "swap" the future obligations and take a fee on the way by.

Derivatives! Little understood by most everybody in the world, they can be fatal even when handled by professionals. Letting futures trader Nick Leeson run a derivatives portfolio unchecked in far-off Singapore would bring down Barings in 1995. When they saw Alexander's memo, some long-time Confed employees feared for their own professional future and the financial health of their firm. Frank di Paolo, who had started with Confed as an actuarial student in 1956, regarded the previous culture as a "penny-counting, conservative investment outlook [with] puritan work ethics and cautious and disciplined planning in relation to growth and geographic expansion." That was all changed with the arrival of the new culture, one that he described as "a 'go-get-it' and 'go-for-broke' type of mentality brought into the executive suites of the Toronto head office by a group of misguided incompetents."

Di Paolo worried that derivatives were "just Las Vegas." He was in Toronto during the fall of 1991 for an actuaries' conference. In the past, he would also have been invited to attend the annual Confederation Life planning meeting on the same trip, but di Paolo was retiring in November. He had already passed on his responsibilities to his successor, George Powell, so di Paolo only went to a banquet for the forty attendees of the two-day planning session.

Because of his years of long service, di Paolo was given a seat of honour next to Pat Burns at the dinner held at a downtown hotel, and di Paolo took the opportunity to warn Burns against getting into derivatives. Burns was dismissive, saying there had been no decision, but if they did go into the business, it would be through a subsidiary.

"So what?" asked di Paolo. "It's all Confed money, whether lodged in a subsidiary or not." "I wouldn't worry about it," said Burns. Within a year, CTSL had derivatives with a notional value of $10.2 billion on its books.

The new entity handling derivatives wasn't just a subsidiary, it was a subsidiary of a subsidiary. Perhaps Burns thought that made things twice as safe. And who was the head of CTSL during this early period when everything was put in motion? Why, the founding president was none other than Bill Douglas, whose idea CTSL had been. Burns was also on the CTSL board and, initially, there was a staff of two: Bill Alexander and Bill Benton. By 1992, CTSL employed thirty-five.

On February 20, 1991, Douglas appointed Alexander to replace him as president of CTSL. Douglas continued as chairman. Alexander had started at Confed as a summer student in 1959 and worked in the actuarial department for seven summers. He was a University of Toronto maths-and-physics grad, who had worked from 1966 to 1973, mostly in group life insurance, then joined Excelsior Life Insurance Co. in 1973 and was there for fourteen years, during which time it was acquired by Aetna.

Alexander returned to Confed in 1987, joined the investment department, reporting to John Watson, and looked after Canadian insurance funds, then commercial paper activities. At Confederation Treasury Services Ltd., Alexander's role was to run treasury operations. Although he was highly regarded, he was not part of the inner circle, the seven-member president's advisory council. That connection was left to Douglas and Mike Regester, Pat Burns's protégé, who was also CTSL vice-chairman.

As if Confed weren't in enough trouble in businesses it was supposed to know something about, CTSL began supplying hedging services through derivatives such as interest-rate swaps, foreign-currency exchange, short-term investments, and securities repurchase* transactions both to the various Confed divisions and to others in the financial community through counterparty deals.

---

* Repos, as they are known, are agreements to sell a security and then repurchase it an agreed-upon future date and price.

But of all the crazy schemes run out of CTSL, none was crazier than the set-up involving funds from the Michigan trust. Crazy like a fox, that is. Unlike Canada, where insurance regulation is for the most part a federal matter, each state in the United States sets its own rules, although there is much cooperation and similarity of procedures through the National Association of Insurance Commissioners (NAIC). Canadian life-insurance companies use Michigan as their state of entry into the United States, and it has generally been accepted practice that the Michigan Bureau of Insurance keeps an eye on such "alien" firms, as they are known, on behalf of other states. Confed designated Michigan as its state of entry in 1964.

All alien companies are required to file financial statements in March that cover the previous year. This NAIC statement, as it is known, is a detailed, quantitative report on American operations and is designed primarily to show that a company has sufficient assets to provide for its U.S. liabilities. The NAIC statement reads, in part: "The most important fact conveyed by the Statement is whether the Company has a sufficient amount of admissible assets to meet all known liabilities of its United States business including statutory deposit."

In other words, Confed had to maintain assets in the trust account in the United States that were equal to the liabilities owed to policy-holders. The reason, of course, is that if a company went bankrupt, there would be sufficient assets to cover debts.

The scheme for CTSL to get at funds in the Michigan trust was first discussed in 1990, when the United States investment division migrated from Toronto to Atlanta. The first formal description of the idea was set out in a memo dated September 24, 1990, from CTSL assistant vice-president William Benton to Larry Rae, assistant vice-president, United States corporate actuarial and statements. Benton, who had joined Confed in 1988 as an assistant vice-president and had moved into CTSL at its founding, became senior vice-president in 1991.

The one-page memo began: "Larry, as we discussed, I would like to be able to access the funds in the [United States] short term pool.

Brent Campbell's operations will be left unaffected* as I will match the rates and terms they now achieve. With the money, I can reduce my borrowings in the capital markets. Overall, Confederation Life's consolidated balance sheet will look better – there will be fewer liabilities and profitability ratios will thus improve.

"The big problem is that the trust requires physical delivery in the [United States]. I am unable to do this on a day-to-day basis. I suggest that you talk to the trustee and ask him for a solution."

Benton offered two possibilities: a flexible note with rates and amounts that could be adjusted by a daily phone call; or a note "that is much larger than the S.T. Pool is envisioned to become," with monthly interest payments and an annual adjustment.

CTSL's specialty was centralized cash and short-term investing. This scheme Benton proposed would gather all cash in the Confederation Group rather than have one arm of the operation out borrowing in the short-term money market while another arm was investing surplus funds with some brokerage house.

Prior to CTSL, such internal activities had been handled by accounting; CTSL was to be the specialist department using experts like Benton. But it started to grow a life of its own once the era of swaps arrived. Those early discussions about the new arrangement culminated in a February meeting that was summarized in a May 30, 1991, memo from Alexander to Clive Curtis, vice-president, investments, in the United States, that stated baldly: "CTSL will 'manage' the United States Short Term Pool for you. In essence, we will be borrowing the funds and paying you LIBID† for their use . . . with the benefit to you being that you always have your funds invested and you will not have the administrative costs associated with a trader to do this for you."

In fact, the system had already been up and running since early in

---

* As director, insurance investments, Campbell was the resident actuarial expert in Atlanta, who kept the duration of liabilities and assets matched because the United States was selling long-term structured settlements that required intricate offsetting activity in the futures market.

† The London Interbank bid rate, which was higher than the offer rate and meant that the United States received rates based on the top interest rate that day.

the year. The May memo merely formalized the reality that had seen CTSL's activities expand geometrically beyond cash management. Alexander's concluding sentences read: "If you or Brent have any questions or problems with the process, please give me or T-bill a call. As I mentioned yesterday, we seem to have things working pretty well at present."* For the United States, getting rid of excess funds was something of a relief; they didn't have to worry about money coming in more quickly from GICs than what was going out on mortgages. Excess funds simply went to Toronto and were managed. An internal attempt later to do a forensic audit found the system so complex that Atlanta gave up trying to figure out what Toronto was doing and just let them get on with it.

A document dated March 1, 1991, gave further validity to the whole intercorporate scheme. Called an "agreement of setoff" and signed by Alexander, Benton, and Confed vice-president, corporate accounting, Borden Rosiak, the five-page covenant in effect created a scheme by which Confed and CTSL agreed that any intercorporate borrowings between the two would be offset *without any obligation for actual repayment* from one company to the other. The effect was that the CTSL notes were all short-term, or demand, notes but, in fact, they were not really payable when due but were "offset" by Confed. That was because CTSL had no real money of its own; it just acted as a central treasury for Confed. An agency agreement covering repos, dated November 11, 1992, signed by Brent Campbell and Clive Curtis, again validated in writing what had long been practice.†

While all of the sluicing about was going on, Confed was continuing to reassure clients, both current and prospective, of corporate financial health. Typical was a forty-two-page publication the size of the annual report, entitled *Financial Profile*. The 1993 edition lists four

---

* Because both Bill Alexander and Bill Benton were in Toronto, Benton was called "T-bill" to differentiate the two; the nickname arose because he was the short-term money expert.

† The amounts washing back and forth became huge. On August 11, 1994, $1,060,218,000 was owed by Confed to CTSL, set off against $1,259,809,000 owed by CTSL to Confed, making CTSL a net debtor in the amount of $199,591,000.

elements under the reassuring title "Multi-Level Consumer Protection." The first level was general government regulation, including numerous state insurance departments, each state's Secretary of State, the United States Securities and Exchange Commission, the state securities departments, and the National Association of Securities Dealers.

The second level was even more explicit. "[B]ecause Michigan is our state of entry into the United States, Michigan law requires Confederation Life to deposit its United States assets in a trust account with a United States domiciled bank. These assets are expressly held to meet our obligations to United States policyholders. The Michigan Insurance Department audits the trust account to ensure that we are, at all times, more than solvent when comparing United States trusteed assets to our United States liabilities."

And, if that wasn't enough, many states in which Confed did business could require their own funds on deposit – and some of them were supposed to be watching the Michigan account, too. "Other states require a certificate from the Michigan Insurance Department evidencing the deposit of the trusteed assets described above. The purpose of these deposits is to ensure immediate access to company funds by the respective insurance departments *in the unlikely event Confederation Life suffers serious financial difficulties* [emphasis added]."

Oh yes, and on top of that, the "Federal Department of Insurance in Canada requires that all Canadian insurers be prepared to support and satisfy liabilities in any country with the *total* assets of the company. In other words, Confederation Life's Canadian and United Kingdom operations may be used to support and satisfy United States liabilities."

This document, given to prospective and current Confed clients in the United States, couldn't have been more specific and reassuring. Not only was there a Michigan trust account covering all United States liabilities, there was backup from Canada and the United Kingdom.

In fact, there was no such money in the trust at all. In addition to its treasury and derivative activity, CTSL assets included items due from Confed and Confed subsidiaries, a circle that took money from the

Michigan trust, placed it in the hands of CTSL, which in turn owed it to Confed, which had been the original owner anyway. From time to time, short-term promissory notes were also put into the trust fund by CTSL in order that assets equalled liabilities. These transactions were called "topping up."

But no new money was created, no new capital raised, the whole process was just a mockery of a legitimate creditor-debtor relationship. CTSL could not pay off any loans; it had no funds other than what it borrowed. All CTSL could do, was expected to do, and did do, was shuffle money from one pocket to another and roll over the notes as they came due.

The system CTSL had created was rather like the national debt. Just as governments and society became addicted to spending, so did Confed. Just as government thought for a time that deficits could pile up to the sky, so did Confed think it could consume its internal funds and create new businesses without worrying about the cost or eventual repayment of those funds. "Regulators could take the position that striving for growth and diversity was to the detriment of the company," says Alexander. "You can make a business argument that it was for the good of the company."

Here's another way to look at the monster Confed created. Imagine you have two personal bank accounts. You move $1,000 from account A to account B. Normally, the bank statement that arrives at month's end describing the balance of A would reflect a drop of $1,000. What if, at the time of withdrawal you give the bank an IOU for $1,000 – signed by you – promising to pay account A $1,000. For its part, the bank considers your paper IOU as good as cash, so the bank statement shows a debit of $1,000 for the transfer and a credit of $1,000 for the IOU. As a result, the bottom line doesn't change, the balance in A is still $1,000, even though $1,000 was removed. Account B, however, has a balance that's been increased by the real $1,000. Eureka, a veritable money machine; cash created out of thin air!

The method of getting at these funds in the Michigan trust was just about as simple. Every day, CTSL calculated how much money was in the trust, withdrew that cash – "cash sweeping" they called it – and issued a promissory note in return. After a while, just withdrawing cash wasn't enough to fund Confed's needs. In May 1991, Alexander established an even more aggressive method to get at the value of United States Treasury bonds on deposit in the Michigan trust. CTSL sold the bonds held in the trust and made a simultaneous commitment to repurchase those bonds from the buyer at a predetermined price, sort of another "offset" arrangement. When the cash was received after the sale, the money was wired to CTSL's bank account at a Canadian Imperial Bank of Commerce (CIBC) branch in Toronto and a CTSL IOU note was issued.

When the repurchase agreement matured, the original buyer could liquidate the bond or CTSL could buy it back – but the cash did not go back into the trust. The IOU remained. The effect was for Confed to cash in bonds early, get at the monetary value immediately, and never replace that value in the trust.

At first, the conduit for all this cash flow was Hartford National Bank and Trust Co. and its successor company, Connecticut National Bank. Starting October 22, 1992, the trusts were moved from Connecticut to Illinois, where they were maintained by Harris Trust and Savings Bank, the Chicago-based American arm of the Bank of Montreal. The eighteen-page agreement was signed October 22, 1992, by Confed assistant vice-president David R. Lee, who was head of securities accounting, and Bob Eagleson, an investment accounting manager. Vice-president Maureen Waldron signed for Harris Trust. The document set out who was the sheriff and what could happen if the sheriff's watchdog barked. Noted subsection 11 (b): "If at any time the Trustee shall be notified in writing by the Commissioner of Insurance that the said Commissioner shall have determined that the company is insolvent, *or that its trustee deposits are below the minimum amount prescribed by statute* [emphasis added], and that due notice of the Commissioner's findings to that effect have been forwarded to the Company, such notice shall suspend disbursement." In other words, until the regulator says "stop," Harris and Confed have conveniently assumed they can do what they want and they are both off the hook.

A second contract, called an agency agreement, was signed on November 11, 1992, between CTSL and Confederation Life Insurance

Co., for its American investments portfolio. The arrangement gave CTSL unlimited powers to enter into repurchase transactions with United States Treasury securities with third parties of CTSL's choosing and "invest the cash in such manner and at such times as CTSL, in its discretion, shall determine." In other words, a free hand over all the empire's holdings. The four-page understanding was signed by Brent Campbell, Confed's director of insurance investments, and Clive Curtis, the Atlanta-based vice-president of United States investments.

The system was amazingly simple. A Harris officer would fill in pre-signed, blank CTSL notes with the amounts to be transferred and with the rates provided by CTSL. The process was not a sometime thing; it produced reams of paperwork. From October 22, 1992, through August 11, 1994, CTSL issued more than seven hundred notes with face amounts totalling more than US$54 *billion*. Of that amount, less than 2 per cent was ever paid off; the rest was merrily rolled over for another day, the never-never land of non-payment, using new CTSL notes.

A procedures committee was set up under Alexander and Benton, and a six-page set of instructions to traders was drawn up and issued on October 30, 1992. A diagrammatic version of procedures was included that showed up to fourteen steps in the repo process, not including various side options that could be taken.

Why didn't Michigan regulators spot the scheme? The two-hundred-page filing Confed made each December 31 is far more extensive than what's known as the OSFI 54 required in Canada. United States authorities require, among other items, specific details about every mortgage, equity holding, T-bill, bond, and other investment in the United States. Trading activity during the year must also be recorded. The whole point of this, of course, is that, under subsection 411(4) of the Michigan Insurance Code, Confed had to warrant that there were enough assets housed in the United States to cover American liabilities.

At a quick glance, which is probably all such forms get by harried regulators facing an avalanche of paper every year, everything appeared on the up and up. Under the heading "short term investments," the 1990 filing shows US$83.9 million in United States government bonds, term deposits with Barclays Bank and the Bank of Nova Scotia, and commercial paper from Exxon Corp. and GE Capital Corp. All were appropriate investments for a company like Confed.

However, in the December 31, 1991, filing, the items listed as short-term investments show a dramatic change. The three-page section shows one Barclays term deposit worth US$2.9 million, then twenty-three separate items called "Confederation Treasury Services Ltd. term deposits" in amounts varying from US$1.1 million to US$88.8 million. All of them have maturities in the first five months of 1992. The total value of these short-term investments is now US$340,755,702. The notarized filing was signed by Pat Burns, corporate secretary Mark Edwards, vice-president, corporate accounting, Borden Rosiak, and actuary Michael Rosenfelder.

In the December 31, 1992, filing, the pattern changes once more. CTSL is still listed as the issuer, but most of the items are no longer shown as term deposits, they are called promissory notes, and the total dollar amount involved has almost doubled from the previous year to US$606,429,445. The three-page section shows US$15.2 million in CTSL term deposits, with the rest consisting of twenty-one CTSL promissory notes, all held by Harris Trust.

In December 31, 1993, the terminology is again altered. The CTSL items are now on a single page, they're called "fixed-rate loans," and the borrowings have been gathered into six such loans for a total of US$757,154,962. A line elsewhere in the filing clearly declares: "Excess of United States admissible assets over United States admissible liabilities and statutory deposits, $86,578,286." As for Confed's declaration that there was an excess of assets over liabilities, that wasn't erroneous, it was just that the assets weren't actually in the United States. Nor were they readily available.

As president of CTSL in 1989 and 1990, and chairman of CTSL in 1991, Douglas would have known everything that was going on, especially about transactions as sizeable as these. On the one hand, he accepts general responsibility. "The manner in which CTSL was managed, I take full responsibility for that." As for the specifics, he claims no knowledge, because he was more interested in the leasing company. "To the extent that there was a transaction in calendar '91, and I don't know if there was or wasn't, of the sort that the Michigan commissioner is asking about [in the lawsuit filed in 1995], I did not know about it at the time," says Douglas.

The best explanation for Confed's motivations is that the "borrowings" would have been repaid when the economy and real-estate values improved. "I don't think there was a focused strategy by management to say, 'Let's keep the ball rolling an extra six months or a year by raiding the cash in the United States trust. We think we can rip off these regulators by slipping them these notes, pulling the cash out, and that will keep us going,'" says David Murray, senior vice-president at Deloitte & Touche Inc., the accounting firm that handled CTSL during its first eighteen months in liquidation.

"Maybe they were too arrogant, but their perception was that this is all going to work out. [They said,] 'There's some liquid cash over here, I can use that, I'll put an IOU in.' I don't think they saw themselves as ripping off the trust."

———◆◆◆———

Confed needed to keep the ball rolling, because regulators were making corporate life more and more difficult. Since the 1989 meeting, OSFI had been urging Confed to reduce real-estate holdings, improve asset quality, and put better financial controls in place. There had been insufficient response. "More and more we kept on saying, 'You're not delivering. This is not coming along as it should,'" says Michael Mackenzie. "I was getting more and more testy, more and more concerned that there were no controls over this guy. Jack Rhind thought [Burns] was the greatest thing in the insurance industry."

"Some of the remedies that Confed had put in place weren't as effective as management would have thought they would have been," says John Thompson, deputy superintendent, insurance and pensions. There was also the problem of span of control. "Confed was a very, very complex company," he says. "In a complex company like this, it's typical that you run across situations where the management of the senior entity is not as aware of what's going on in subsidiary companies as they should be."

OSFI escalated its action to what it calls a "stage-two" intervention: they were not yet predicting outright failure, but they were becoming nervous. Trends that had been brought to management's attention over a two-year period had not been reversed. At stage three, solvency is threatened, and OSFI presses harder for new capital and additional sources of funding, a change in senior management, even a merger partner or sale. At stage four, OSFI takes control of the assets or winds up the institution.

At the time, Mackenzie was oblivious to Confed's manipulation of the Michigan trust. He did, however, have other concerns to raise with the board. An October 25, 1991, visit was supposed to be a wake-up call to management and directors. Mackenzie, accompanied by Robert Hammond, deputy superintendent, insurance and premiums sector,[*] presented the findings of OSFI's examination.

With Burns sitting at one end of the board table and Mackenzie at the other, the antipathy between them was palpable. The problem was a combination of personal chemistry and Burns's general contempt for all regulators in general and Mackenzie in particular. Although Burns said little in front of the directors and Mackenzie, directors knew the CEO was angry. "You could just feel it," says a director. "Pat had a bit of a short fuse."

Mackenzie had three areas that worried him. First, he said, he wanted to see Confed's forecasts of capital, because he was concerned that capital could drop below safe thresholds. He urged that new capital be injected. Second, he expressed concern about the deterioration of asset quality in real estate, and asked for a business plan to show how the situation would be turned around. Third, OSFI worried that management oversight of financial and investment controls was weak.

A second meeting, between Mackenzie and those outside directors who were there that day, followed the first. Despite the supposed freedom they were supposed to feel with management absent, there

---

[*] Hammond departed in May 1992 to become general manager of the Canadian Payments Association in Ottawa and was replaced later that year by John Thompson.

was little apparent, stated concern. Directors had heard similar information in the past, given to them by management. Such reports have
a "pro forma" ring, says Mike Regester, with no particular problems
underlined. "A pro forma presentation often engenders a pro forma
reaction. In a mutual company that would be probably even more
true." As far as directors were concerned, Mackenzie's message that
day was not much different from what they already knew. He had
raised their awareness levels a little, but not much.

Later, outside the room, Burns accosted Mackenzie, asking why he
had to bring such matters before the full board. "Why didn't you just
speak to me about it?"

Replied Mackenzie, "Look, Pat, we've been to other [insurance
company] board meetings and this hasn't been a problem. I don't
know what you're talking about."

Burns returned to the meeting and told directors that Confed was
in good shape; according to him, it was OSFI that was the problem.
"Pat was able to put a spin on it [saying,] 'They're not taking any
chances. It's a typical bureaucratic thing. We're okay,'" recalls a director. "It's personal," Burns would say. "I don't like Mackenzie, and
Mackenzie doesn't like me."

In conjunction with the face-to-face meeting, Mackenzie
dispatched a two-page letter to each director, restating his concerns in
the three areas. He also sent each director a copy of Hammond's
longer letter detailing the examination results. Mackenzie attached his
card to the material he sent Adam Zimmerman and jotted a note
saying, "Call me about this." Zimmerman and Mackenzie had known
each other since birth. Both sets of parents had been friends before
that. The two men had joined Clarkson Gordon (the precursor firm
to Ernst & Young) as young university graduates in 1950. Mackenzie
had been a history major, Zimmerman, in philosophy, so the two
were a different breed than the usual commerce-and-finance types
who populated the firm.

Zimmerman telephoned – he was the only director who did – and
told Mackenzie that he had not made a particularly convincing case.
Said Zimmerman, "Mike, you've got to realize this guy Burns is a
crackerjack." Replied Mackenzie, "Read the letter again."

Other directors were equally loyal to Burns. "I don't know that I would subscribe to the 'crackerjack,'" says one, "but I wouldn't challenge it." As for the letter, he was dismissive. "It was an ass-saving device." Directors saw Burns as an untouchable. He was an industry leader, had been 1989-90 chairman of the CLHIA, and was the founding chairman of CompCorp, the industry's self-financed consumer-protection scheme. What did the regulator know?

Mackenzie was familiar with the reaction. In such circumstances, directors are like patients told by a doctor that they have a disease: They go into denial. "We observe a general unwillingness by directors to accept our criticisms of management action," says Mackenzie. "If there is a perceived difference between the regulator and management, they seem to prefer to take management's side rather than look hard at the issue. They often do not insist on getting the kinds of information that management may be loath to provide. I think this pressure is a function of the boardroom culture of Canada."

But perhaps there was something else at work as well. If Mackenzie's meetings with other life-insurance boards during the same period are any criteria, he was delivering too muted a message. Other once-grand Canadian companies had also suffered from the contagion of declining asset values and dumb-headed management. At the time, Mackenzie was also nervous about North American Life, Imperial Life Assurance Co. of Canada (the Toronto-based arm of Quebec's Desjardins empire), and Crown Life Insurance Co.

He was meeting with other boards to discuss their troubled circumstances and the difficult economic environment in which they were operating. Yet the message he delivered was often surprisingly benign given capital insufficiencies and their failure to strengthen their balance sheets. Mackenzie's words, according to those who heard him on the boardroom circuit, were more feel-good than failure-predicting. He would say that they were not alone in their parlous state and that he understood how hard it was to raise capital.

Crown Life serves as a particular example of Mackenzie's *laissez-faire* approach. The company had profits in 1990 of only $18.8 million (down from $50.4 million the previous year) on assets of $10 billion. Much of the problem was caused by a depressed real-estate market in

Texas and other sunbelt states. Twenty-eight per cent of Crown's United States assets were in mortgages, with huge dollops of that total either in non-performing loans or repossessed properties. But real estate wasn't Crown's only American calamity. In 1988, it had lost $20 million in the fiercely competitive United States group life- and health-insurance business, and sold out to Great-West.

In fact, Crown had been lurching along for years. In 1982, former Canadian National honcho Bob Bandeen was brought in as president and CEO to revitalize Crown, and he promptly fired one-quarter of the staff and closed one-third of the sales offices across the country. At the time, Crown was known as "the abattoir," because of all the employee blood running in the hallways. After Bandeen departed in 1985, former John Labatt Ltd. executive Robert Luba took a run at getting the place set right, only to be replaced as president in 1988 by Fred Richardson, a former insurance consultant.

Crown Life's majority owner, conglomerate Crownx Inc., finally put Crown up for sale in early 1990, but couldn't arouse much interest. Help came at last in 1991 in the form of an injection of $250 million in capital by Haro Financial Corp, run by Regina businessmen Paul Hill and Charles Knight.

Haro's 42-per-cent interest in Crown was backed in turn by an election-eve loan guarantee from the province, then headed by Progressive Conservative Premier Grant Devine. The deal (which had been code-named Project X by the government during the lengthy negotiations), wasn't enough to save Devine at the polls. The NDP under Roy Romanow won, but went ahead anyway with the agreement that called for Crown to move its head office from Toronto – where it had resided since the firm was founded in 1900 – twenty-four hundred kilometres to Regina.

Despite government support, Crown remained financially frail. In 1993, independent rating agency TRAC Insurance Services Ltd. ranked Crown near the bottom of its death-watch list, along with Confed. Even so, Mackenzie's visits to Crown Life's board of directors in that era hardly smacked of the stuff of a worried regulator. "He'd talk about ratios," says Stephen Paddon, who first heard Mackenzie's annual messages to the Crown board in his capacity as

Crown's vice-president, general counsel, and secretary, then as a director after his appointment to the board in 1993. "I expected fire and brimstone, but there was only a little heat. He'd end by congratulating management."

Such a lacklustre performance was unlikely to bedazzle directors and propel them into action. If the country's most senior regulator shrugged his shoulders and seemed satisfied, why should directors bother to rouse themselves from their torpor? If the police chief says there's not much crime, won't officers just continue to nap in their squad cars? "For some reason, Mackenzie mellowed the board [and] made them feel comfortable with a management team that was running the company into the ground," says Paddon, who did not stand for re-election to the Crown board in 1994 and is now practising law in the Toronto office of Calgary-based firm Bennett Jones Verchere. He thought Mackenzie should have read the board something from the statutes about directors' responsibilities. "The directors didn't go away scared – and they should have been scared. I didn't think it was blood-curdling enough. I could see this company going down and down."

Just like Confed. Mike Mackenzie's "warning shots" might just as well have been fired from a pea shooter.

CHAPTER 7

Once More into the Breach

"It was déjà vu all over again."

– Yogi Berra

Whether Mike Mackenzie's phrases were tough enough or not, Confed directors were beginning to rouse themselves. "Boards may not want to do what we think is necessary for them to do. On the other hand, we may feel that such measures are critical to the success of that company," says John Thompson of OSFI. "We could then issue a direction to carry out our wishes. Those powers are there." No such powers were invoked.

Even the most unaware director could see that Confederation Trust was a disaster. It was only on the occasion of that October 1991 visit, claim Confederation Life directors, that they belatedly learned about the pay-for-performance bonus arrangements in the subsidiary. "It's really rolling the dice when you put people in that blank-cheque situation," says one director. "It's not prudent." It's even less prudent for a director not to know what was going on in a key subsidiary.

Conveniently, Barry Walsh's contract was coming up for renewal. His status had diminished, confidence in him was gone. As long as the good times rolled, everyone was willing to put up with the fact that Walsh had been running Confederation Trust part time from Vancouver. After the regulators visited the board, Walsh's contract was not renewed.

Zool Samji, who had recently returned to Toronto after working for Confed in the United Kingdom for seven years, was assigned to move into the trust company as president to try and clean things up. Mike Regester was named chairman.

Regester was Burns's choice to succeed him as CEO of Confederation Life. Regester had been elevated to executive vice-president in 1990, a sure sign that he was tipped for the top. Born in Britain, Regester became a chartered accountant and arrived in Canada in 1965. He worked at Clarkson Gordon for two years, then went into estate planning for Confed before moving to Atlanta as marketing vice-president. He was appointed vice-president, individual operations, for the United States and Caribbean in 1984, then returned to Canada as senior vice-president, Canadian operations, in 1989. The fact that he was parachuted into Confed Trust showed that much was expected of him.

At the same time, the Ontario regulator also imposed new requirements. In December 1991, Ontario reduced Confed Trust's borrowing multiple from 15:1 to 12.5:1. A 15:1 multiple means that, for every dollar of capital, a company can borrow fifteen dollars from the public in deposits. The reduction meant, in effect, restricted growth. Ontario also demanded $50 million in capital be injected into Confed Trust by Confed Life – and said that the new capital could not be used as leverage for lending. Confederation Life complied and put $35 million of capital into Confed Trust in December 1991, adding a further $15 million in March 1992. Coopers & Lybrand was hired to do a forensic audit on the trust company to see if there had been any fraud. Says Regester, "They said the odour wasn't very good, but there was nothing they could find, because the paperwork was so bad."

Confed Trust adopted a more stringent set of policies and guidelines, including tighter procedures covering investment and lending policies invoked by OSFI and OMFI. The firm would concentrate on single-family residential mortgages and personal lines of credit.

Commercial-mortgage funding was restricted to restructurings, reso-
lutions of existing mortgages, and renewals that were absolutely
required.

Despite all the new capital, however, the problem just got worse.
When OMFI projected the trust company's numbers, it saw continuing losses. When Ontario regulator Brian Cass met the board of
Confederation Trust in September 1992, the four Halifax-based
directors had by then been replaced by Jack Rhind, Pat Burns, former
Ontario health minister Dennis Timbrell, a Progressive Conservative,
and former Ontario energy minister Robert Wong, a Liberal.

Cass was delighted at the appointments. He thought Confed Trust
had been "one of the worst companies I've ever seen. [They] put stuff
on their books at a time when there were four lawyers acting as directors, and so help me, I'm positive they didn't understand what they
were into. It resulted in a carnage."

Cass told the newly constituted board of the trust company that
they were getting close to being offside on capital. "You've got to
have a plan to deal with that," he told them. "Because if you don't, the
moment you have inadequate regulatory capital, you will notify
the public before you accept any future public deposits." At that point,
the company would have two choices: issue a press release so that
everybody knew or get each depositor to sign an acknowledgement
of awareness.

The company had a different view; it claimed a return to profitability was coming. "A lot of companies say, 'We're going to be
profitable,' but what they do is base it on the non-performings coming
back to life," says Cass. "Regrettably, that didn't happen." To buttress
his concerns, Cass left a copy of the two pages containing the items he
raised with the members of the board. In October, Confederation
Life injected a further $20 million of capital into Confed Trust.

"The other fellow's business always looks easy. The Confederation
Life people put inordinate trust in the Confederation Trust people,"
Adam Zimmerman said later. "These fellows got to thinking they
could walk on water, and they couldn't."

"The eighties were a peculiar decade in Canada," says Bob Astley,
CEO of Mutual Life Assurance Co. of Canada, of Waterloo, Ontario.

"We created the illusion of increasing prosperity, while actually creating a sharply increasing debt. Asset values rose, creating the illusion of profitability and increasing capital, which enable companies which were in fact eroding their real capital base to publish results which appeared to be buoyant."

No financial institution was immune to the changed environment. In 1992, the six largest banks in Canada made provision for $6.9 billion in bad loans – and half of that total was caused by commercial real estate. Foreign banks had net losses of $380 million, the first such loss since they'd arrived in 1980. Trust and loan companies lost a total of $1.2 billion from 1991 to 1993.

But, although the banks' bottom line suffered, they managed to increase their market share. As panicky Canadians weathered the recession, they made sure their personal assets were in the hands of the strongest institutions. The market share of the ten largest financial institutions rose from 71 per cent of total assets at the end of 1991 to 86 per cent of total assets only two years later.

Insurance was not as well positioned. In January 1992, Les Coopérants Mutual Life Insurance Society collapsed, the result of imprudent real-estate investment in Canada and the United States, leaving its 160,000 policyholders in the lurch. The economy was beginning to bite. This was Canada's first-ever insurance company failure.

Les Coopérants, like Confed, suffered from head-office syndrome. In 1988, the company moved into a new $125-million tower on de Maisonneuve Boulevard, with a marble lobby, private dining room, and museum. "Our head office mirrors our evolution and our corporate culture," sang the 1989 report to shareholders. "It reflects our strength, our originality and our vision of the future."

By 1991, Les Coopérants was six times larger than it had been just seven years earlier, with $3 billion in assets, more than two-thirds of which were invested in businesses outside the core life-insurance business, which had begun in rural Quebec 115 years earlier. The forays into uncharted territory included a trust company, real estate, financial planning, and a savings and loans. Cash shortfalls were covered by loans, profit fell, and the company lost $31 million in 1990. There was a management shake-up, but action came too late. Losses would have been $60 million in 1991, but the firm went belly up before they were reported.

On that occasion, Pat Burns, wearing his white hat as chairman of CompCorp, sounded as if trouble was something he'd neither thought much about nor believed would ever arrive. Suddenly, the regulators just might have a role after all. "We feel quite strongly from the standpoint of CompCorp," said Burns, suddenly a fan of OSFI. "We'll have discussions with regulators to make sure we don't have another one of these."

Confed's twelve-month results to December 31, 1991, were equally disastrous. Profit fell from $106 million in 1990 to $17 million in 1991, well below the $100-million profit that had been expected. Moreover, the profit level was Confed's skimpiest since 1977, when assets were one-tenth the size. Return on average surplus fell to 2.1 per cent from a healthy 12.5 per cent in 1990 and 13.9 per cent in 1989.

Directors now realized that maybe Mike Mackenzie was on to something when he visited in October. Non-performing assets had grown to $695 million. Even the holy of holies – Canadian insurance operations – lost $13 million. But the situation was far worse than it appeared. Confed was stretched in all directions and did not have enough capital to withstand the serious real-estate losses it was incurring. In addition, there was a liquidity crisis. Confed had managed to create the worst possible situation any financial-services company could: a funds mismatch. Confed had invested primarily in assets of long-term duration, but many of its liabilities were of the short-term variety. That meant the company might not have cash to meet its obligations as they came due.

The circumstances were so altered from expectations at the beginning of the year that Ernst & Young had to extend its audit examination. Confed's audit committee had asked for some of the additional work; the rest was done because of the unexpected circumstances, increased risk, and the worldwide deterioration of the real-estate market.

The proposal for the 1991 audit originally saw E&Y partners Bob Lord and Sheryl Teed attending only two audit-committee meetings, in June 1991 and February 1992. They ended up attending three others as well, in April, September, and December. Auditors inspected the books in London, Toronto, and Atlanta. They reviewed a sample of Confed's private-placement investments. Following the Mackenzie visit, the board ordered Ernst & Young to do more verification on actuarial reserves. The unexpected work by the two dozen people involved in the audit meant that the original fee estimate of $310,000 for the 1991 audit grew to a bill submitted of $514,330.

Auditing is a peculiar profession. Examinations are not, for example, necessarily designed to find errors or fraud. Auditor's tests may detect such problems, but basically, argue the beancounters, uncovering errors or fraud is the responsibility of management.

Tony Griffiths was the first director to become disenchanted with management. "He'd seen these kinds of things before, and he knew that this was the tip of the iceberg," says a director. Griffiths's view was, in effect, "If this [item] wasn't brought to the board, what else was there?"

He had, indeed, seen similar desperate corporate circumstances. Born in Burma to Australian parents, Griffiths twice ran Mitel Corp., of Kanata, Ontario. In the mid-eighties, during his first incarnation, he hauled the high-tech firm, which makes telephone switching equipment, back from the abyss of bankruptcy by closing three plants, selling off assets, and slashing employment by 20 per cent. When a new management team arrived in 1987, Griffiths was elevated to chairman, the fourth person to hold the post in a fifteen-month period.

But Mitel was soon in trouble again, and Griffiths returned for a reprise as CEO in 1991. This time, the turnaround was not quite so simple. Two years later, Mitel was still losing money, and, when Griffiths's contract expired in January 1993, he was replaced as CEO, although he again stayed on as chairman.

If Mitel were a revolving door for Griffiths, his efforts at Toronto-based Ondaatje Corp. were like being caught in a tornado. After serving for two years as a director of the merchant bank, which had interests in Southeast Asia, in early 1995 Griffiths accepted an invitation from the controlling shareholder, Christopher Ondaatje, to become president and CEO. Griffiths suddenly departed that June after serving only four months.

Griffiths loved to take on troubled situations, but that quick in-and-out suggests a remarkable lapse of judgement, considering that he had known the mercurial Ondaatje for forty years. Griffiths says that the two men "agreed to disagree" about the general direction of the company. "He's always controlled his company. He has a history of doing things on his own. I made a mistake by agreeing to go in," says Griffiths.

A Confed director since 1975, Griffiths had been a member of the audit committee since 1988. Once Mackenzie had lobbed in his 1989 warnings, Griffiths would sometimes raise questions about strategic direction and prod management about the need for action. Griffiths saw Rhind as not only dismissive to the point of arrogance, but overly protective of Burns. After all, Burns had been Rhind's personal choice for successor. He could not admit failings by Burns, his own anointed.

At the January 16, 1992, board meeting, Griffiths suggested that directors take steps to discover the depth of the problem "by retaining outside advice to make an assessment." The executive committee of the board decided not to go ahead, because Confed already had assessments upon which to draw of "two regulators, various Coopers [& Lybrand] reports, and the external auditors." After Confed director David McCamus, chairman and CEO of Xerox Canada Inc., resigned from the board in February 1992, Griffiths became chairman of the audit committee, and that winter met several times for breakfast with OSFI superintendent Michael Mackenzie to discuss action. The audit committee was itself going through other membership changes as well. Thomas Ladner, a lawyer with the Vancouver firm of Ladner Downs, had been a director since 1968 and joined the audit committee on June 20, 1990. Poor health plagued him, however, and the last meeting he attended was September 18, 1991. Ladner was not replaced until February 1992, by which time he was seventy-five.

Management was at least beginning to go through the motions. Deputy superintendent Robert Hammond wrote to Bill Douglas on January 30, 1992, expressing his pleasure "that Confederation Life will take steps to remedy the problems we have identified." Specifically, Hammond cited Reemark, capital, and control over investment policy. Hammond did note, however, that action had so far been outlined only in brief, and said that OSFI expected more extensive plans.

Steps to date included: lending in the British bank and Confederation Trust had been halted; mortgage commitments in the United States would be cut to half of the 1991 levels; equity worth $200 million had been sold, with a further $200 million to be unloaded in 1992; Coopers & Lybrand had been hired to look at ways of disposing of up to three-quarters of Confed's real-estate investments; and a workout program had been set up in the trust company and in the United States to deal with foreclosures.

There was nothing wrong with what had been put in motion, except that lending restraints were about two years late. As for real-estate sales, there were no buyers. The board also began to ask for more specific reports from management on other subsidiaries, such as Confederation Treasury Services Ltd., and management agreed to circulate financial statements.

At the February 5 meeting of the board, directors also took a moment to increase their pay, as if the extra workload required a reward. Total annual compensation, which had been set in 1988 at a maximum of $475,000, was given a new ceiling of $600,000.*

Word was beginning to circulate in select circles within Confed that financial strength was deteriorating. In March 1992, Dave Hare, who had moved to Atlanta in 1982 to be vice-president, group marketing, as part of the early wave of settlers, delivered a speech in San Francisco. An American firm, Executive Life, had recently gone under, so Hare's message was about the need for financial stability. Among the attendees on that occasion was Bill Allison, Hare's boss as senior vice-president, United States operations.

---

* Annual fees for each director were $15,000, plus there was a meeting fee of $900 and expenses. Committee chairmen received up to an additional $3,000. Jack Rhind received a fixed $60,000 annually in his role as chairman of the executive committee. Total annual compensation to directors was $519, 934 in the final year the company was alive.

Later, Allison took Hare aside and said, "I'd be a little careful. I just found something out and we may not be as financially stable as we should be." Then he quickly added, "But don't worry. We'll be all right."

No one in the know was admitting anything in public. Geoffrey Jarvis, who ran Canada's largest independent life agency, with five hundred agents representing thirty companies, had begun to worry about the safety of policies placed with Confed on behalf of clients. A regular attendee at annual meetings, Jarvis found both the other attendees and the management surprisingly blasé about the troubling profit level announced at the February meeting.

The fact that there were no questions from the floor "showed a lack of knowledge, lack of interest, and a lack of integrity," says Jarvis. As for Rhind and Burns, "both were intolerant of suggestions or advice. Burns was arrogant; Rhind was unresponsive."

Jarvis began to place new business with companies other than Confed and began to make noise in public through his column in *Canadian Insurance/Agent & Broker*, a trade magazine. He might as well not have bothered. "The industry," he says, "wanted a conspiracy of silence."

In March 1992, Mackenzie again met with the board and declared his disappointment with the lack of action. As commercial paper and other short-term instruments were coming due, cash was flowing out to repay those matured instruments. But less revenue was coming in from real estate, so Confed was beginning to suffer from liquidity problems.

OSFI staffers had been receiving monthly updates on this dilemma. Some of the directors now began to challenge Mackenzie, complaining that his earlier messages hadn't been particularly strong. They pointed out that Mackenzie had only indicated that there were worrisome trends, not that the company was headed for any danger zone.

Satisfied that he had finally gained the full attention of the directors, Mackenzie chose not to escalate possible action. He had substantial powers, but used none of them. For example, regulators can revoke an auditor's appointment or enlarge the scope of an audit, order a special examination of an institution (paid for by that institution), order a special actuarial valuation, have assets appraised, increase frequency of the regular annual examination, order capital to be increased, impose conditions on how a company carries on business, issue a direction of compliance if an institution is committing – or is about to commit – an unsafe or unsound business practice. Ultimately, OSFI can take control of the institution or its assets.

Moral suasion is the first step, but, if that gets nowhere, the superintendent can seek a letter of undertaking, signed by the CEO and approved by the board of directors. Undertakings could include restrictions on investment or lending activities. OSFI did demand to see a business plan, but the projection that Burns and Rhind gave Mackenzie in his office that winter saw Confed quickly returning to health. Mackenzie thought the projections were too optimistic, and told Rhind that either Burns had to be replaced or the company would continue to deteriorate. Rhind was flabbergasted. "Mike, you can't be serious about this. Pat's a great guy." Replied Mackenzie, "We've lost confidence."

It was about then that Bill Douglas decided the time was right for him to leave Confederation Life and move to Newcourt – as the leasing company became known – a switch Douglas says he'd been planning since 1989 when he became chairman of the leasing company. Confed, he claims, wasn't a fulfilling place to work. Yes, his ideas, such as the trust company, the leasing company, Confederation Treasury Services Ltd., structured settlements, and group-mortgage benefit, had been adopted, but that wasn't enough.

"Not sufficient of my ideas were implemented to leave me with a feeling that they were even tested," he says. "To move into a role where they could be tested in a unified or coherent pattern, I thought was fun. I wished I'd moved quicker to get involved in a company like Newcourt has become. It was my vision that Confed could and would become similar in character to what Newcourt is. I was just wrong in the judgement, and I wished I'd realized I was wrong earlier and started in a different direction."

As far as trouble in the trust company or real estate or anywhere else, Douglas would have run things differently, and problems, presumably, would not have arisen. "My ideas were used far more in getting things established than in managing them in the way that I thought I'd like to see them managed. There's a difference between establishing things – a lot of my ideas were accepted and implemented, many by me – and the ongoing management philosophy in terms of focus and rewards. I thought it was a step forward to move into the leasing company, where I could have more influence."

The key word in that tortuous explanation is *reward*. Douglas had looked after his own reward. He had put in place a plan – with the approval of Burns – to buy shares. In 1990, Douglas had borrowed money from Confederation Life to buy his 5-per-cent stake in the leasing company. By the time the board learned of the arrangement in 1992, principal and interest owing had grown to $1,677,137. Directors were discovering the depths of the symbiotic relationship between Burns and Douglas, as well as Douglas's powers over the CEO.

Douglas's loan to buy shares in the leasing company was brought to the board "late in the day," says a director. "He had a conflict of interest. Do you expect a person to blow the whistle on himself?" Admits Douglas, "I did approve every large loan made by the leasing company, which, to me, was important to protect Confed's interest and to protect my interest."

Throughout, Douglas stoutly maintains there was no conflict that should have caused concern. "There are conflicts all the time," he told the *Globe and Mail*'s John Partridge in 1994. "When you ask for a salary increase, your interests are in conflict with those of your employer. The issue is not whether there is a conflict, but whether the conflict is properly managed and controlled." But what if the individual is employee and boss both?

Douglas convinced the board of Confederation Life to agree to a departure deal that saw him sell the shares, then repurchase them with a loan from Confed once he'd become chairman of the leasing company. Douglas pocketed a profit of $950,630, then took out a $2.7-million loan to repurchase the shares he'd recently dumped.

For Douglas, the departure meant not only that he didn't have to wrestle with Confed problems anymore, but also that he enriched himself. In 1993, his total compensation was $793,839. In 1994, his annual compensation rose 37 per cent to $1,086,720. On January 3,

1995, after he left Newcourt, he was paid a further $1,460,355 to cover both the severance agreement and the remaining term of his employment contract, which had been set to expire later that year.*

On May 27, 1992, Pat Burns finally came clean with his board of directors. In addition to a capital problem, he told them, Confed also faced a potential liquidity crisis. The cause: Confed had invested in assets of long-term duration, but many liabilities were short-term. The mismatch meant liquidity problems paying the short-term liabilities as they came due. He told the directors that Confed was about $1.5 billion short of covering potential demands with liquid assets.

Tony Griffiths reported that his audit committee had met with the auditors, Ernst & Young, who advised management to pursue any and all possible options to avoid a liquidity crisis. Griffiths, who had been working behind the scenes for several months to topple Burns, had convinced enough directors that Burns must be ousted as CEO. "So much had gone on. Pat had just been swept along," says one director. "We had to make a change. There had to be a fireman brought in. [Burns] saw the inevitability of it. He was very depressed. I don't think

---

* Douglas fared even better with Newcourt shares. When Newcourt went public in February 1994, the initial 5-per-cent interest he had acquired while still at Confed had become, according to Newcourt's share registry, 766,050 shares. At $13.50 per share, they were worth $10.3 million. He purchased an additional 32,470 shares at the time the company went public, then in December 1994 sold 200,000 shares at $14.50 per share for gross proceeds of $2.9 million, leaving him holding 598,520 shares. In January 1995, he exercised an option to buy 86,541 shares at $12.15 to hold 685,061 shares, then sold 20,918 shares in April to hold a total of 664,143.

In an interview in March 1996, Douglas said he then held 450,000 shares. Since he is no longer a director of the company and therefore not required to reveal his trading activities, the exact price for the approximately 214,000 shares he must have sold between April 1995 and March 1996 is impossible to determine. However, during that period, share price rose from about $15 to about $25. Assuming he sold at the mid-point, $20, his pre-tax proceeds would have been $4.3 million. In August 1996, share price had reached $32, making his 450,000 shares worth $14.4 million.

he was up to fighting all the things that were coming out of the wall at him."

Two years earlier, directors had conducted a personnel inventory and management review. Mike Regester was seen as the likely heir. They now decided not only to speed up Burns's departure but also jettisoned the idea of elevating someone from within. Fresh blood was needed to revitalize Confederation Life.

For a time, directors believed that they had convinced Burns to step aside, retire immediately, and not wait until the following year, when he was due to go at age sixty-five. But they had misjudged the feisty CEO. He wasn't going to give up quite that easily. He rekindled his fighting Irish spirit, and he began to resist any move to push him out early. The "crackerjack" was not yet spent. Burns holed up to fight for his corporate life. Other loyal members of management supported him; they did not relish the thought of bringing in an outsider; that was too much of an admission of their own failings.

The board pressed on regardless. A search committee, headed by Adam Zimmerman, with Tony Griffiths and George Mara as members, was established. The directors wanted better internal audit information and financial controls, so Wendy Watson was recruited as vice-president, internal audit, reporting directly to Zimmerman. Watson had been in a similar role at Sun Life for fifteen years and had checked Confed carefully before accepting the job. As part of her personal due diligence, she conferred with Mike Mackenzie, who told her flat out, "There are some big issues – but nothing that can't be dealt with." Senior Sun colleagues were equally sanguine, saying that, yes, Confed was having problems with its trust company and had taken on mortgage and real-estate business that other companies had turned down, but wasn't every company in the same pickle?

The first thing Watson did upon arriving at Confed in mid-July 1992 was to review the previous year's board minutes. What she read recorded there neither heightened her concern about the financial condition of Confed nor made her wish that she had not joined. What she did see, however, was animosity between Burns and regulators that came through even in the formal record of board proceedings. "The tone was very different [from Sun]. The regulators were not our favourite people, but we certainly were incredibly polite to them and did all the nodding in the right direction," says Watson. "I was surprised in the [Confed] boardroom where it was made very clear to them that they were not welcome and that their comments were not welcome."

In her experience, as dicey as it got at Sun was for CEO John McNeil to schedule his sessions with OSFI early in the morning, so all he had to do was serve coffee rather than lay on a lunch that would prolong his time with the regulators. The relationship Burns had with Mackenzie was entirely different. When Mackenzie met with Burns and management that July, September, and October, Burns would disagree loudly and violently with Mackenzie as the superintendent prodded him to act. In response, Mackenzie did not avail himself of the increased powers handed him under the revised Insurance Act, which had just passed in June. Mackenzie could, for example, have examined officers under oath, requested asset valuations, and directed that a special audit be conducted.

Watson's internal audit turned up items that had previously been repressed. In the past, bad news hadn't always been passed up the ranks. "A lot of the financial problems stemmed from [the trust company], and you could say it snowballed, but there were problems in other parts of the organization," she says. "The funding for this trust-company problem had to come from somewhere. Any company that grew as quickly as that one did, something had to give."

As the pressure on him grew that year, Burns's alcohol consumption became more obvious. "Pat liked to drink. He'd always liked to drink," says George Powell. But when Burns visited Atlanta that May, something had changed. Powell didn't know that directors wanted to get rid of Burns, but he could see the result when he and Burns and two others went for lunch at a nearby club. "He seemed to need a drink badly," says Powell. "That was when I thought maybe his problem had gone a bit far. I thought that he might not have had the same control."

"It was no secret that he drank and could become belligerent," says Bill Bowden, director of United States agencies. "I can't understand why no one said anything. It was like the case of the emperor has no clothes. What do you do if you do say something and nothing changes. Do you walk?"

That summer, Confed employees on coffee break in Greenwin Square, the retail mall across Huntley Street from head office, saw Burns on more than one occasion coming out of the liquor store shortly after its 9:30 A.M. opening. They'd watch him take the just-purchased bottle out of the brown paper bag and tuck it in his pants pocket. He'd then adjust his suit jacket to try and make sure that the bottle wasn't obvious, throw the bag in the trash, and head for the office. "He was the first or second customer, along with the winos," says a long-time employee who regularly watched Burns make his purchase and go through the stealthy steps that followed.

There was a widespread view that alcohol had been a problem for Burns for years. "One of the major causes of the destruction of Confederation Life is the alcohol dependency of the chief executive officer," says Frank di Paolo, vice-president, financial. "He had delirium tremens, and from eight o'clock in the morning he was shaking until he could get hold of a glass of whisky. I don't think he really had control of the wheel during the last five years of his tenure, and that's when the problems started."

Di Paolo often saw Burns go through three double whiskies at lunch. "Everyone knew that he was an alcoholic. He lost complete control of the company. His underlings took on the company," says di Paolo. For di Paolo, this was all familiar ground. Old J. K. Macdonald himself used to get into the sauce. At the 1957 Christmas party, di Paolo's second year at Confed, Macdonald had been so badly under the weather that his speech was an embarrassment.

Others say that Burns's problem only became full-blown once the board lost confidence in him. "When does it become a problem?" says Jack Rhind. "He could hold an enormous amount. I've seen people like that. Wally McCutcheon was the most incredible.* He just got

---

*   A director in nearly two dozen companies, McCutcheon was a cabinet minister in the John Diefenbaker government and a candidate for leadership of the Conservative Party in 1967. He died in 1969.

sharper and sharper. Burns didn't drink in that sort of obvious way that some people like McCutcheon might."

"He was always a pretty good drinker, but he wasn't a drunk," says a long-time director. "In the latter stages, Pat didn't look well. He looked like he hadn't been sleeping and had been boozing. His appearance is unfortunate. He has that nose. In the six months prior to his departure, he drank quite a bit. He looked shaken."

No wonder. He was in a desperate battle for his status and reputation. There are many theories of management, but the plain fact is that no one can really predict how someone will do in any top job until they actually occupy the office. Worse, when boards of directors go looking at the available talent in an organization, all too often they realize that there is precious little from which to choose. In most companies, the organizational pyramid really does come to a point at the top.

Certainly that was the case at Confed; there was no other choice than Pat Burns – twice – in both the seventies and the eighties. Some observers of the corporate scene argue that you take office with a certain well of strength from which to draw. From day one, that inner strength diminishes, until there's nothing left. Others say that individual growth is possible, that people will visibly become more than they were before the appointment.

Whichever theory is true, Burns came to office with too little talent and did not grow during his time. During the easy eighties, Burns and Confed were swept along on the wave of Bill Douglas's ideas in an economy where even fools could make money and often did.

When trouble came, Burns was ill-prepared. "Pat was a very strong chairman," says Mike Regester. "In easier days, boards were prone to listen to strong chairmen." He was not a modern man, he was more like a throwback from the sixties than someone equipped for cyberspace. When trouble arrived, it was then too late for conservatism, and conservatism was the only other management style he knew.

Even Jack Rhind began to wish for a *deus ex machina*, a saviour who would come along as they always do in Greek tragedy, literally lowered onto the stage out of the blue with the power to punish wrongdoers, reward the righteous, and generally clean up the tangled mess created by the playwright. Says Rhind, "So many times, I have said to myself, 'If Harold Lawson were here, we'd get out of this.'"

"[Lawson's] talent was an incredible brilliance and a way of being able to surmount obstacles and say, 'Well, it can be done, if we just do this.' He could make things fit that other people couldn't seem to. He made things happen. He brought National out of being just a mundane, small company that nobody knew much about. He put it on the map." The depth of Rhind's desperation in wishing for his old mentor from National Life is both palpable and pathetic.

But there was something else at work here. Confed's background as a family-centred company had functioned well for decades. The paternalistic approach, with subsidized cafeteria lunches and summer picnics, was typical in the banking and insurance industries in Canada until the eighties. Then the world changed, and some institutions, such as the Bank of Montreal under Bill Mulholland, were modernized. They became tougher, less-caring places, but more profitable and more likely to survive.

If the eighties hadn't been so easy, Burns's management style would have caught up with him far sooner. Lack of financial controls, decentralization to the nth degree – all that worked in simpler times. "Pat gave people their heads, and I felt that was one of his strengths," says Al Morson of CompCorp. "If you gave somebody their head and they don't do their job right, that could be a problem."

"Pat was a very aggressive man. He put in the computer system in the sixties, which, at the time, was a model for the industry," says Regester. "He liked to make things happen, but it was a different environment in the eighties than the sixties. A lot of us were naively out of our depth as a management group. A good businessman will have an innate caution about the direction he's going. We were putting in controls, but not fast enough."

"Pat Burns had a tremendous capacity, ability, and tremendous accomplishments, and he also had some weaknesses," says Bill Douglas. "One of the biggest was absolute trust in people to get involved in the trust-company affair or the real-estate investments that Confed did without adequate controls. He had sufficient confidence in the people who were involved in these operations – and confidence in humanity in general – that was overplaced. That was his biggest weakness. It's very frequent that your biggest strength is also your biggest weakness."

At the board meeting on June 24, 1992, Ernst & Young was retained, in the words that the recording secretary included in the minutes, to "identify and quantify a survival plan or a repair program." Ernst & Young had been doing Confed's books for years, going back to the days of its precursor firm, Clarkson Gordon. There is no question that the firm has depth and talent. E&Y has sixty-seven thousand employees in six hundred cities in one hundred countries. The firm audits twelve of the fifty largest banks in the world, more than any other firm.

Still, the choice of E&Y to review strategy was a baffling one. Rather than hiring the fox to watch the henhouse, this was more like hiring one of the hens. E&Y had been part of the process by which Confed had so badly lost its way, and had approved all that had gone before. It hardly seemed the likely place to turn either for fresh thinking or a bold rescue plan.

In any event, the advice Ernst & Young did offer was not earth-shattering. In August, it urged the board to take "vigorous, immediate action," and recommended several merger partners that Confed might pursue. A year would pass before that idea, as obvious as it was, was actually under way.

Wendy Watson established a new program called key control reviews, an internal system that was meant to do daily what an external audit firm does annually: conduct risk-based assessments and try to identify areas where material financial errors had arisen or could happen. In particular, the reviews focused on corporate actuarial, Canadian operations, and information systems.

"The very strong growth that Confed achieved, the seed of that growth, did not carry with it the consolidated control system that should have been there," admits Regester. "Those of us who were autonomous were part of the autonomy. The corporate side didn't stress the need for centralized control enough. We just weren't aware of it, innocently. Maybe we weren't as clued into the needs of management of a large corporation as we should have been."

By August, the board's search committee was down to a short list

for a new CEO, so it hardly seemed appropriate to do anything precip-
itous just yet. Directors decided that Confed should focus on strong
business franchises, which might result in divestiture of some business
units. But any action taken now would only tie the hands of the new
man, so the directors – in their wisdom – decided to wait. Four
months had now passed since Pat Burns had finally admitted the
liquidity problem, and all that had occurred during the summer heat
was that the board had found yet another reason to do once more that
which it did so well – nothing.

Elsewhere within Confed, some restorative action was under way,
however. Changes in the Insurance Act, which became effective
June 1, 1992, allowed a mutual company to strengthen its balance
sheet by issuing debt obligations that would count as capital for regulatory purposes. Confed wasted no time. Two Eurobond issues were
successfully floated: the first on June 10 for $100 million at 9.5 per
cent; the second on July 30 for £100 million sterling (about C$196
million) also at 9.5 per cent.

The second issue was no doubt aided by a letter Ernst & Young
submitted July 23 that put Confed's books in the best possible light.
Although the firm admitted that it had audited no financial statements
since December 31, 1991, E&Y said it had read board minutes, studied
interim financial statements provided by Confed, and discussed those
statements with management. Said the letter, used to support the
attempts to raise capital on the Euromarket: "We did not find any
change in total shareholders' equity or loan capital . . . or any decrease
in the net assets . . . or in the total surplus funds" compared with the
previous year-end six months earlier.

Inside the company, some areas were simply being shut down. On
July 20, 1992, D. Wayne Joyce, Confed's director of agencies for
Canada, sent a memo to all the company's agents, telling them to stop
selling guaranteed accumulation annuity plans. Such plans, similar to
bank term deposits or guaranteed investment certificates, had been
big business for Confed. But when the plans were sold, Confed was
taking on a future liability. As a result, the firm had to have an asset
with sufficient value to ensure the customers could eventually be paid.
Confed now had nowhere to invest client money at high rates, so

moved to cut off the inbound flow of funds. In order to make sure agents listened to head office, interest rates paid were made uncompetitive and agents' commissions on that business were slashed in half.

In public, Burns continued to put the best face on his situation. "Until a recovery comes, you are going to see other companies hit with the same problems," he said in August. "We just might have been a little earlier and a little more acute than others." How much worse off he was than the rest of the world was about to be revealed.

CHAPTER 8

The Search for a Saviour

"How did you go bankrupt?" Bill asked. "Two ways," Mike said.
"Gradually, then suddenly."

– Ernest Hemingway

On September 2, 1992, TRAC Insurance Services Ltd., of Toronto, released its first report on the financial strength and solvency of the Canadian life-insurance industry. Confederation Life received the worst ranking of any company and was found wanting on six of its eight tests of financial well-being – the first time there was any public fingerpointing drawing attention to the fact that, maybe, just maybe, there was a problem. Others in trouble, according to TRAC, included Crown Life and Sovereign Life.[*]

Bill Andrus, president of TRAC (which stands for tests, ratios, analysis, and charts) certainly has the background to be an industry scold. As an actuary for more than two decades, Andrus previously worked

---

[*] In December, regulators concluded that Calgary-based Sovereign had slipped so badly that it had no capital at all and seized the company, thereby confirming TRAC's view about at least one firm.

at the Ontario Department of Insurance, plus several private-sector firms, including Pilot Insurance, Empire Life, and Canadian General Insurance Co., as well as Fairfax Financial Holdings, owners of general-insurance firms.

Andrus set up TRAC in 1980 as a part-time task, working out of his house. The service issued reports that rated the corporate health and claims-paying abilities of three hundred property-and-casualty-insurance firms. His partner, Don Smith, has been at the whistle-blowing game almost as long. In 1981, Smith tried to clean up Pitts Insurance Co., of London, Ontario, from the inside as executive vice-president and was later hired by the superintendent of insurance to help with that wind-up.

Despite the fact that TRAC had been producing credible reports on the property-and-casualty-insurance firms for more than a decade, the 1992 findings on the life-insurance business were roundly denounced by Confed and the industry. Mark Daniels, president of the Canadian Life and Health Insurance Association (CLHIA), wrote to TRAC saying, "The potential for misunderstanding is uncomfortably high." Daniels said that any suggestion that consumers should use TRAC to assess companies was "fraught with danger and is, we believe, irresponsible counsel."

In a September 4 letter to employees and agents, Pat Burns claimed that TRAC's information was misleading, because it underestimated Confed's capital by 60 per cent. He argued that TRAC had failed to take account of $200 million in capital gains that had been deferred for tax reasons. Burns wrote, "Let me assure you that Confederation Life Insurance Co. is financially strong and continues to build on this strength. We are capitalized comfortably above the levels required by the Office of the Superintendent of Financial Institutions (OSFI) and continue to obtain strong ratings from industry recognized rating agencies."

Ratings are crucial to a financial-services company. Good ratings give comfort to policyholders, customers, and investors. When ratings are lowered, or downgraded, questions arise and policyholders become nervous and demand cash-surrender values. Specific products such as corporate-owned life insurance (COLI) and bank-owned life insurance (BOLI), where companies take out policies on behalf of employees, require ratings of a certain level. If ratings fall below that, corporate treasurers must automatically find other coverage with a similar umbrella, but from a company in better health.

Rating agencies had become ever more important in the scheme of things, with growing power and awesome responsibility. A. M. Best Co., founded in 1899, is the oldest rating agency, and its particular focus on the insurance industry makes it a power in the sector. The best known is Moody's Investors Service, founded in 1909 by John Moody, who established the simple ABC rating system to advise potential investors about the health of United States railway bonds.

Little change had come about by 1958 when Moody died. Bonds were still a pretty stable commodity, but the Vietnam War rendered prices more volatile in the sixties. In 1970, when Penn Central defaulted on $82 million in commercial paper, investors suddenly began paying attention.

There are four major rating agencies in the United States that matter: A. M. Best, Standard & Poor's, Moody's, and Duff & Phelps. In Canada, there are three: Canadian Bond Rating Service (CBRS), Dominion Bond Rating Service (DBRS), and the aforementioned TRAC. Their written reports, usually running three to four pages, focus on institutional investors (Moody's) and consumers and insurance producers (Best and S&P). The media, regulators, brokers, and the public also watch – particularly for downgrades.

"Financial strength is clearly a competitive advantage. Ratings are a simple way of communicating this to the public," said Mike Lombardi, principal in the Toronto office of Tillinghast Towers Perrin, an actuarial consulting firm. But the agencies are far from perfect. "A high rating is not a guarantee that the company will survive, and a low rating is not a guarantee that the company will fail," says Lombardi. Most of the information gathered by agencies comes direct from management, usually in lengthy sessions at which the company presents its case and the agencies ask pointed questions.

The agencies are paid by the companies they analyse. Ratings cost $20,000 in Canada, two or three times that in the United States. For decades, there had been no failures. The industry was dominated by large mutual companies and several closely held stock companies that rarely issued shares or debt instruments. As a result, Canada was not exactly propitious territory for the agencies.

In the fall of 1992, TRAC was alone in its negativity. All the rest continued to say that Confed was healthy. A. M. Best maintained Confed at A+ (superior) throughout the year. Standard & Poor's had rated Confed's claims-paying ability AAA until January 1992, when it was cut to AA+ then to AA in September. According to the explanation with that rating, AA meant "excellent financial security. Capacity to meet policyholder obligations is strong under a variety of economic and underwriting conditions." On October 26, Duff & Phelps dropped Confed from AAA to AA+. But, even with those changes, Confed retained better ratings than the big six Canadian banks.

In an interview at the time, Burns admitted that Confed's capital base had eroded, but denied there was any difficulty. "I would not say difficulty. What I would say is you always wish it was maybe higher." In order to preserve capital and increase surplus after a year when profits were low, Confed would "slow down the growth of certain product lines and . . . look at our investment portfolio and shift the profile to lower risk into corporate and government and bonds and away from mortgages, real estate, et cetera.

"We've experienced a period of rapid growth . . . so that tends to erode capital," said Burns. "None of this comes as a surprise. We were monitoring it, and we basically said we would always want to keep our capital at a level that matched the [regulatory] requirements with some comfort level."

That fall, Confed disposed of about $100 million in real estate, including $30 million worth of properties in Edmonton, Saskatoon, Winnipeg, and Toronto, through the first-ever auction by a major financial institution. Another $100 million in property, acquired through foreclosures, was also dumped. In many cases, Confed had to do vendor take-backs just to close the deals. Still, there would be some cash flow into the coffers from the new owners. A five-year target had been set to reduce the exposure in real estate to 46.5 per cent of assets, while almost doubling bonds from 16.5 per cent to 29 per cent of the total investment portfolio.

Although TRAC looked as if it were sticking its neck out, there was a more ominous, official measurement that was not publicly revealed. OSFI had instituted a new ratio intended to measure the health of insurance companies, called the minimum continuing capital and surplus requirements (MCCSR).

For public consumption, Burns said he was still studying the new requirements, so he could not say how Confed was positioned in relation to prescribed levels. But he did admit that the company was not operating at what he called its preferred position: twenty-five percentage points above the designated level. In fact, at the time MCCSR was launched in 1992, Confed's ratio was a sorry 125 per cent, barely above the 120-per-cent minimum prescribed by OSFI.* The average among all Canadian companies in 1992 was 159 per cent. Foreign life companies operating in Canada were at an even healthier 233 per cent. Confed was badly lagging, and OSFI had further substantiation of Confed's poor performance relative to its peers.

By September 1992, Burns had spent four months resisting the wishes of his directors to replace him, but the combination of the unsettling MCCSR and TRAC results aroused the board for the final assault. The short list included one insider, Mike Regester, and two outsiders, Paul Cantor, formerly of the Canadian Imperial Bank of Commerce (CIBC), and Dominic D'Alessandro, president and CEO of Laurentian Bank.

If Confed had been healthy, Regester would have been the logical choice to succeed Burns. Now he stood little chance and was simply kept on the list as a formality. Fifty at the time, Regester knew full well that the next logical step for him was "either CEO or out." He claimed he was "not by nature an ambitious person," but admitted he was working sixty-hour weeks and worried he was too approachable

---

* The percentage expresses a ratio of the capital available to the capital required, so 100 per cent would be exactly equal to the capital required, but OSFI erred on the conservative side and used 120 per cent as the working minimum. In some cases, firms slipped well below the minimum level before action was taken. Equitable Life Insurance Co. of Canada, of Waterloo, Ontario, sank to 70 per cent, hired a new CEO in 1992, and took drastic action that brought MCCSR up to 130 per cent two years later.

to be a boss. "I think I get a little too close. I'm too sensitive to people's personal problems." He said he believed in giving underlings their head "within firmly set parameters. If they get outside the parameters, then I would be asking critical questions. But I don't usually have to." The style sounds uncannily like Pat Burns's pick-'em-and-leave-'em approach.

Among staff, Regester was by no means a unanimous choice as heir rampant. "Mike was not universally viewed as the right horse," says George Powell, who had seen Regester up close in Atlanta. "Was [Ronald] Reagan a great president or was Reagan in the right place at the right time? Operations were successful under Mike, and he had something to do with that. But the higher up the totem pole you go, the more you need to be well rounded and to be able to manage in all environments."

In the end, directors decided that they did not want Regester; they wanted a clean break from the old ways. They had settled on Cantor, but he'd been put on hold for months. He had spoken at length to Mackenzie and the auditors about Confed and had been ready since July to take on the role. "I had to fight for that job," says Cantor. "It was a widely sought after role in the Canadian business community. Nobody suggested it wasn't going to be a challenge, but everybody believed it could be turned around."

Directors hoped to make the announcement that summer, but Burns wouldn't step aside. The situation was all too familiar – exactly the same as the one Confed directors had found themselves in the mid-seventies when Craig Davidson, ill and abusing alcohol, refused to leave and finally needed a shove before another outsider, Jack Rhind, could be brought in.

In October, the opportunity for the putsch finally came when Burns and Regester travelled to Washington, D.C., to attend the annual meeting of the Life Insurance Marketing and Research Association (LIMRA). Forces in Toronto chose that moment to make their move, as if Burns were some potentate from an emerging nation who was out of the country on a state visit. Rather than call in the army to conduct a coup, however, the chosen method was bloodless and more adroit. News was leaked that Cantor was being brought in to replace

Burns. On October 20, Barry Critchley wrote in his *Financial Post* column that Cantor's appointment as the new president and CEO of Confed would be announced later that same day. Burns, said the article, was retiring.

The *ancien régime* was ended. Regester was scheduled to host a lunch that day, but cancelled the event at Burns's request to hole up in his hotel room and call key Confed people around the world in order to put the ouster in the best possible light. The official announcement followed as predicted. Paul Cantor was the new president and CEO. Burns would retain the title of chairman as a way of saving face.

Cantor would later complain to friends that the delay in his being parachuted in cost him dearly. He would blame Burns for holding back his turnaround plans for Confed, but, at the time, Cantor believed that he couldn't lose. If he pulled off a rescue, he'd be a hero; if he didn't, the debacle would be Burns's fault. In addition to resurrecting Confed, maybe this new role could also mean a little personal redemption. Like Burns before him, Cantor had some people – in this case his unappreciative bosses at the CIBC – to whom he wanted to demonstrate his mettle. Unlike Burns, however, Cantor arrived at Confed already a member in good standing of the York Club. J. K. Macdonald would have approved.

Paul Cantor was born in Edmonton on January 8, 1942. His grandfather was an Orthodox rabbi who emigrated to Canada from eastern Europe around the turn of the century. His father was a biochemistry professor at the University of Alberta and chief coroner for the province. A summer working as a hospital orderly convinced Cantor that he was not cut out to follow his father into a career in medicine. "I realized," he told writer Charles Davies in 1988, "that I was uncomfortable having human life in my hands." Cantor did his undergraduate degree at the University of Alberta. There, he joined Delta Upsilon fraternity and said to his new brothers, "I'd like to be involved in campus affairs." As with anyone who so magnanimously volunteers, there was suddenly a host of jobs. "The next day, I was head of fund-raising for World University Service of Canada (WUSC), was arts-and-science rep to the national federation of Canadian University Students, and the director of publicity for varsity guest weekend."

After graduating from the University of Alberta in 1962, he started law at the University of Toronto, but left after first year to work full time at WUSC for three years. There he got his first hands-on business experience, importing handicrafts from around the world for sale on campuses across Canada. After that, he returned to law school, graduated in 1968, and then joined the Department of Finance in the international-programs division, helping to arrange project financing in Asia, Africa, and the Caribbean.

He liked international development, but one day someone in finance said to him, "You were a lawyer; we need a lawyer to study other countries' tax laws and how they affect Canadian trade policy – and you're it." At thirty, Cantor was suddenly part of the team put together in response to U.S. President Richard Nixon's protectionist trade program called the Domestic International Sales Corp. (DISC). Next, he worked at Polysar Inc. for two years as taxation manager, then in 1976 joined the tax department of the Canadian Imperial Bank of Commerce (CIBC).

At the bank, Cantor was soon seen as a fast-tracker. CEO Russ Harrison liked Cantor and put him in charge of Treasury operations. But though Cantor aspired to be president of the CIBC, he had his doubts that the board would pick a Jew. Such an elevated position would be a first for any Jew in a Canadian bank. In the early eighties, Bill Neville, an Ottawa lobbyist who had run unsuccessfully for Parliament, was working at the CIBC as a vice-president, advising Harrison, and would talk to Cantor about their respective career paths. Recalls Neville, "We used to ask each other which two of the sixty-eight vice-presidents are not going to be president." Their conclusion, according to Neville, "The Jewish tax lawyer and the exotic plant from Ottawa."

Cantor liked to describe himself as a strategist, not a banker, but he did well at climbing the corporate ladder. By 1986, Don Fullerton was chairman and CEO of CIBC; he gave his three likely heirs equal status.

Warren Moysey ran individual banking, Al Flood was in charge of corporate banking, and Cantor headed investment banking. Cantor played a key role in 1988 when the CIBC bought two-thirds of investment firm Wood Gundy Inc. for $190 million, then oversaw the merging of the bank and Gundy's investment-banking divisions.

Cantor had a reputation for being about the least pretentious senior banker in the country. He was intelligent, did not stand on ceremony, and would often show up unannounced at the office of an underling rather than summon the minion to his lair.*

While Cantor's office was situated on the bank's executive fifth floor of the Commerce Court West in downtown Toronto, he didn't partake of all the amenities available to him. Cantor is an inveterate junk-food lover, so, rather than ride up on the elevator to the bank's fifty-sixth-floor dining room or order sandwiches to be sent down on a silver tray, nothing made Cantor happier than to slip out on his own to a nearby McDonald's and bring back lunch in a paper bag. The greasy smell of French fries wafting about did not endear Cantor to his colleagues in their wood-panelled world.

That's not to say Paul Cantor doesn't like fine things. He owns an electric blue 1340cc Harley-Davidson Electraglide and a 650cc Suzuki Tempter and has participated in an annual event in which people known as RUBs – rich urban bikers – don their leathers and play outlaw.

On a summer's day in 1993, for example, after he'd arrived at Confed, he tooled around on what's called the president's ride, a day-long outing in which two dozen "bad" actors on their $20,000 "hogs" travel in a pack and have lunch at a country inn. The posse included: Stephen Bebis, then president and CEO of Aikenhead's Home Improvement Warehouse; Colin Watson, then president and CEO of Rogers Cablesystems Ltd., and Gordie Tapp of "Hee Haw" fame.

---

* Such surprise visits did have their embarrassing moments. Once, Cantor found himself sitting opposite a junior's wall calendar, which featured scenes from the Second World War. That month's giant photo showed the Führer of the German Third Reich addressing his troops at the Nuremberg rally. Cantor made no mention of the lapse in taste.

For Cantor, owning a Harley was the realization of lifelong dream. "I'd been thinking about it for a long time, and one day said to myself, 'Time is going by, and if you don't get on with living life you never will.'" Mind you, the first time Cantor took his test for the motorcycle licence, he failed. He was driving too slowly.

Cantor also revelled in his role as an "owner" of the Toronto Blue Jays. The CIBC had purchased a 10-per-cent founder's share in the Jays in the mid-seventies. As a result, Cantor was able to supply friends with tickets – and not just for home games but also for hard-to-get dugout seats at stadia in other cities.

Don Fullerton replaced Russ Harrison as CEO in 1985 and, like Harrison before him, was tough on potential heirs. Warren Moysey had been tipped for the top, but Fullerton abruptly turned on him in the fall of 1990. Fullerton called Moysey in and told him he wasn't happy. When Moysey asked why, Fullerton declared that he was immediately leaving to travel for a couple of weeks in the Far East and didn't have time to explain. When Fullerton returned from his trip, there still was no explanation forthcoming. It was almost as if Fullerton had suddenly decided he didn't like the cut of Moysey's jib. Moysey departed and Cantor's stock rose.

But when the time came to replace Fullerton as CEO, the board wasn't ready for someone like Cantor, who might have new ideas. Fullerton had already taken the bank through a lot of reorganizational change. The institution he'd been handed by Harrison wasn't in as good shape as the Bank of Montreal had been when Bill Mulholland had given way to his successor, Matthew Barrett, in 1990. Fullerton had reorganized the bank in three parts under three different presidents, and chopped five thousand employees. Fullerton liked Cantor and was even said to favour him as his successor, but he was only one vote at the board. The rest of the board felt that the bank had been through enough change for a while and wanted a rest, a period of consolidation.

For that, Al Flood was a better fit. He had run the United States operations in New York under Harrison, and the two were similar characters, both outspoken. Harrison and Flood would argue heatedly about all manner of things on a regular basis, and Harrison would just as regularly threaten to fire Flood, but never quite got around to it. For the board, selecting Flood was like a step back to the days of Harrison, a retreat from all the activity that Fullerton had dragged them through. So, in 1992, they picked Al Flood as CEO, as a transitional figure at the top.

Flood merged corporate banking with the investment division, of which Cantor had been president, and gave both entities to John Hunkin, who had been head of Wood Gundy, the brokerage subsidiary. As a result of that shuffle, Cantor had no power base and quickly concluded that his best shot at becoming chief executive of CIBC was gone.

Flood did not want his former rival waiting around for him to stumble. In one of his first steps as incoming CEO, Flood fired Cantor, who departed on June 5, two days before Flood was set to take over. Cantor received a year's salary (about $350,000) as a golden handshake, and the bank paid for an office in a classy holding tank on Toronto Street, set up for just such similarly downsized executives.

Cantor then did what all defrocked executives do; he telephoned everyone he knew. On the network was George Mara, who was looking for a CEO again, just as he had in 1976. To the Confed directors, Cantor seemed like the bright fellow they needed to restore credibility and credit: hard-working, with a good reputation and a background in investment banking that might mean he could tap new sources of capital for Confed.

As Cantor did his due diligence, the picture he saw was not pretty. Not only was the company too far into real estate, there was too much geographic concentration. In the United States, where total holdings were US$3.67 billion, one-third were in just two states – California and New Jersey. Add three more states – Texas, Virginia, and Florida – and Confed had invested more than 54 per cent of its total portfolio in just five states. So much for diversification. Even in a large company like Confed, such investments caused substantial pain. If a state's economy weakens, Confed's portfolio takes a hit. Moreover, more than 57 per cent was invested in just two categories: office and retail, the first sectors to go into free fall.

Some insiders were worried about less-visible problems. George

Powell, the man who had replaced Frank di Paolo as financial vice-president in the United States, didn't like something he spotted on Confed's 1992 statement. Under liabilities, there was an item called "deferred net capital gains" showing $246.3 million. Powell believed that the figure was far too low, perhaps understating reality by as much as $200 million. If he were right, that would reduce surplus – stated that year as $900 million – by $200 million, knocking it down to $700 million.

Surplus is the key to an insurance company's financial stability. The size of an insurance company, measured by assets, has nothing at all to do with the safety of the firm or the ability to meet policyholder obligations. Confed's assets in 1992 were $18 billion, up 50 per cent from 1988. Problem loans *in the United States alone* were equal to two-thirds of surplus – 84 per cent if Powell was right – the safety cushion of corporate strength and endurance.

When Powell put the question to company actuary Michael Rosenfelder, he got nowhere. "They didn't answer me. This is the junior asking the senior," says Powell. "Rosenfelder wasn't a mentor; he wasn't a great one to share what was going on. Knowledge is power. I was not an initiate into the practices."

The disregard for Powell demonstrates the closed-shop culture that was Confed. The higher-ups did not encourage questions, and definitely discouraged dissent, and with fast asset growth and high staff turnovers, there were always new employees coming along who learned to fall into line. Only the views of a select few really mattered. Anyone else was not "an initiate."

In fact, Powell was no junior. He had been at Confed for fourteen years. Born in Edinburgh, Scotland, educated at McGill and the University of Illinois, he taught at the University of Guelph for three years before joining Confed in 1978 and working his way up in actuarial services. He moved to Atlanta in 1982, in 1986 he was named vice-president for information services, and in 1991 he became financial vice-president.

As far as Powell was concerned, the questions he raised were matters of common sense and classic morality. The actuary has the most responsible role in the company; if he doesn't like what's happening, he can go straight to the superintendent. "I do think that you get into some issues of ethics. It's not that it's dishonesty, but it's degrees. What are the rules of the game that you're playing? I'm very much a spirit-of-the-law man, not a letter-of-the-law man. I think theirs was a letter-of-the-law mentality, and [they] skated through the loopholes sometimes," says Powell.

OSFI's Michael Mackenzie also saw Rosenfelder as a weak link. "The one problem that [Confed] didn't respond to very well was our concern about the actuary." Rosenfelder, who had Canadian and British citizenship, had joined Confed in 1956 and was named vice-president, corporate actuarial and finance, in 1988, rising later to corporate actuary. "[Rosenfelder] was a nice guy, but there was a fundamental lack of independence," says Mackenzie. "He'd been part of Burns's team; he'd been involved with all of this in the eighties. When I say a lack of independence, he was part of the action. Actuaries play a fairly influential role in management. Once you start down the road of not being as conservative as you should be, you're kind of locked in. It's very hard if things aren't going well to shift gears."

Moreover, Rosenfelder was poorly regarded within the insurance community. "He's an actuary's actuary," says Claude Lamoureux, president and CEO of the Ontario Teachers' Pension Board. Lamoureux, himself an actuary, does not offer the description as a compliment. "Like a lot of actuaries, he tended to be very narrow. If he was asked a question, he'd give you the right answer, but beside it there could be a bomb and he would not even want to touch it."

Such internal lassitude did not slow down external activity. The real estate-market might be dead, but the corporate-owed life insurance (COLI) business in the United States was growing by near-geometric proportions. In 1992, Confed had its biggest COLI sale ever when one corporate client paid a US$100-million premium, all in one lump sum. There were two other huge sales as well, one with a premium of US$80 million and another for US$50 million.

The $100 million was supposed to be paid at 11 A.M. on December 31, 1992; by 2 P.M. there was still no sign of the money. It was New Year's Eve day and banks were beginning to close, employees were departing. The early closings mattered, because Confed wanted the $100 million invested; a cheque couldn't sit on someone's desk for three or four days not earning interest. At 2 P.M., Confed's banker, Harris Trust, shut down its wire-transfer capability.

There was another potential embarrassment. The $100 million had already been "invested" at 10 A.M. that morning, even before it was actually in hand. As a result, that account was now overdrawn by $77 million. Finally, about 3:30 P.M., the $100 million became available. Confed scrambled around, found a New York bank that was still open, and the sum was wired from the client to New York, then on to Toronto to cover the overdraft.

No amount of due diligence by an outsider like Cantor could ever turn up all these goings-on. The Confed that Paul Cantor had signed on to save was riddled with weak management, behind-the-scenes juggling, and an inbred culture that neither listened nor learned. For all the due diligence he'd done, Cantor was no better off than the gullible investor who buys land in Florida sight unseen. It would be months before Cantor would realize that he was mired in a swamp out of which there was no safe passage.

CHAPTER 9

---•◆•---

A Secret Revealed

"If you can keep your head when all about you are losing theirs,
it's just possible you haven't grasped the situation."

— humorist Jean Kerr

P at Burns's last public act as CEO was to declare One Mount
Pleasant Place officially open at a special ceremony on
October 27, 1992. Burns and Tom Pitts cut a ribbon, and a few
pleasantries were uttered, but no one was paying close attention.
Everyone knew Burns had been drummed out. No one feels more
bereft than a CEO who has lost his title; the world moves on and he
suddenly discovers that those associates, bankers, and clients didn't
really care about him as an individual or a businessman. It was the
office that mattered.

At the board meeting the next day, directors reviewed what was
called a business-franchise analysis. The work had begun earlier in the
year with a series of studies into liquidity forecasts. The analysis,
which was to be ready for Cantor's arrival, looked at the various lines
of businesses that made up Confed, with a view to selling them off
separately. Information exchanged with the regulator was discussed.
Grumbled Adam Zimmerman, "OSFI's concerns seem to be with

what did not happen over the past year rather than what was happening today." Five of the seven outside directors did not attend the meeting, as if they could not face the music. Burns was there, but by then his views were rarely sought. He had become a wallflower at the dance that spun towards corporate death.

Paul Cantor officially took up his duties November 16 and met with the directors for the first time at the board meeting on November 25. He spent the first few months of 1993 in the usual new-boy pursuits: visiting departments, glad-handing the troops, and making courtesy calls on people like J. P. Sabourin, president and CEO of Canada Deposit Insurance Corp. Regulators were relieved by his very presence. "The relationships between ourselves improved when Cantor arrived," says OSFI's John Thompson. "He was very open in the way he dealt with us and was very interested in the observations and comments that we had to make about the way the company was being managed. He faced up to the issues and started working towards solving them."

Cantor travelled extensively, visiting regional offices and branch headquarters, such as Atlanta. His message was simple: poor management had caused overexposure to real estate. He intended to set new standards, particularly in non-insurance subsidiaries, and reduce real-estate holdings. Cantor told staff that he wanted to move from width to depth and focus on the insurance business. Just how he would go about that was not yet clear.

He was not universally seen as a welcome saviour. Many of Confed's employees were upset that not only had the firm gone outside their ranks for a chief executive, but they'd hired a *banker*. They'd refer to him as a banker, and from their mouths it sounded like a slur. Cantor noticed the slight. "People only refer to me as a 'banker' now that I've left the bank. But no one ever called me a 'banker' when I was at the bank. They may have called me a lot of names, but 'banker' was not among them." He'd ended up with the worst of both worlds.

Cantor added two key executives, one of whom was also a banker and a man very similar to himself in style. Michael White, who had his CA from Price Waterhouse and was a former senior credit officer at

the Bank of Montreal, arrived in March 1993 to become senior vice-
president, corporate, and chief investment officer. Michael Mackenzie
briefed White on February 3 before he agreed to take the job, just as
he had met with Cantor. In June, Chris Davis, former president of
commercial real-estate services at Royal LePage Ltd., was named vice-
president, real estate, of Confederation Life and chairman and CEO of
Confed Realty Services Ltd.

Cantor fired Mike Regester, the pretender to the throne, just as Al
Flood had dumped him. Burns had warned Regester of this likely
outcome, saying, "There won't be room for Paul Cantor and you."

"I would have used a Regester," says Regester. "But we had different styles. [Cantor] was held out as the great communicator. I don't
believe he was. The message was: 'Senior management has caused the
problem, so you've got to change the culture.'"

In Ottawa, officials were watching the proceedings with deepening
concern. "Paul was faced with a dilemma," says David Dodge, deputy
minister of finance. "He needed capital if he was going to survive. But
he also had a much bigger management problem than he or anybody
else realized." According to Regester, management was not all that
interested in pitching in to help Cantor, because they thought that,
"This guy didn't listen." Perhaps Cantor didn't even know the right
questions to ask. The cause hardly mattered. What did matter was that
the amount of helpful information exchanged was minimal. As a
result, his learning curve became a flat line.

The hope that this banker would raise capital to save Confed soon
foundered. A preliminary prospectus was filed with the Ontario
Securities Commission to issue subordinated debentures, with RBC
Dominion Securities acting as the lead firm. It would be the first such
direct debt issue by any Canadian insurer, a method now allowed
under the Insurance Companies Act that had just been passed. The
deal went nowhere; the market was not interested.

Nor were there any buyers for Confed Trust. Burns Fry Ltd. had
been retained in November 1992 to dump the troubled firm, but
discovered that the trust company had little value, because of its poor
portfolio. Burns Fry approached several possible investors over a six-

Peter Redman / *Financial Post*

The Pat and Jack Show: Jack Rhind (left) was brought in as CEO of Confederation Life in 1976 and later picked Pat Burns as his successor. While Burns (bottom) boasted to a Canadian Club audience in 1990, "We are ready to take on the world," Rhind was equally growth-oriented. Upon learning that a competitor had bought a trust company, Rhind said, "I'm going to be the only kid on the block without an electric train. Get me an electric train."

Peter Redman / *Financial Post*

The master builders:
(facing page, top left) Barry
Walsh, left, and John Heard
ran Confederation Trust, while
(top right) Bill Douglas, left,
and Steven Hudson headed the
leasing company. (Below) The
lavish marble lobby of head
office, including time capsule.
(This page, bottom) The official
opening by Canadian operations
head Tom Pitts and Pat Burns.
Says director Adam Zimmerman
(this page, top), "I can't imagine
why they built that building."

Peter Redman/Financial Post

The sheriff's posse:
Federal watchdogs
included: (facing page,
top) John Thompson and
Suzanne Labarge; (below)
insurance superintendent
Michael Mackenzie; (this
page, top) Michigan
insurance commissioner
David Dykhouse; deputy
minister of finance David
Dodge (bottom left); and
Victor Palmieri (bottom
right). "A child could
have told them that the
strategy *had* to result in
disaster," says Palmieri, a
liquidation specialist
based in New York.
"The problem is that
there is never a child in
the boardroom."

Clarence Tabb/*Detroit News*

Fred Chartrand/Canapress Photo Service

Peter Redman / *Financial Post*

The rescue party: Canadian CEOs who failed to form an industry con-sortium included John McNeil of Sun Life (top), Dominic D'Alessandro of Manulife (bottom left), and Tom Di Giacomo (bottom right), who acted as lubricator.

Jeff Wasserman / *Financial Post*

Peter Redman / *Financial Post*

Gordon Cunningham of London Life (top left), Bob Astley of Mutual Life (top right), and David Nield of Canada Life (bottom). The free-marketers became cripples who cried out for the crutch of government support.

David Zalubowski/Toronto Star

The wheeler-dealers: Orest Dackow (top) of Great-West Life spent seven months in futile negotiations with Confed's Paul Cantor, seen here (bottom, right) with real-estate vice-president Chris Davis on their hogs. Says Cantor, who once clambered onto a boardroom table to make a point, "I'd rather be remembered for my Harley than my table dance."

Peter Redman/Financial Post

month period, but found no appetite for healthy trust operations, let alone for those loaded with non-performing loans.

CEOs like Cantor, who are hired to achieve turnarounds, usually cut back on expenses as a first step. Entertainment is always an easy target, and sets an obvious example for the troops that times have changed. Yet the annual meeting, held March 24, 1993, certainly didn't look like Cantor was trying to tackle problems relating to excess. Geoffrey Jarvis, the Toronto-based general agent who sells for several insurance companies, attended and thought the event was lavish in the circumstances. "The sumptuous buffet, complimentary cocktails, and glossy handouts were in stark contrast to the dismal – and ominous – financial report," he said.

Cantor assured policyholders that Confed would soon be getting "back to fighting the battles we know how to win. Over the next few months our Confederation Life management team will be . . . identifying specific opportunities and changes for the company." Results for 1992 were terrible, even though growth had been slowed from the runaway days of 25-per-cent annual jumps. Assets were now $18 billion, up 11.4 per cent from 1991, when the increase had been 14.9 per cent over 1990.

Profit, a slim-pickin's $17 million in 1991, slipped to $1.9 million in 1992. Canadian operations did slightly better, with a $3-million profit versus a loss of $13 million in 1991. Confed Trust and Confed Financial Services combined to lose $35 million – about the same as the previous year. Head office, a handy catch-all category, had a loss of $46 million (in real-estate and restructuring charges) versus a loss of $2 million in 1991.

At the annual meeting, policyholders seemed oblivious. There were no questions from the floor. At the press conference that followed, Jarvis asked, "What action will be taken to reduce losses?" He was stunned at the lack of announced action. No staff cuts were planned. As for real estate, he was told that the market was stabilizing and all would be well.

Not publicly revealed at the time was the warning issued by Ernst & Young after its completion of the 1992 audit. "Troubled and non-performing real-estate based investments remain at high levels and show some indication of growth in the near term for the industry. The Company is exposed to further deterioration in real-estate values, particularly in the near term while the economy remains depressed."

The warning came despite some improvement in the black hole that was real estate. Invested assets (excluding segregated funds) at the end of 1992 were 59 per cent in mortgages and real estate. That level was an improvement over the 74 per cent at the height, but still a long way from the better-run Sun Life, for example, where the equivalent figure was 40 per cent, about the same as the industry average.

Confed was doing so badly that some life-insurance agents had better earnings in 1992 than the company. Alan Buerger, chairman, The Coventry Group, of Fort Washington, Pennsylvania, and the leading individual insurance producer in the United States, phoned Bill Bowden, director of agencies in Atlanta, to rub it in. "Bill, I can't resist teasing you," said Buerger. "I made more than Confed did last year."

In conjunction with the annual meeting, Cantor made two appointments to the board: Kenneth Field, president of real-estate developer Bramalea Ltd. from 1979 to 1988, and lawyer Daryl McLean, a specialist in corporate acquisitions and reorganizations with McCarthy Tétrault, of Toronto. Two other invitees declined to become directors: Jalynn Bennett, a former Manulife executive then running her own consulting business; and William Etherington, president and CEO of IBM Canada Ltd.

Cantor shuffled the executive committee, dumping Burns, Rhind, and Albino. Zimmerman was elevated to chairman, as Burns lost the last vestiges of power. Cantor also carried out a minor staff housecleaning. In addition to firing Regester, he got rid of two other executives: Doug Newman in Confed Realty Services and William "T-bill" Benton.

Among Cantor's early clean-up tasks was to approve the severance pay and departure of Bill Douglas from the life-insurance company en route to his full-time role as chairman of the leasing company. On March 23, 1993, Confed reduced its interest in the leasing company to 22.5 per cent by selling its holdings to employees of the leasing company and to Mutual Life. The sale had the effect of not only increasing capital but also of increasing liquidity, because the leasing company repaid $200 million in interim funding that had been provided by Confed.

If only Cantor had consulted Douglas, who knew where the bodies were buried, he would have learned all he needed to know about the magnitude of the task he'd undertaken. Douglas attended a March meeting in Barbados of several Confed subsidiaries. The session, held there annually, allowed participants to hear financial results, gossip about the business, listen to speakers talk about new tax wrinkles in leasing, and take a break from the rigors of the Canadian winter. At dinner one night, Douglas turned to Confed investment vice-president Barry Graham, who was sitting beside him, and admitted that real-estate operations of the life-insurance company and the trust company would each end up dinging Confed for losses of $250 million.

The total, $500 million, was a huge sum that would wipe out more than half the surplus, slashing it from $900 million to $400 million. The $900-million figure was already too low for a company of Confed's size; at $400 million, Confed would be as weak as a kitten. By contrast, Sun Life, which was half again as big as Confed, with $32.4 billion in assets, had a surplus of $4 billion, more than four times Confed's cushion. Such losses meant Confederation Life was all but doomed even then. Cantor would take months to discover the size of the hole, let alone figure out a way to fill what had become the Grand Canyon.

Initially, Cantor had naively believed a few tweaks here and there to the balance sheet would be enough. "As we got into it, it became increasingly clear that the challenge was going to be bigger than that, and additional resources would have to be brought to bear," he says. "Overall, the exposure to real estate was going to have a bigger impact than had been expected. We simply had too much exposure. You had a quantity problem in the insurance company coupled with a quality problem in the trust company, which combined turned out to be a lot for the company to bear."

On April 28, the ghosts of the past were finally exorcised, as Confed said goodbye to Pat Burns. The occasion was a dinner at Rosedale Golf Club, an awkward affair for two reasons. First, this was not the usual fond farewell; Burns had been turfed out of office early. Second, Paul Cantor was very much on hand, preening as if this were a welcome-aboard event in his honour.

Mike Regester, Burns's choice for successor, was not among the attendees. The planning was conducted with such lack of aplomb that Burns was told to phone Regester, who was himself in the process of leaving Confed, to tell him he wasn't welcome.

Regester was lucky. Most of those who did go that night can't remember a thing said or done in Burns's supposed honour. They really didn't want to be there, and, once it was over, they expunged the send-off forever from their minds. As his departing gift, Burns was presented with an oil painting of a Canadian winter scene, the very painting that had hung in his office, as if no one wanted even the slightest reminder left behind of his days at the top.

Burns's parting words, printed in the annual report, were tinged with melancholy and might-have-been. "It seems only a short while ago that I walked through the doors of Confederation Square in downtown Toronto on my first day with the Confederation Life," he began. "On that day, some forty-seven years ago, I never thought that I would become chairman." Those were the days, he recalled, when all they did was sell "plain vanilla life insurance."

"As I look into the new century, I sense a return to those older values that drove people to be self-reliant, to undertake the responsibility for their own future and that of their families," he said. "The future is bright, and there are exciting opportunities on the horizon . . . strong management is in place to lead [Confederation] well into the next century."

Burns's view of the future was a tad effusive, even given his attempt to go out on a high note. After all, he'd been the one to expand from plain vanilla to Burns' and Douglas's thirty-one flavours. Confed would be bankrupt in sixteen months. That year, the company sponsored a book, written by specialists at a hospice to be read by people who were about to be or had recently been bereaved. The title: *I Can't Stop Crying*.

◆·••·◆

Paul Cantor went on the Grand Tour. In April, he visited Confed offices and employees in Vancouver, Calgary, and Edmonton. In June, Ottawa, Montreal, Stevenage, London, and Glasgow. In July, London, Ontario, and Halifax. In every city, the message was the same. Confed was focusing on three things: consolidating operations in the core businesses, concentrating resources on supporting those businesses, and committing to high levels of customer service. The "three Cs" became Cantor's mantra. "Survival," he'd say, "is the issue."

However, after more than six months on the job, and countless such meetings and speeches, Cantor seemed to have made little progress with staff. Whereas Burns dealt only with senior officers, Cantor had made an effort to meet employees at all levels, but the contact was not always positive. For example, Cantor told the Atlanta-based George Powell at one point that expenses in Toronto had been cut by 10 per cent. "I tried to point out to him that he hadn't really done that, he'd cut expenses by maybe 6 per cent and transferred the rest to the United States," says Powell. "He told me I was wrong."

For Powell, Cantor was just more of the same. "I actually saw a lot of Pat Burns in Paul Cantor. I was told never to say that to Paul Cantor. He didn't always listen; sometimes his mind was made up. It was a posture rather than a reality. He's done a very good job of controlling his own PR. He worked long, hard hours, but I don't think he necessarily had the right team. Paul put some good people in place. But he didn't put anybody in place who knew the insurance business."

To Cantor and Michael White, the entire liability side of the balance sheet, those billions of dollars in items that were due to policyholders decades hence, remained a mystery. When White made his first visit to Atlanta shortly after joining Confed, he got into a lengthy discussion with staff in the investment division. White just couldn't seem to understand why anyone would take on such long-term items. They, in turn, couldn't believe his lack of perception about the insurance sector.

Cantor's banking experience had rendered him equally ill-prepared for such long-tail issues. "With his background, I'd say it was very difficult for him to sit down and have a view as to what a particular liability was worth," says John Thompson of OSFI. "With little understanding of the life-insurance field, and in particular the actuarial aspects of the business, it was very difficult for him," agrees Roger Cunningham, who as vice-president, human resources, reported to Cantor. Adds David Murray of Deloitte & Touche, "The first year he probably didn't realize what was going on. In the second, he couldn't figure out what to do about it." Says Michael Mackenzie of Cantor, "It was only three or four months before he was overwhelmed."

Little wonder. The news just kept getting worse. Between 1990 and 1992, Confed had purchased US$45 million in bonds issued by Towers Funding Corp. At first, the bonds, to be used to purchase qualifying health-care receivables from hospitals, were highly rated and secure. Then there were allegations of fraud, the companies involved filed for bankruptcy in March 1993, and legal actions were filed against the trustee, auditor, and rating agency. OSFI recommended that Confed take a provision of US$20 million, leaving a net exposure of $23.7 million. Even the investments that were supposed to be solid seemed to be unravelling.

Confed also lost the services of a key officer. That spring, Tom Pitts, senior vice-president, Canadian operations, was stricken ill so suddenly that his legs buckled on nearby Huntley Street and he had to be helped away. In June, he invited four of his senior colleagues to his west-end house to tell them the fatal diagnosis: cancer. After that, he was not in the office again, and died in January 1994.

Despite the company's continuing downward spiral, Mackenzie continued to find a lack of cooperation at the board level. Even as late as July 1993, Mackenzie made a note to himself that Jack Rhind was not being helpful. It wasn't that he was being an obstructionist, he just said he'd do things and then didn't. Says Mackenzie, "Jack Rhind was a senior insurance executive. He had years of experience at Confed and at National Life before that. He should have been more helpful. He knew what had to be done, but he just wasn't putting his back into it."

Some tasks that Cantor tackled simply backfired, none more resoundingly than his efforts to deal with Confed Investment Counselling Ltd. For years, the employees had been trying to buy a 40-percent share in the subsidiary that managed pension-fund assets for corporate clients, Confed's equity holdings, and some portions of the corporate surplus.

The staff had what's known as a "phantom" stock scheme, but it wasn't really working and they wanted the real thing – ownership, just like their peers in the funds-management business at other companies. Efforts to achieve ownership predated the arrival of John Watson as president in 1990, but at one point or another over the years, both Burns and Regester had each negotiated a buy-in deal, only to renege at the last minute.

When Paul Cantor arrived, he summoned Watson from the investment division's office at 350 Bloor Street, where Confed leased several floors, and told him, "I want you to get this deal done." Watson was delighted by the prospect, but a week later Cantor called to say that he'd changed his mind. He'd decided to take a closer look at the company before coming to any arrangement and had hired a consultant, Stephen Donihee, to help.

Donihee, a former Royal Trust employee, showed up claiming he had a mandate from Cantor to look at the books and try to cut costs. Officers and portfolio managers soon concluded that what he really had in mind was to become president of Confed Investment Counselling. Watson complained to Cantor, but Cantor insisted that the review process continue. After several months of the consultant being in his face daily, rather than fight Cantor on the issue, Watson up and quit in July.

In response, Cantor called a meeting with the senior staff to be held in the fifth-floor boardroom of Confed Investment Counselling to explain his side of events. He showed up with two colleagues in tow, White and Cunningham, to meet with about half a dozen portfolio managers. Everyone sat around the triangular boardroom table, the one that the counselling firm had always enjoyed owning because people never knew where to sit when they first saw it. They'd enter the room, then walk round and round, trying to figure out where the head of the table was, then finally give up and just plunk themselves down somewhere, anywhere.

The portfolio managers, loyal to Watson, were irate at the turn of events and railed against Cantor for precipitating the abrupt departure of their boss. Cantor became just as cantankerous, and what came to mind was a similar occasion twenty years earlier when he was at Polysar. Cantor's superior, Mel Erlindson, was giving Cantor a performance review, and Cantor kept disputing what his boss was saying. Finally, Erlindson climbed up on his own desk and said, "Have I got your attention now?"

It struck Cantor that a similar stunt would make the portfolio managers sit up and listen. So he hoisted himself onto the table and walked across the triangle, all the while shaking his finger at the managers and shouting, "I'm running this goddamned company." His audience, dumbfounded at the display, which seemed to combine ridiculous bravado with boyish rage, could only muster mumbles. Cantor, embarrassed to find himself playing king of the castle, clambered down from his perch and soon left.

So did the entire international division. They joined Watson in exile, established Sprucegrove Investment Management Ltd., and took $1 billion in profitable pension accounts with them. One attendee later said he'd wished he'd tucked a five-dollar bill in Cantor's pants as a tip for his performance at what became known internally as "the table dance."

The five bucks wasn't the only money Cantor failed to collect that summer. A wealthy German investor was visiting Toronto in June 1993, with his wife and his financial adviser. The investor already owned some property in Toronto and was driving along Mount Pleasant Avenue with his wife. She spotted the recently opened Confederation Life building and immediately fell in love with its soaring architecture.

He called in some Toronto deal-makers from McLean, McCarthy (now part of Deutsche Morgan Grenfell Canada Ltd.) to help: Kenneth

Field*, Terry Whelan, and Gord Robb. Confed vice-president of investments Barry Graham was approached, and Cantor authorized Graham to start negotiations. Graham and Whelan dickered for most of the summer over the selling price and finally came to a verbal agreement on terms that would have meant the purchase of the building for $115 million, with Confed taking a twenty-five-year leaseback. What a deal! Confed would more than get its construction costs repaid, gain a patient owner, and have fixed-price rental premises. For a firm in desperate need of cash, an angel had arrived who was prepared to bail them out in a sinking real-estate market.

In September, three months after they first sighted One Mount Pleasant Place, the investor and his wife were back in Toronto. The genteel investor of polished European manners announced that, before he signed any agreement of purchase and sale, he wanted to meet the president of Confed personally. For him there were niceties involved in business that were above and beyond just sending in henchmen to craft a deal.

A meeting was duly arranged in Cantor's boardroom. After ten minutes of pleasantries, the investor explained to Cantor that, before putting the lawyers to work on the final documents for signature, he had wanted to meet Cantor, shake his hand, and get to know him a little.

Cantor tried to be genteel in return, but his message was bald. "We have a bit of a problem. We can't actually go firm on the transaction." It was as if a screen suddenly fell across the visitor's face. Cantor's frank admission, given without an explanation, was not welcome news.

Stilted conversation continued for another five minutes, then the German bid his farewells. Going down on the elevator, the would-be buyer exploded with rage: "I will never deal with this company again as long as I live." As far as he was concerned, Confed had not been bargaining in good faith. There were lots of other deals out there; his wife

---

* Same name, same industry, but not the Bramalea Kenneth Field who had joined the Confed board earlier in the year.

could choose another bauble. For Confed, it was a lost opportunity to raise cash. For his part, Cantor had concluded that he did not want to tie Confed to a twenty-five-year lease. "The whole objective was to have the widest possible range of options available to the company," he says. "To have entered into a proposition like that would have substantially reduced the options available."

Meanwhile, the real-estate market was continuing to deteriorate. In 1992, Confed had managed to offload $200 million worth of properties. Now there was no market for further sales. The only possible transactions were internal. In order to clean up Confederation Trust's portfolio and reduce the number of non-performing loans, a transfer was planned to satisfy the regulators. Bad assets would go to the life company in return for good assets into the trust company. Explains Ontario superintendent Brian Cass, "The life company used to come to me and say, 'Trust us.' I say at the end, 'You wear the problems.' If you were the ones responsible, you can deal with the losses."

In fact, it didn't matter to Confederation Life where the bad loans were booked. Everything was consolidated on the Confed Life balance sheet anyway, so the life company would be no worse off. But the process tangled up dozens of people for the better part of a year, as each mortgage and related property was carefully evaluated. The regulator has different rules when it comes to evaluating real estate in a trust company versus a life company, so there was a great deal of procedural nonsense.

By the end of November 1993, the transfer was complete. Confed Trust sent Confed Life $199 million of its non-performing loans. In return, Confed Life moved onto Confed Trust's books $41 million in cash and $158 million worth of mortgages from its group mortgage benefits (GMB) plan.* Confed Life continued to administer the complete GMB portfolio, which was so healthy that there were only

---

* This was a business Confed launched in 1987 aimed at large-group clients who might enhance employee benefits by subsidizing staff mortgage payments, usually by two or three percentage points below going rates. Confed employees could also partake. In addition to the $200 million in third-party mortgages, there were 1,094 loans worth $106 million to staff at the life and trust companies.

six loans, with a book value of $500,000, in arrears. Three of those loans were insured by Central Mortgage and Housing Corporation. Still, the non-performing loan problem had largely been dealt with.* The offspring had shifted its problems to the parent.

Although Cantor had undertaken to return Confed to its core business, life-insurance sales, he was eager to alter the long-standing arrangements that had made them Confed's celebrated centrepiece. He arranged a strategic alliance with Equinox Financial Group, an insurance and financial-services marketing organization. The deal meant Confed agents selling life insurance in Canada moved under the Equinox umbrella.

Equinox had been formed by Aetna Life Insurance Co. of Canada in 1990 and employed about five hundred full-time agents in more than two dozen franchised offices across Canada. Under Equinox, the fixed costs of distribution – previously paid by the company – are picked up by franchisees, who own and operate the branches. Other members of the alliance were Commercial Union and Westbury Canadian Life, so Equinox agents had a full portfolio of insurance products, including property-and-casualty items.

Confed was to receive an immediate payment of $2.4 million, a 25-per-cent stake in Equinox, and hoped to save $15 million a year by dropping its costly network of three hundred agents. Cutting the deal took months and was a drain on management resources. The first announcement was made in July 1993, but the sales agreement wouldn't be signed until January 31, 1994, and the transaction wasn't completed until February 11.

The cost to the Confed culture was dear. The heart of the organization, a national network of twenty-one branch offices staffed by career agents who sold only Confed products, was no more.

Less contentious was the May 1993 sale of Confed's 9.8-per-cent stake in brokerage firm Midland Walwyn Inc. that had been bought in

---

* When seizure occurred in 1994, the total assets of Confed Trust had been reduced from nearly $1 billion two years earlier, with more than one-third of that non-performing, to $770 million, with only $42.2 million non-performing.

1988. Bill Douglas's dream of building a financial-services empire was slowly being dismantled.

In August 1993, the leasing company, no longer controlled by Confed, moved out of its offices at 321 Bloor. Steven Hudson was happy to be gone. Water for the toilets came from rooftop tanks. At the end of the day, as water levels grew low (they were refilled at night), pressure for refilling toilets dropped. "You had to choose your time carefully to go to the men's room," says Hudson. Employees in the know used the facilities early in the day. Confed was cutting back on the water supply because Canadian operations had moved next door into the new building, and employee numbers at 321 Bloor had fallen. "That was probably my first sign that things were a little tighter than I'd been told," says Hudson. "I knew it was time to move."

Newcourt relocated to three-and-a-half floors in downtown Toronto's BCE Place. To show off how well it was doing, despite its association with Confed, it spared no expense. The 90,000 square feet of facilities included a resident chef, a 10,000-square-foot client centre with audio-visual display systems, three monitors in both reception/waiting rooms showing stock-market quotations, and Canadian art on the walls, ranging from native works by Benjamin Chee-Chee and Norval Morriseau through landscape artist Horace Champagne to abstractionist Jean-Paul Riopelle.

In September, Cantor announced that Confed Trust's nine storefront branches would close in November to be replaced by five financial centres in the same cities: Vancouver, Calgary, Toronto, Montreal, and Halifax.

But such steps were just dribs and drabs. Cantor had to tackle the big picture. In June, OSFI completed an on-site examination of Confed and directed the company to find some means of ensuring long-term health. The options were: manage themselves back to profitability, sell major business units and use the proceeds to fix what was left, or find a strategic partner and sell control.

Rating agencies were now making known their discontent. A. M. Best downgraded Confed from A+ to A. Standard & Poor's dropped Confed one notch to AA−. The agencies told Cantor that they expected to see an increase in capital and a return to profitability in

1993. If there were no such improvements, went the message, they would have no alternative but to conclude that the problems with real estate were more severe than had been admitted, and they would be forced to further downgrade Confed's claims-paying and debt ratings. Such a step would have an accelerating aspect, particularly for institutional and corporate investors in the United States. When investors saw such further downgrades, they would begin what's known as a "flight to quality" by moving out GIC money when the instruments came due or transferring lines of business to healthier companies.

Cantor was also getting red-flag signals from Ernst & Young. A 1993 review of Confed's complete mortgage portfolio painted a horrific picture. Of the total book value of $7.2 billion in mortgages, $501 million were more than ninety days in arrears, a further $506 million were on the watchlist, $242 million were being renegotiated, and there had been $226 million in foreclosures. Twenty-one per cent of the entire portfolio was in trouble. Mike O'Regan, the partner in charge of audits of both Confed and Confederation Treasury Services Ltd. (CTSL), told Cantor that Confed could not handle any more problems with assets of any size. The boat was beginning to list badly.

Cantor finally realized that the quick turnaround he had hoped to achieve was not about to happen. At the June 23 board meeting, Cantor admitted to directors that, at best, there was "a wait-and-see attitude" as the marketplace looked for better earnings, growth in capital, and a move out of peripheral businesses. "Internally, he indicated there was growing concern and that morale was decreasing," according to the minutes of the meeting. "He said that recruiting was difficult in this environment."

On June 7, Cantor had retained investment bankers J. P. Morgan & Co. and CIBC Wood Gundy Inc. as financial advisers. The two firms had given Confed the code-name "Frontier," so they could talk about their client and prepare charts without worrying about revealing the actual name. Morgan managing director Kenneth Froewiss told the board that a preliminary assessment suggested there was adequate time for a systematic evaluation of options. He cited two reasons: first, there was no risk of an imminent "run on the bank," and, second, Confed appeared to have sufficient liquidity.

However, his presentation also included a dire warning. Although some American insurance companies, such as Equitable, Travelers, and Mutual Life of New York, had survived similar difficulties, he pointed out that Confed "is in a weaker condition than several recently distressed Canadian insurers."

Froewiss outlined three possible strategies: raise capital from selling major businesses or pursue a hybrid approach by selling businesses and reducing real estate; find a strategic partner for a sponsored demutualization; or seek a merger, partner, or acquirer.

One of the suggestions, demutualization, was studied for months. Legislative changes by Ottawa in 1992 had made it possible to convert policyholder interests in mutual companies, such as Confed, into share ownership, thus leading to new capital that could strengthen the balance sheet. In September 1993, Cantor finally put in place a process to analyse demutualization thoroughly.

Cantor designated two men to conduct the study: Jay Richardson, who had recently retired as director of annuity products in the United Kingdom after thirty-seven years as an actuary with Confed, and Ron Till, a CA with international expertise as a consultant with Peat Marwick Stevenson & Kellogg. Morgan urged Cantor to hire an outside, independent team of actuaries. The suggestion was not well received at Confed, because Cantor didn't want to lose control of the study; he seemed to want to have the smallest team possible, not for the sake of economy, necessarily, but just so that he had tight hold on the reins.

He eventually agreed, however, to hire Milliman & Robertson Inc., of New York, and Eckler Partners Ltd., of Toronto, for actuarial advice. Cantor then instructed the two companies that nothing was to happen concerning demutualization until the end of October because, Cantor said, he first wanted to develop a five-year strategy for Confed. The actuarial advisers assumed there must be no serious threat to Confed, otherwise why wouldn't Cantor move with more haste? Finally, when the two consulting firms were allowed on site in November, Confed made it clear that it would call the shots in terms of what assumptions the consultants would use.

That became a very different project from the "independent" study that J. P. Morgan had in mind. "They said it would be their report, and we agreed we would tell them how an investor company might look at Confed – but Confed was responsible for the [actuarial] assumptions," says Paul McCrossan of Eckler. "Cantor, even late in 1993, did not realize the precarious state of the company and how quickly events were closing in."

The study concluded that demutualization would cost $50 million and take twelve to eighteen months. Cantor decided not to go ahead. He had believed, right from the start, that demutualization wouldn't help. "You still don't have any new money, because all you've done is converted a mutual company into a share company," he says. "You have the same people who are now shareholders instead of policyholders, but no new money has come in." Cantor was cutting off his escape routes.

There was, however, a successful contemporaneous example carried out in 1991 and 1992 from which Cantor might have taken heart. Richard Jenrette, a founder of Wall Street securities firm Donaldson Lufkin & Jenrette, sold the brokerage firm to Equitable Life, a venerable American insurance firm. He became chairman of the firm just when real-estate problems hit both Equitable and Confed. Jenrette negotiated an injection of US$1 billion via a private placement from Axa, the giant French insurance company and, in addition, raised US$450 million from an initial public offering. For their part, policyholders received US$272 million in cash and stock as a result, and Equitable ended up among the strongest publicly traded insurance companies. To be sure, the process wasn't cheap. Fees paid by Equitable in 1991 and 1992 to lawyers, actuaries, and bankers totalled some US$150 million, but the company survived, and Jenrette later returned to Wall Street.

There was another possibility that Cantor passed over, too. Other troubled companies were selling what are known as "surplus" notes, a debt instrument that counts as equity. Prudential Insurance Co. was the first, but, since 1993, more than a dozen insurance companies have sold some US$6 billion of these notes in the private-placement market, creating what are, in effect, a new flavour of junk bonds. Investors snap them up, however, and, as a result, insurance companies not only survive but also prosper.

Cantor seemed to be wearing blinders. For him, the only way ahead seemed to be to find a strategic partner. "Our conclusion was that the approach of incrementalism, $50 million here, $100 million there, ran the risk of doing a little bit more a little bit too late," Cantor says. "The way to provide policyholder protection was to get way ahead by looking for a significant investor and making sure that we have a cushion of support. The rating agencies were nipping at our heels. There was a continuing exposure to continuing downgrades."

On October 8, Cantor called on Michael Mackenzie with the one-hundred-page document that Cantor was showing to any potential partner. The hope was that, with globalization, many firms would be interested in acquiring Confed's business in Canada, the United States, and the United Kingdom to gain new footholds or add to their market share. Cantor asked Mackenzie to keep the document to himself.

Regulators were buried in other problems. In March 1992, Shoppers Trust Co. was placed in liquidation. In November 1992, Dominion Trust Co. merged with Security Trust Co, only to fail a year later. In March 1993, Royal Bank had agreed to buy Royal Trust, thereby preventing a huge collapse. Prenor Trust Co. was liquidated on December 3, 1993, and Monarch Trust Co. on February 8, 1994. The regulators were relieved when Desjardins Group, Quebec's largest financial institution, took over rival Laurentian Group Corp., including its insurance operations, in October 1993, in a deal worth $625 million. That meant another firm went off the watch list. Mackenzie was happy that Cantor seemed to have the situation in hand. For a time, Mackenzie did keep Cantor's secret document locked in a desk drawer before showing it to OSFI colleagues.

If Cantor thought he had plenty of time to search for the best partner, the situation was about to change. A secret had finally been uncovered. On October 12, Michael White met in Detroit with officials from the Michigan Insurance Bureau. The purpose of the meeting was twofold: White shared Confed's business plan with them, including the hunt for a strategic partner; Michigan reported on its examination audit.

Michigan conducts such audits every three years, and the previous examination, in 1990, conducted by bureau staff, the actuarial consulting firm of Tillinghast, and a zone examiner from Georgia, had found no problems. Margaret A. Oberle, examiner in charge, stated in her report that year, "We tested extensively for unrecorded and under-recorded United States liabilities. Also, Section 411 of the Michigan Insurance Code requires that alien insurers must place enough qualified assets (as defined in Chapter 9 of the Michigan Insurance Code) in trust to cover United States liabilities. We evaluated these trust agreements and the underlying assets to ensure that they are properly valued and that they comply." Indeed, examiners found that Confed had an excess of assets over liabilities of US$147,622,682, the biggest safety net Confed had ever recorded.

Thus fortified, Confed had trumpeted the trusteed assets as it continued to sell in the United States. A March 1, 1991, letter from vice-president W. T. Knechtel to Confed's general agents was typical. In it, he sought to settle any qualms anyone might have about Confed's financial strength by pointing out that United States policyholders "enjoy fourfold protection."

First, Michigan required a deposit of funds with immediate access by regulators in the case of company difficulties. Second, trusteed assets were maintained (at that time by Connecticut National Bank, in Hartford, Connecticut) so that "we are, at all times, more solvent when comparing our United States assets to our United States liabilities. (The second point seems awfully like the first, but no matter.) Third, and over and above that, "Canadian and United Kingdom assets support and satisfy United States liabilities." Fourth, "Confederation Life is a strong and viable corporate citizen and is heavily invested in the United States."

In 1990, Republican John Engler had defeated the Democratic incumbent, James Blanchard, to become governor of Michigan.* In 1991, Engler appointed a new insurance commissioner for the state, David Dykhouse. Dykhouse had previously served as commissioner – from

---

* Blanchard was appointed by President Bill Clinton as the American ambassador to Canada in 1993.

1966 to 1969 under Governor George Romney – when he was in his early thirties. For this second go-around, Dykhouse took a huge salary reduction from his job in the private sector. The commissioner's salary is about US$75,000 a year, one-tenth of what Dykhouse had been making at the New York law firm of Shearman & Sterling.

Engler said he was looking for an activist in the role, so Dykhouse was proactive, making much of the fact that he was revoking certificates held by insurance companies that were not active in state. He became something of a consumer champion, chasing down complaints about an insurance company known as American Way.

He also attracted some unwelcome publicity. Although the Michigan commissioner is a gubernatorial appointment (in some states the post is filled by election), the role is supposed to be non-partisan. But Dykhouse, who is a Republican, agreed to let his home near the Lansing Country Club be used for a fund-raiser at which guests could meet Republican senators at an early evening reception on March 9, 1994.

Once the $100-per-head invitations were issued by Dick Posthumus, Senate Majority leader, and Dan DeGrow, chair of the Senate Republican Campaign Committee, Democrats and journalists alike took after Dykhouse like hounds at the hunt. Dykhouse insisted that he had no plans to attend the event and claimed that ownership of the house was not supposed to be mentioned on the invitation. The fund-raiser was cancelled. "We were looking for a nice house for the event," said DeGrow. "That's all there was to it. But with hindsight, it was stupid on our part. We screwed up." Added Engler spokesman Rusty Hills, "It flunks the smell test. The governor says it won't be at Dykhouse's house and that Dykhouse won't be there."

The regular Michigan field audit of Confed for the period January 1, 1991 to December 31, 1992, began June 1, 1993, and continued through the summer into September. The previous situation, with assets greater than liabilities, was no more. Examiners found the CTSL notes that had been listed as short-term investments and concluded that they were not permitted investments. That didn't mean that the notes could not be in the trust, but they could not be counted as assets required to offset the U.S. liabilities.

Michigan raised the notes with White at that October session. He explained the notes as part of the company's practice of running cash management on a North American basis. "It was all passed off to the Michigan regulator as an efficient way to manage their liquidity on a centralized basis," says Michael Mackenzie, who has come to think that the removal of funds by Confed from Michigan was in response to his pushing for sounder liquidity levels.

There was no point in Michigan demanding that Confed replace the IOUs; Confed had no means of making such a repayment. The money had all gone into operations, to finance the leasing company, the trust firm, and to build the new head office. If Michigan had required immediate repayment of the notes, such action would precipitate the collapse of the company. Confed had no place to turn for US$606 million listed as promissory notes in the 1992 return. Both sides agreed to work out a plan over time that would restore asset values in the trust. Meanwhile, the IOUs would be officially listed in the 1993 filings as fixed-rate loans, not promissory notes.

For his part, White outlined Confed's business plan to find a strategic partner, and Michigan agreed to monitor the situation. White apparently did not bother to inform his boss of what was a serious regulatory deficiency with the trust, because Cantor claims he didn't know about the notes until Dykhouse told him in early 1994 – even though Cantor, White, Dykhouse, and Michigan's deputy commissioner, Robert Bailey, met for dinner at Toronto's York Club on November 19. Cantor regarded the evening get together as a bridge-builder; he says neither side raised any serious issues.

The Michigan situation made the need for a "going-concern" situation even more urgent. A company that's a going concern is like a seaworthy vessel under full sail. In such circumstances, it has value on the open market. If the same vessel is either discovered to suffer dry rot, or becomes becalmed by bankruptcy, selling off the parts has substantially less total value.

In order to scope out investor interest, Cantor, Zimmerman, White, and executives from investment banking firms Morgan and Wood Gundy had personally called on a dozen potential investors during a three-week period in September and October.

A short list of about eighteen insurance companies, banks, con-glomerates, and other financial institutions was drawn up and each was visited to see if there was any interest.

Cantor's style as he went the rounds was nothing if not direct. In September, for example, when he approached Sun's John McNeil, he complained that he had no idea when he joined Confed the trouble that would ensue. He told McNeil that he'd initially believed that his job at Confed was to make the company prosper and grow. Instead, he found such resounding problems with asset quality that he had been driven to seeking someone – anyone – to take over the company. Says McNeil, "I was either his first choice or his last hope."

Cantor told McNeil that Confed would be setting up a "data room" at the Toronto office of law firm McCarthy Tétrault, where financial information about Confed could be studied by interested parties. McNeil said he'd also want Sun executives to be able to talk to Confed officers as part of the scrutiny. "That's a round-two event," replied Cantor, "not round one." McNeil appointed Sun president John Gardner to head the team looking at Confed.

Many of the hopefuls who visited the data room also trooped to Ottawa and called on deputy finance minister David Dodge to check out possible tax consequences and regulatory hurdles. Dodge had worked with Cantor in the seventies in the department and was a fan. His message to any tire-kicking executives was positive. "We're not going to give the store away, but we're not going to make your life hard. Negotiate the deal and come back." Although his main interest was the minister's February budget presentation, Dodge monitored proceedings.

Out of the eighteen firms that showed initial curiosity, only five professed any interest. "International institutions were not necessarily interested in coming to Canada, nor were Confederation's operations large enough in the United States that they would be considered a beachhead," said James McSherry, vice-president of Wood Gundy. "In this particular case, globalization did not help as we tried to solve their problem."

The possibles included: BAT Industries plc, a British conglomerate that sells insurance, has a stake in Imasco (controlling shareholder of

Canada Trust), and owns American Tobacco (Lucky Strike, Pall Mall, and Kent among other brands); Metropolitan Life Insurance Co., a United States mutual company; Liberty Life Association of Africa (the largest on that continent, capitalized at US$6 billion, which makes it slightly larger than the Bank of Montreal); and two Canadian firms, Sun Life and Great-West Life.

After further consideration, the foreign firms dropped out. Sun was also fading fast, for two reasons. First, Sun didn't want an alliance so much as it was willing to bid on portions of Confed, specifically group insurance and the operations in the United Kingdom. Second, Sun CEO John McNeil was battling health problems that meant the company was less likely to take a major strategic step, given the uncertainty of his leadership.

McNeil had been plagued for months by back pain of undetermined origin. An initial CAT scan on his spine in October showed no probable cause, but a follow-up scan showed he suffered from an internal growth that was a rare abdominal fibrosis. In addition to causing excruciating pain, the growth sapped his energy. Kidney failure in December hospitalized McNeil for a month, and he spent much of 1994 going through various surgical procedures, steroid treatments, and periods in the hospital. "McNeil's disablement was a real negative," says Adam Zimmerman.

The field had narrowed quickly. Cantor phoned McNeil and said, "I've got to figure out which girl to dance with and it isn't you." Great-West Lifeco Inc. president and CEO Orest Dackow had spent a week examining the financials in the data room and told his colleagues that Confed faced considerable trouble, but he urged further investigation.

After months of searching the world for a partner, Confed was left with Great-West as the only company that was interested in a comprehensive deal. When Cantor offered to open discussions, Great-West demanded exclusive negotiating rights. Cantor agreed. The way ahead narrowed again. Still, Confed executives all told themselves, if there were going to be only one possible partner, Great-West appeared to be sturdy enough. Sixty-nine per cent owned by Paul Desmarais's Power Corp. of Canada, Great-West was the third-largest life-insurance company in Canada, with $25.3 billion in assets, and the largest stock life-insurance company. If it acquired Confed, the fourth largest, with $19.2 billion in assets, the new combined entity with assets of $44.5 billion would be number one.*

Great-West itself had twenty subsidiary companies engaged in property ownership and management, as well as employee benefits. Confed and Great-West were both major group-life-and-health insurers; combined they would have had about 20 per cent of the market share. Any union of the two would almost certainly hurt employees. According to a secret Government of Ontario estimate at the time, at least a thousand Confed employees, most of them in the Toronto area, would lose their jobs.

On December 15, Mackenzie and Thompson met with the Confed board to present OSFI's findings after the annual audit of the company that had been carried out during the summer. Confederation Trust was in better shape, due to the asset transfer, but the rest of the message was the same as it had been for the previous three years: poor asset quality and lack of management controls. Cantor told them that numerous potential investors had now reviewed Confed, and the net effect of their work was to convince him that a strategic partnership with Great-West was the only way to save the company.

Mackenzie was questioned closely about the extent of government support for the deal that might be forthcoming, and the regulators told Confed not to count on anything, but that help had not been totally ruled out. The possibility is reflected in the carefully – if awkwardly – worded minutes of the meeting: "[T]he question as to whether there could be no financial back stop by the government was still on the table and that Confederation Life should know that if, and he said it was a low probability if, the Company ran into financial difficulty, there could be no government back stop."

As if to underline the need for a partner, on December 17 the rating agency TRAC announced that Confed had again failed to meet six of its

---

* At the time, Manulife was the largest, with assets of $38.5 billion; Sun was second at $34.1 billion.

eight solvency tests. TRAC's findings were based on 1992 results; the numbers at December 1993 were even worse. After making a bare profit of $1.9 million in 1992, Confed lost $29 million in 1993 on assets of $19.2 billion. The net rate of investment income earned was 7.74 per cent, the result of declining rates generally and Confed's poor performance in particular. For all the company had been able to achieve with its investment portfolio that year, the money might as well have been socked away in Canada Savings Bonds.

On a positive note, the percentage of assets in real estate and mortgages was going down. From a peak of 73.8 per cent in 1989, real estate and mortgages were now 50 per cent of total assets, a level that was still more than twice as high as it was in the 130 largest American life-insurance companies.

Asset quality had continued to deteriorate; non-performing assets now totalled $807 million in bonds, mortgages, and foreclosed real estate. Policyholder loans were up more than 50 per cent, from $619 million in 1992 to $958 million in 1993. Some of that may have been caused by the recession, as individuals exercised the option available to them of generating low-interest loans, but some of it must have also been due to nervousness. Getting cash value out of a policy makes more sense when a company is still a going concern. After liquidation, the death benefit will still be paid, but policyholders looking for cash-surrender value join the creditor queue.

The company certainly could not complain that policyholder deaths cost too much in benefits and were a drain on resources. In 1993, 1,869 Canadians went to their graves holding Confed life-insurance policies worth $112 million – about half the value of bad mortgage loans in Ontario alone.

Operating expenses had been trimmed $54 million, down 10 per cent from the previous year, and among the savings yet to be realized was a $1-million cost reduction expected in 1994 now that 321 Bloor was empty. The executives were the last to move in December into One Mount Pleasant Place, where Cantor tried to set a modest tone by using rented furniture in his new environs. The old home office, with its infamous carpet, was abandoned on December 17, 1993, less than forty years after it was first occupied.

Despite the terrible results, the board of directors blithely pro-
ceeded to set aside funds for salary increases and merit bonuses in
1994. As the year came to an end, the human resources and compensation committee, headed by George Albino, recommended that half
of the twenty-two hundred employees in Canada receive salary
increases in 1994 and that $870,000 be earmarked for merit pay. In the
United States, the committee said that merit pay of $1.3 million
should be shared among 70 per cent of the twelve hundred employees. In the United Kingdom, 90 per cent of the employees would split
£450,000. Supplementary pensions were to be expanded to others
beyond the current roster of executive officers. The board unani-
mously approved all the recommendations.

Cantor's first year at the helm had not turned out the way he had
hoped. The future of the firm was now in the hands of a competitor,
Great-West Life, a company known for its hard-nosed ways. The
good ship Confed was sailing towards the shoals, with brigands in
pursuit, yet all the while many of those aboard were being hand-
somely rewarded for their savvy seafaring ways.

CHAPTER 10

Slow Dance:
Doing the Deal

"What a strange game, the only winning move is not to play."

— from the film *War Games*

O nce the proposed merger was on, the lives of everyone at
Confed changed forever. Typical of how the news was
announced and the project launched was the breakfast
meeting called just prior to Christmas, when about twenty middle
managers were summoned on short notice to the Marriott Hotel, two
minutes away from the Atlanta branch. After an initial briefing, each
Confed employee was introduced to a counterpart from Great-West,
then took the new "buddy" back to the office to open the kimono on
Confed's secrets. Russ Friend, vice-president, legal, described the
mood best when he quipped, "It's Great-West or bust."

Similar meetings to set up the due-diligence "buddy" system were
held right across Confed, from California to England. Top-level talks
were conducted at One Mount Pleasant Place in Toronto. At the table
for Great-West was Orest Dackow, president of Great-West Lifeco,
the overall holding company. An actuary by training, Dackow had

been with Great-West thirty-five years; he ran the company's United States operations out of Denver.

For Confed, it was Paul Cantor and Mike White, aided by a thirty-member Toronto-based advisory group that met daily at 8 A.M. for an hour. Officers from the American head office in Atlanta and from Stevenage in England participated by phone, and the group was regularly buttressed by lawyers, actuaries, and financial advisers.

Cantor began the process with a sense of "foreboding and loneliness. I became acutely aware that a lot of people and their futures were riding on how well I did at the negotiating table." Confed's capital (net worth after subtracting liabilities from assets) at December 31, 1993, was $1.1 billion. Cantor wanted $500 million to $600 million more capital to cover any losses that might be discovered and to get the important minimum continuing capital and surplus ratio (MCCSR) up from 125 per cent to a healthier 150 per cent.

In order to facilitate negotiations, Dackow was given an office on the executive floor of One Mount Pleasant Place, down the hall from Cantor. The meeting rooms on that floor take their names from Canadian geography and contain oil paintings of various regions by Canadian artists. Dackow was in the Klondike Room; his desk was a section of an exotic-wood dining-room table. The rest of the table was in the St. Lawrence Room, where it was used by Cantor and Dackow as a neutral meeting-ground.

Cantor saw a certain humour in assigning Dackow to the Klondike Room with its painting showing men on their way – or so they fervently hoped – to moil for gold. Cantor had studied the paintings carefully and switched some of them around after he arrived, giving pride of place in his own office to a prairie landscape with a figure in the foreground meant to be trader and explorer Henry Kelsey in 1691, when he was in his early twenties.

The down-the-hall arrangement did not help the two twentieth-century explorers, however, because the real decisions were not made by Dackow. Dackow was run on a string from Montreal by Robert Gratton, the Jesuit-trained president of Power Financial. Says Finance's David Dodge, "It was a bit like negotiating with an automobile salesman who says, 'I've got to go and see my manager.'" To make matters worse, Dackow is the first to confess that he is "addicted to formal processes." As a result, every step in the negotiation took far longer than it would have if both sides had been represented by decision-makers.

Coincident with talks in the second week of January 1994, Milliman/Eckler reported to Cantor and told him that any game plan to help Confed by selling more insurance wouldn't work, because the company couldn't stand the strain of all that new business; Confed did not have the capital base to support such a strategy. Another possible door to health was closed. Cantor was surprised by the information and asked his product-development staff in the United States why he hadn't been told previously about the detrimental outcome of such an approach. Cantor was also surprised to learn from the actuarial advisers that Confed wasn't meeting its budgeted expense levels.

The external environment provided further reminders. On January 18, 1994, A. M. Best put Confed under review with negative implications, a loaded phrase that didn't mean downgrade but the next thing to it. Confed had become the most ratings-sensitive company in Canada. The company's United States business – structured settlements, GICs and COLI/BOLI – were particularly tricky. For example, if GIC holders don't want to do a rollover as GICs come up for renewal, then Confed has to produce cash. That's fine as long as there's lots of money on hand, but as more and more demands are made for cash, liquidity becomes a problem. If those GICs are backed by real estate of decreasing value, selling the assets behind the GICs becomes counter-productive. If that real estate is in free fall, it fetches fire-sale prices.

Imagine the balance sheet, with assets and liabilities on separate sides. On the liability side, there are three fingers – notes, corporate mortgages, and derivatives – linked with three fingers on the liability side – GICs, structured settlements, and COLI/BOLI. Remove one liability "finger" by taking something off the books and suddenly the asset "finger" is without its mate. The balancing act is destroyed. How to untangle one side without touching the other? What a Gordian knot there was to undo.

The initial scrutiny by Great-West had led them to disturbing

conclusions about Confed's sorry state. Key conversations between
Cantor and Dackow about Confed's capital would go something
like this:

Cantor: "I've got $1.1 billion. I know $500 to $600 (million) is
gone, but I think I've got $500 (million) left."

Dackow: "I think you're high. The number is between zero and
$250 (million)."

Precise evaluations in such circumstances are always elusive. First,
both sides adopt negotiating positions. Second, real-estate assets can
only be priced when something sells; anything else is guesswork.
Because there were no buyers, who knew what those asset values
really were? But whose number was right mattered less than achieving a deal that the market agreed would work. Otherwise, policyholders – both institutional and individual – would flee, and the firm
would collapse, despite all the effort.

Both sides concluded that a market-conscious solution meant
Confed had to shrink to fit its new financial reality. As a result, much
of January and February was spent trying to find a balance among
needed new capital, asset sales, and other business steps in order to
satisfy both regulatory requirements and the rating agencies who
were taking the pulse daily.

The Great-West approach to bargaining was to put something on
the table during an intense two- or three-day period of negotiation,
then go away and caucus for up to a week. Says Cantor, "It became
quite common here to say, 'They also serve who only stand and
wait.'"

Cantor took to working out daily at 6 A.M. in the company fitness
centre with his associates, not to plot strategy but to build cardiovas-
cular strength and stamina. Capacity and competence among
Confed's management differed greatly. "Some grew and strengthened
and flourished under the duress of the situation," says Cantor. "Others
had difficulty coping with the changes that were taking place and
became impediments to doing the deal."

Confed employees had every reason to be perturbed. Their
assigned "buddies" from Great-West could show up any time they
chose and receive whatever information, financial or otherwise, they

wanted. The Great-West representatives took considerable pleasure in acquiring client lists and would appear at social events where Confed was entertaining clients and blatantly hand out their own business cards. For many at Confed, the due-diligence process was more like rape than a prelude to marriage.

On February 28, Cantor and Dackow visited Michael Mackenzie to present a letter summarizing a merger. The understanding included new capital, asset sales, and a series of administrative steps to reduce operating costs. They aimed for an announcement March 9. On the one-page balance sheet that they showed to Mackenzie, there was a huge item: inter-company loans worth US$620 million, the Michigan money.

Mackenzie's forbearance was crucial. That month, Ernst & Young had informed the Confed board that it would not sign the auditor's report approving the 1993 financial statement until Mackenzie confirmed that he supported the deal with Great-West – and a letter of intent was actually signed between the two companies.

The missing funds from the Michigan trust did not seem to bother anyone at the time. "It didn't matter to us that the United States regulator was short US$600 million or whether Canada was short," says Dackow. "In liquidation, it becomes very important as to where the funds are, whether they're in your left pocket or your right pocket. Under a going-concern solution, it didn't matter whether the funds were in your left pocket or your right pocket. All that was important is, how much is there, the amount of the funds. We were going into the arrangement on the premise that we would keep everyone whole."

Great-West also made a lot of noise about the synergies that could be created between the two companies and how back-office administrative costs would be slashed. While such savings didn't translate into capital, there would be an ongoing improvement in the balance sheet. Great-West claimed savings would be $24 million in the first year, rising to $40 million in 1995, and continuing at that level every year until 1998. In total, savings would range between $144 million and $186 million. "I frankly didn't believe the number, but if it was half the size, it was still a big number," says Confed chairman Adam

Zimmerman. As for the overall package, "Our sense of what Great-West were offering was skinny," he says. "But they believed that their presence and the substance of Confed was sufficient to stabilize the situation."

Cantor, Dackow, and Zimmerman called on five rating agencies to explain the tentative agreement. The agencies were supportive, but a bit dubious, and wanted Great-West to put in more capital. On March 7, after phone calls from Zimmerman and Cantor to Mackenzie asking for his help, Mackenzie called Standard & Poor's in New York to make reassuring noises and try to get them to hold off any public declaration about Confed's situation that could unnerve the investment community. His pleas only delayed the inevitable; on March 16, Confed was placed on a "ratings alert." Great-West agreed to add a standby feature to the deal that meant up to $150 million was available if needed.

By this point, negotiations had been going on for three months, fourteen hours a day, seven days a week. "I've been stuck at my desk lately," lamented Cantor in a memo to staff. "I'll be glad when these discussions are behind us." Morale was scraping bottom. Change is never easy at the best of times, but now a competitor was poking about Confed's inner workings, and the fun had gone out of the business. There were rumours that Cantor had received a death threat and, in response, hired a bodyguard. He denies the story, but security was tightened on the executive floor. "The size of the change that was going through here was overwhelming," admits Cantor.

He tried keeping communications open by launching a regular memo for employees, called "Straight Talk." He conducted "town-hall meetings," at which the quarterly results were issued, and organized seminars for managers on the trauma of the "change process." Still, Cantor – the table dancer – seemed to relish his role as tough guy with his colleagues. At one point, he said to Bill Alexander, "I'm a real prick, aren't I?" Replied Alexander, "Yes, you are."

Then, just when staff was feeling most beleaguered, Confed publicly announced executive compensation for the first time in the company's history. Cantor had earned $700,000 in 1993; Bill Allison, senior vice-president in charge of the United States, $431,582;

Michael White, $320,200; and George Willman, senior vice-president in charge of the United Kingdom, $288,923. For those toiling in the trenches, and battling a "buddy" from Great-West, the sums seemed astronomical. Life was looking more and more unfair.

The morale problem was becoming an important issue, because it was blocking the upward flow of information. In March, Eckler Partners advised Cantor that he needed to get a better handle on the liability side and told him that long-serving Confed staff were not telling him how bad the situation was. The corporate culture never did include delivering the straight goods; Cantor had had no success changing that eternal verity. "If you stayed at Confed, you stayed by keeping your head in the foxhole," says Paul McCrossan of Eckler. "Cantor was more open. He wouldn't have shot the messenger, but he never convinced senior executives of that."

For example, Cantor had only recently become aware of the existence of the CTSL notes in the Michigan trust, since the information had been kept to an inner circle at Confed. The Milliman/Eckler team, likewise, was unaware of the notes until mid-April, even though it had been advising Confed for six months. The notes first came up during a conversation among employees and Milliman/Eckler staffers over coffee when one of the Confed people said, "Just think of the trouble we'd be in if we hadn't got the money out of the trust."

There was another issue that was also mysteriously buried. According to a March letter signed by Eckler partner Paul McCrossan, his firm had concluded that Confed was on the verge of insolvency and, as a result, should not continue to sell blocks of business as if everything were normal, because it would be in contravention of the Insurance Companies Act.

Cantor says he forwarded the letter to OSFI for the information of regulators, although he did not necessarily concur with the view presented. Says Cantor, "Paul McCrossan has his own campaigns that he's waging, which are directed to the role that consulting actuaries ought to play in the review of insurance companies." Neither Mike Mackenzie nor John Thompson have any recollection of the letter or its contents. Thompson further maintains that a thorough search of OSFI files in 1995 turned up no copy of the letter.

Solvent or not, sales continued unabated. "Confed was surprisingly successful in selling new business," says Bob Astley, CEO of Mutual Life, "even when the negotiations [with Great-West] were going on." Individual policyholders and institutional investors were equally oblivious. "For the life of me, it's a mystery as to how they continued to sell commercial paper throughout the period," says Sun's John McNeil.

As March progressed, Great-West's interest appeared to be flagging. Cantor complained to Dackow and was granted leave to seek another partner. Cantor approached Sun again, and this time McNeil insisted that they be able to talk to Confed management. Cantor agreed, and Sun dispatched a dozen people, who spent ten days studying the books and concluded, as before, that it was only interested in buying the group business – particularly Canadian group – and the British operations. The Sun team also concluded that Confed was in such rough shape that it needed a capital injection of $800 million to $900 million.

No deal was ever officially presented by Sun, nor did Cantor bother to follow up and ask for Sun's response. The sideshow just disappeared as if it had never occurred. Great-West was now Confed's only hope, and Dackow was jubilant. He could drive an even harder bargain over as long a period of time as he liked. The tempo of the rescue had been set all along by Great-West; now the tone and texture would be, too.

Meanwhile, Cantor was fighting internal fires, desperately trying to get Confed's costs in line. New rules that were instituted April 5 included: any purchase order had to be approved by CFO Borden Rosiak; there would be no more free parking, everybody would pay $103.50 monthly in the underground garage; the company would no longer purchase publications – as subscriptions ran out, they would not be renewed; no personal stationery would be authorized, except for business cards; all staff travel required senior-management approval; technology purchases would be frozen; sports and entertainment tickets were eliminated. The Blue Jays Skybox, beloved of Burns, was no more.

The deal with Great-West was nearing final form. Despite the fact that they knew the alliance was in the works, some of the rating agencies dealt further downgrades anyway. The AA from Duff & Phelps that had been unchanged since July 1993 was altered April 14 when Confed was put on a watch list and reduced to AA–. A. M. Best lowered Confed's rating from A (excellent) to A– (excellent) citing recent below-average earnings that weren't likely to improve soon.

For the majority of observers, such levels were more than good enough. "Most of us went through a school system in which 'A' was perfect. Yet, in the insurance industry, 'A' denotes a company on the precipice," says Senator Marjory LeBreton, a consumer activist who complained that ratings didn't tell the real story.

If the rating agencies were apoplectic, Michigan was becoming apocalyptic. What if the strategic alliance didn't pan out? How would Michigan protect American policyholders? Dykhouse hired some high-powered help: Victor Palmieri. Dykhouse briefed Palmieri, for whom the situation had an all-too-familiar ring. Said Palmieri to Dykhouse, "If you've got inter-company notes, look out."

Palmieri was well known in financial circles as an insolvency expert. Born in 1930 in Chicago to immigrant parents, he grew up in Beverly Hills, California, graduated from Stanford Law School, and was recruited by Warren Christopher (later President Bill Clinton's secretary of state) to work at the Los Angeles law firm O'Melveny & Myers. After five years there, he got into real estate in Los Angeles and was a millionaire before he turned thirty.

After riots tore apart nearly two dozen American cities in 1967, Palmieri became involved in his first crisis-management situation when he was named deputy executive director of the National Advisory Commission on Civil Disorders (known as the Kerner Commission, after its head, former Illinois governor Otto Kerner).

In 1969, he founded The Palmieri Co. and was called in to help with the bankrupt Penn Central. His salary was a hefty $25,000 a month. Palmieri was so successful at selling off real estate and unwinding a complex maze of tax shelters that, two years later, he was appointed chairman of the Pennsylvania Co., as well as chairman of all Penn Central's non-rail subsidiaries. Among the assets were amusement parks, now operating under the name Six Flags Inc. Total fees for Palmieri and his firm were US$33 million.

In 1980, President Jimmy Carter appointed Palmieri ambassador at

large and United States coordinator for refugee affairs at the State
Department to handle the Vietnamese boat people and the influx of
Cubans into Florida. In 1981, he married his second wife, Rhonda
Martyn – a dance-troupe director, and, at thirty-five, a woman twenty
years his junior – at his secluded forty-acre home on California's Big
Sur. Festivities lasted two days.

Over the years, Palmieri has developed a list of six common
elements that he says inflict all troubled companies, whatever their
size. He grandly calls them Palmieri's Laws:

• The law of collective incompetence: Put a group of successful,
experienced, and intelligent businessmen in a panelled room, call
them a board of directors, and their individual level of intellectual
acuity and moral courage will immediately plummet to the lowest
common denominator.

• The law of the visionary leader: The salesman genius who
succeeds to top management is almost always too arrogant or too inse-
cure to take financial guidance and too focused on making deals to
worry about the balance sheet. Whenever a super salesman, endowed
by heaven with a "strategic vision," is put in charge of a financial institution, the odds are two to one that the company will be in insolvency
proceedings within three years.

• The law of sudden crisis: No matter how great the sense of
surprise and shock in the financial community when the crunch
comes and the headlines appear, no corporate crisis really happens
overnight. It takes years of intensive effort by a determined management to create the conditions for the failure of a major corporation.

• The law of budgets and forecasts: In a turnaround situation, the
information presented to a newly arrived CEO is more likely to be part
of the problem than part of the solution. If prior leadership had built
an honest management-information system, there would be no need
for outside help.

• The law of creditor relations: The key to a successful reorganization is making all creditor groups equally unhappy, but not so
unhappy that they resort to time-consuming adversarial proceedings.
In short, keep them sullen, but not rebellious.

• The law of external effects (California-style): In the end, macro factors tend to swamp micro factors. Earning a living as a corporate crisis manager is a little like big-wave surfing. You can bring in a team of the best and brightest, build credibility with lenders, cut costs, create a perfect plan, and be a charismatic leader, but if the swells of recession are running against you, you're not going to make it to shore before the sharks start circling.

As the best-known corporate rehabilitator in the United States, Palmieri, who charges US$600 an hour, had been through a few rescue attempts before, including Mutual Benefit Life, of Newark, New Jersey, seized by state regulators in 1991. Mutual Benefit got into trouble after investing more than US$1 billion in four non-insurance subsidiaries: two Florida residential developments and two leveraged buyouts of retail companies (one a baby-wear firm and the other a home-improvement centre). There were also ninety limited-partner-ship syndications.

Palmieri is currently president and CEO of MBL Life Assurance Corp., the successor firm. The bailout plan allows policyholders to collect the full value of their policies, with annuitants collecting over a seven-year period. The plan is guaranteed by the National Organi-zation of Life and Health Guaranty Associations, of Herndon, Virginia, and a consortium of major companies, such as Prudential Insurance (headquartered just down the street from MBL in Newark) and Metropolitan Life, of New York.*

Mutual Benefit was taken over by the state of New Jersey to halt a run sparked by credit downgrades that were in turn caused by a dete-riorating commercial mortgage and real-estate portfolio. At the time, Mutual Benefit had been in business for 147 years, had US$14 billion in assets, 700,000 policyholders, 2,700 employees, 1,200 agents, and a complex financial structure that included thirty-five operating compa-nies and one hundred joint ventures. Invested assets were more than 50 per cent in real estate, more than twice the industry average of 20 per cent. Fully 45 per cent of the portfolio was committed to office

---

* The Palmieri Co. billed US$13 million over four years for its work on Mutual Benefit.

properties; one-third of total loans and investments were in three states – Florida, New Jersey, and California. Sound familiar? Until Confed, Mutual Benefit was North America's largest insurance failure.

Both suffered crisis situations. "Almost by definition, a crisis situation creates an atmosphere of shock and bewilderment, outside as well as inside the organization, often turning quickly to anger and a sense of betrayal," says Palmieri. "Employees lapse into a demoralized trance, key personnel begin faxing résumés, vendors hesitate to ship, customers start cancelling orders, banks call in credit lines, regulators start investigations, legislators schedule hearings, ratings agencies announce downgrades, auditors agitate for write downs, plaintiffs' lawyers file multiple-shareholder class actions, and the directors start sweating about the board's liability-insurance coverage. Meanwhile the media are circling."

It didn't take Palmieri long to size up the situation; Confed and Mutual Benefit could have been twins. "The two are remarkably similar. Both were long-established mutual life-insurance companies, well over a hundred years old in both cases, both flagships in their respective countries. Both were headed by individuals or a succession of individuals who presided over an accumulation of risk which rendered the company increasingly vulnerable to a change in the economic environment. Precisely that change occurred with a crash in the real-estate market that took place in 1990 as a result of the excesses of the late eighties.

"In each case, you had a board of highly successful, powerful civic and corporate leaders sitting around a board table in a semi-conscious state so far as the corporate strategies were concerned, and where it was leading so far as the perception of risk was involved. In short [it was] a total failure of prudential stewardship," says Palmieri. "It's another demonstration of the extent to which boards of directors peopled by individuals – who in their own right are successful and even shrewd businesspeople – can, when they assemble in a boardroom, lose 50 per cent of their IQ points over a long period of time."

With Palmieri as wheelman, David Dykhouse of Michigan began protecting his position. Under the provisions of that state's statutes, Dykhouse could have placed Confed under supervision, a move that would have alerted everyone to the company's parlous state and precipitated a run. Instead, in April, he parlayed the need for his approval on negotiations in Canada to end the use by CTSL of funds in the trust. The total in IOUs was frozen on April 15, 1994. The cash box was closed, US$620 million later. Elimination of the CTSL notes was made a precondition to approval of the alliance.

"Both OSFI and the Michigan department were victimized by the efforts of the management to obscure what was happening," claims Palmieri of the long-running scheme by CTSL to shuffle funds in the Michigan trust. A twenty-two-page document, dated May 13, 1994, and signed by Dykhouse, Cantor, and Maureen Waldron of Harris, would finalize the April understanding. It provided that, if Confed were seized by regulators, Dykhouse could order Harris to pay him those trusteed assets. Negotiations leading up to the letter of intent with Great-West also began to include discussions of how to redirect some of the new money coming into the deal back to Michigan in order to get the trust on side.*

On April 19, Dackow, Cantor, and White met in Detroit to outline the Great-West merger deal to Palmieri and officials from the Michigan insurance commissioner. Dackow went down the list of fundamental errors in management that Great-West had uncovered during its due diligence:

- lack of skills to manage the business outside of insurance;
- a growth program that outstripped capital resources;
- failure to diversify investments;
- over-exposure to real estate;
- inadequate balance-sheet management;
- expense structure out of proportion to the industry;
- weak management; and
- weak product lines.

---

* On May 30, directors were finally brought into the picture about the U.S. trust accounts and the Michigan commissioner's concern. It was the first time the CTSL notes had ever been mentioned in the board minutes.

A thirteen-page letter of intent marked "for discussion purposes" was tabled by Cantor and Dackow. Now that movement had occurred on the trust-account problem, Michigan agreed to the proposed alliance. Moreover, this was the only game in town. If there were no deal with Great-West, Confed was finished. The agreement was delivered that same day to OSFI. The Canadian regulators were fully aware that the trust account had become an issue and that everyone was working to bring it into better balance. "We knew there were remedies afoot," says OSFI's John Thompson.

Confed asked OSFI and the Department of Finance to bless the Great-West deal by noon, April 22. Confed wanted to sign; word was leaking. For most of April, the wider world knew that Confed was negotiating with someone. On April 20, Adam Zimmerman told journalists that the company was Great-West.

Regulatory and political approvals were needed, so everyone assembled in Ottawa, because it was considered neutral ground. David Dodge, quite wisely, takes the view that, if you want to do a deal, you lock everybody together in the same room until there is agreement all round. Finance and OSFI had been briefed on the state of play, but this was the first time everyone had been together – Dodge, assistant deputy minister Nick Le Pan, and counsel Mark Jewett from Finance; Mackenzie and Thompson from OSFI; White and Cantor from Confed; Dackow and Ray McFeetors from Great-West.

The group assembled in Dodge's twentieth-floor boardroom in an office tower one kilometre from Parliament Hill. Watching the proceedings from their framed photos on the walls were fifteen former deputy ministers. The bureaucrats and regulators were there because Great-West was looking for the greatest possible degree of assurance that the rules would stay the same and not change down the road.

Great-West had calculated the levels of risk they were prepared to assume in order for both companies to keep their ratings, and OSFI and finance gave what comfort they could to Great-West. "Probably not as much as they wanted, but more than they had," says Cantor. Officials and regulators bustled in and out, and what emerged was not only the assurance that this deal could go ahead, but also the under-

standing that Ottawa would not impair future industry consolida-
tions. "All the way through the piece, we never appreciated the
difficulty the company was in," says Dodge. "Great-West really knew
more about the company than we did [in Finance], but I think, in
some ways, more than Paul and Mike."

The non-binding letter of intent was signed April 28 and had three
elements: to increase the company's capital base; to reduce the size of
the company and improve liquidity; to have Great-West manage parts
of the ongoing business.

The deal increased Confed's capital base by $460 million, through
a combination of Great-West's capital infusion, asset sales, and various
reinsurance agreements. Great-West would purchase $75 million
worth of preferred shares in Confed, nominate a majority of the
board members, and provide up to $150 million in capital support, for
a total of $225 million. In all, the amount produced by the deal was
only half of what Sun Life had concluded was necessary to resurrect
Confed.

Group life and health in Canada and the United States would be
sold, thereby adding $100 million to capital. Great-West had an option
that expired July 13 to buy both divisions for $52 million; if the option
were not taken up, another party could step in. For an annual fee,
Great-West would also take over most of Confed's administrative
duties – such as claims-paying, administration, asset and liability
management. There would also be some sales synergies. Confed
products could be sold by Great-West's independent broker network
in the United States.

Confed assets worth $1 billion would be sold to Great-West, and
the money would be used to reduce debt, retire commercial paper, or
buy short-term fixed-income securities. (Half the sale was scheduled
to occur before closing, the other half within a year after closing.) The
two sides also agreed to a woolly item called "other measures," said to
be worth $75 million in capital. Ideas included: unspecified financial
re-engineering, leasing buildings currently vacant, selling real estate,
and uncovering other cost savings.

Great-West was not interested in the British operations; they
would be sold at auction. Nor did Great-West have any enthusiasm

for Confederation Trust. According to the letter of intent, Confederation Life would continue to wind down the affairs of its problem child. Everything was subject to further due diligence by Great-West (to be completed by July 23), with a definitive agreement to be signed July 31.

Even the official announcement made the following day managed to capture Cantor's relief that he'd gotten this far. "Linkage with Great-West and its high credit ratings will give our customers and policyholders confidence in Confederation Life's future. We will now have the time and the resources to reshape operating expenses and work out our real-estate problems."

Officials in Finance were pessimistic. They thought the deal had maybe a 55-per-cent chance of succeeding. Part of the problem was that everybody was heavily dependent on what Great-West said about Confed's financial health. Even Cantor admitted that, although he might disagree with some of their evaluations, Great-West had told him of things about which he had been unaware. Officials in Finance also felt as if there was insufficient independent information available and wondered if OSFI had really been "on the case."

The letter was not the end, it was barely the beginning of the end. Two weeks later, Cantor spoke at a breakfast session for financial-services executives at the National Club in Toronto. While he didn't reveal specifics of the deal, he was clearly worried. Someone who knows Cantor well said privately to him during coffee before his talk, "I guess you've just got some t's to cross and i's to dot." "No," Cantor replied, "it's a lot more than that."

Most difficult were three items called "conditions precedent" that had to be achieved before any deal could close. First, both sides agreed that they would review operations in the United Kingdom with a view to selling that business as a block. A decision to sell would have to be approved by both Great-West and Confed. Second, something had to be done about the US$1.1 billion worth of COLI/BOLI business. Other companies had to take on the necessary assumption reinsurance. Third, Confed would seek standby credit in the form of operating lines from the banks.

If all of that were accomplished and the deal closed, Confed would be unrecognizable. Employment would be slashed, since Great-West was handling all the clerical tasks. Initially, some Confed executives would stay on as a transition team, but since Great-West and its parent, Power Corp., controlled the board, Confed's real role would quickly diminish. Cantor had gutted Confed to save it. The name might remain in some form, but the old Confed was dead.

The so-called strategic alliance was, in fact, a take-over. Great-West would not only gain market share in group life and health but also stood to get some of its money back. If, after five years, Confed's capital ratios were healthy, Great-West could redeem the $75 million in preferreds. Moreover, some of the promised funds were only required on a standby basis. The $150-million capital maintenance would only be committed if Confed's MCCSR went into a tailspin below 100 per cent.

The rating agencies gave the deal mixed reviews. On April 29, Duff & Phelps reaffirmed its AA – rating. Dominion Bond Rating Service was less positive and dropped the rating to BBB –.

Cantor hit the road to sell the deal. He arrived in Atlanta on April 30, accompanied by Bill McCallum, president of Great-West Life, en route to Boston, Princeton, New Jersey, and Dallas. Cantor, says Bill Bowden, "looked like death warmed over." Cantor told them that the thrust of the whole exercise was to maximize protection of policyholders. Said Cantor of their new partners, "This is not a deep-pocket unlimited offer, [but] the deal is within their tolerance for risk and reward."

Cantor told the Atlanta staff that he had learned the most about Confed not from all the consultants he'd hired but from companies who considered investing in Confed and had therefore carried out extensive due diligence. He also admitted for the first time that he'd had some difficulty understanding the liability side of the balance sheet. Cantor said he'd talked to Dominic D'Alessandro, former president of Laurentian Bank, after his appointment three months earlier as CEO of Manulife. D'Alessandro had asked his fellow former banker for advice on the life-insurance industry, and Cantor warned him that he would readily understand the asset side, but not the liability side. "I have two pieces of advice," Cantor said to D'Alessandro. "The first is, hire consulting actuaries. The second is, don't take anyone's advice on the subject of hiring consulting actuaries."

Sale of group life and health was not popular in Atlanta, but Cantor was adamant. "Crown jewels or not, they are not the core business lines of a mutual company," he said. "The whole point of the strategy is to give Confed time to work its way through problems by strengthening management and capital, reducing expenses, and increasing liquidity."

The deal, he explained, would inject more than $3 billion in liquidity. First, there would be $330 million in residential mortgages, securitized through the Federal National Mortgage Association. A further $135-million transaction would be done with the Bank of Montreal. Great-West would purchase up to $1 billion in assets such as mortgages and private placements, from Confed. Finally, there was the assumption reinsurance on the COLI/BOLI business. That U.S.-based business had been part of the growth in the eighties, now it was at the heart of the problem. "You folks are both our bane and our breadbasket," Cantor told his Atlanta audience.

On May 30, Confed reported first-quarter results for 1994. There was a loss of $3.5 million, compared to a profit of $5.8 million in the same period a year earlier. The level of non-performing assets rose slightly from the year-end 1993 level of $803 million, to $804 million.

Despite the fact that the take-over meant that many Confed jobs would likely disappear, a poll found that staff at One Mount Pleasant Place had less-weighty matters on their minds. They wanted to have "casual days," when more comfortable clothing was allowed. So, starting in June, Fridays were designated as casual days (with three full casual weeks also set for the summer). There was, however, a list circulated of taboo items. Disallowed were: scruffy or tattered clothing, T-shirts with inappropriate slogans, sweat pants, biking shorts, short shorts or sport shorts, and a welter of worrisome womenswear such as tube tops, Spandex tops, and bikini-style tops.

Great-West's continuing due-diligence process was beginning to turn up more and more surprises. "There was sloppiness in documentation. Transactions would occur, and only one party had a record," says David Murray of Deloitte & Touche. "They didn't document things as clearly as they should have. They blurred company lines."

There were other surprises. Mortgages thought to be in good shape would turn out to be non-performing, with an owner about to walk and leave the insurance company holding the bag. "Desk audits don't tell you a helluva lot," says Finance's David Dodge. "If you took those files and actually went out and looked at the piece of real estate that was there, looked behind it, the quality was a lot weaker than you'd been led to believe."

Adam Zimmerman was even more blunt, saying, "Every time they'd turn over a rock, they'd find a snake." In a company where there is a heavy concentration of non-performing assets, a poor portfolio encourages additional deterioration. Borrowers and mortgage holders take a different attitude towards a lender in trouble. They fail to make timely payments and are not quick to renew leases on the assumption that no one is paying attention.

For example, when the Hong Kong Bank acquired the Bank of British Columbia, a $200-million portfolio of what had been thought of as problem loans suddenly were not problems, because the borrowers realized that they needed an ongoing relationship with a bank – the new owners – and they'd better straighten up.

As a result, whether it was Ernst & Young, Mercer, Milliman, Coopers, or Great-West doing the due diligence, every time someone looked at an asset that had been studied a few months earlier, invariably it was in worse shape, not only because of deteriorating markets but also because of those attitudinal problems. Actuaries slowed the process by engaging in lengthy arguments, even though there was no possibility of consensus.

The COLI/BOLI business was also proving to be a tough sell. When the letter of intent was signed, the hope was that two American firms – New York Life and ITT Hartford – would reinsure this business, so that it would no longer be a source of worry. Both companies subsequently backed off, because the notes lodged in Michigan were getting in the way. The COLI/BOLI business couldn't be peeled off, because there was too little security backing them in the United States. To do something about a liability like COLI/BOLI meant action was required on the asset side – the linked finger. What had originally been Confed's cash cow was now standing in the way of a solution.

With the American firms out, a Canadian approach was proposed in mid-June. Tom Di Giacomo was hired to assemble a consortium of the five largest Canadian insurers, to see if they would take on the COLI business instead. Until August 1993, Di Giacomo had been chairman, CEO, and president of Manulife Financial. That month, after twenty-seven years with the company and six as CEO, he was fired at the board's behest. When he had originally vaulted to the top, the take-charge Di Giacomo seemed just what the fusty place needed. Unlike traditional insurance honchos – counting-room actuaries who lectured rather than led – Di Giacomo was a pugnacious, self-made man.

For two years, Di Giacomo and the Manulife board tried to agree on future strategy and could not. Senior management was split between loyalists and those who didn't like him. Finally, in 1993, the board decided Di Giacomo had taken too long to come up with a strategy; he was gone.

Di Giacomo suited his new role admirably. He knew the players and the issues. The group of CEOs included his successor at Manulife, Dominic D'Alessandro, John McNeil of Sun Life, David Nield of Canada Life, Bob Astley of Mutual Life, and Gordon Cunningham of London Life. This was not an easy job; some of the CEOs knew nothing about COLI, had small United States operations, and couldn't figure out how they'd handle such business. Still, everyone agreed that they'd try to be helpful for the sake of the industry. Over the next month, they agreed to take on the COLI block and share $100 million in losses.

Two other conditions in the letter of intent between Confed and Great-West were also carried out. By June, Great-West had provided $500 million of liquidity support through the purchase of mortgages (no non-performing mortgages were in the package) and private placements of corporate debt. The cash would come in handy for big policy surrenders and the withdrawal of business by major, sophisticated players. For the most part, however, market reaction was supportive. An auction early in July for United Kingdom operations attracted four willing bidders.

On June 10, however, Standard & Poor's lowered its rating from AA to AA −. This was becoming like death by a thousand cuts, as rating agencies kept drawing a little bit of blood here, a little bit there, but never enough to cause death.

Meanwhile, Michigan was continuing to press for its pound of flesh. Bill Alexander, president of Confederation Treasury Services Ltd., held two meetings in the spring with the Michigan Insurance Commission and exchanged correspondence with Victor Palmieri in July, all trying to sort out how much money would flow to Michigan. Depending on how much cash went into the deal, Michigan was expecting about $400 million.

A June 15 letter to Robert Bailey, Michigan's first deputy insurance commissioner, outlined a draft understanding of how that payment to Michigan might be achieved. Among the items: a cash transfer from Confed of $181 million; Newcourt Credit, the former Confederation Leasing, would repay $200 million in advances owing (of which Michigan would get $178 million); and Canadian real estate from Confed's portfolio with an appraised value of $31 million.

At the policyholders meeting in Toronto on June 22, Paul Cantor put on a brave front for a man with little manoeuvring room remaining. "There have been a lot of rumours about our circumstances and considerable speculation on what it all means to each of us," he told those assembled. "In the next few minutes, I will put those rumours and speculations to rest, and replace them with facts, and a clear vision of a strong, secure Confederation Life which will sell personal financial protection in the years ahead." But all the numbers he gave were months out of date. Policyholder protection was his main concern, he said, not just as "a financial issue" but as "a moral issue" as well, but he added ominously, "I do not believe this or any company is immune to disaster."

Privately, both Confed and Great-West were admitting that the end-of-July closing date might be a bit optimistic. In a June 1 presentation to the Hemisphere Group, one of Confed's independent

marketing organizations, at the Marriott Hotel in Burlington, Massachusetts, Paul Cantor and Bill McCallum said that the deal might take
as much as two months longer to complete than they originally
thought.

Great-West was finding a pattern that had become a cultural
problem at Confed. In the eighties, decentralization had put power in
the hands of regions, pushing responsibility well down into the organization. The result was a mish-mash of accounting methods, where
figures kept in the regions didn't always jibe with head-office
numbers.

There was also an inherent sloppiness, described as "close enough
is good enough" by one insider. "If you have a $100-million account
and you're constantly out by $3 million to $4 million, that was good
enough," said the source. Junior staff tried to solve problems and
tended not to inform middle management until things had gone too
far to fix. Senior managers were never told about these black holes,
nor did they ask. It was these sorts of repressed items that Wendy
Watson had found once internal-audit procedures were tightened
upon her arrival in 1992. For Orest Dackow, such sloppiness was
unforgivable.

But the problems weren't only with Confed. Everyone – the industry, Ottawa, and the regulators – remained wary of Great-West. The
general view was that Great-West really just wanted to get the one
trophy division, group life and health. "There was a concern that they
would buy the group – pick up the bowl of cherries – and walk," says
Mackenzie. "That was one of the risks, and it was concluded that it
was a manageable risk and it wouldn't happen."

Mackenzie stayed in touch with the negotiators, but he was coming
to the end of his seven-year term as superintendent. For months, he
had told Ottawa he would brook no extensions beyond June 30; they
should be ready to replace him. He took the unusual step of publicly
recommending as his successor one of his deputies at OSFI, Suzanne
Labarge, a former Royal Bank executive. Dodge pleaded with him to
stay and see the deal through but, when the end of June came,
Mackenzie had departed. After he had watched Confed's tailspin for
almost five years, and with the deal set to close in a month's time, his

indifference seemed bizarre. Explains Mackenzie, "I was scared like hell that if I stayed on, because I've seen it before, [you] stay on for a month, then it's two months, then it's three months, then it's Christmas." Retirement beckoned.

Paul Cantor was continuing his efforts to keep his various constituencies at ease, because financial services is all about faith and confidence. "That's why you can never be angry. You can never be stressed," he says. "You can never be tired. You can never be overwhelmed by the complexity of it all. You must always be bright, positive, self-assured, and confident – no matter how you really feel inside."

Perhaps this Dr. Feelgood philosophy explains why, on July 5, the major rating agencies received a ten-page fax updating them on progress. Information was given in "bullet" form, but two smoking guns were not highlighted – Confed's growing losses as identified by Great-West and the gaping hole in the Michigan trust. On the same day, Great-West and Confed met at the CLHIA offices with the five other industry CEOs – McNeil, Astley, Nield, Cunningham, and D'Alessandro. Dackow outlined some of the findings to date, noting that the problem was larger than he had originally believed, but indicating that Great-West was still intending to close later that month.

Equally typical of the chipper chatter was a meeting called by Cantor to reassure the six-hundred-member Independent Brokers Association of Canada. President Jim Bullock had met with his executive to discuss how brokers could talk honestly to Confed policyholders. What if, for example, a policyholder asked about Confed's health? Were brokers supposed to be honest, say there could be a problem, and urge that they switch to another carrier? Or would such advice cause panic in the streets?

Cantor invited Bullock and Bob Barney, president of Compulife Software Inc., a Kitchener, Ontario-based supplier of comparative pricing systems to the industry, to meet him July 19. Also attending were Nick Villani, president and CEO of Aetna Life Insurance Co., the firm that handled Confed's individual life sales through its Equinox subsidiary, and Denis Devos, Great-West senior vice-president, individual operations.

The mood was tense. Barney entered the boardroom, looked

under the conference table, and quipped, "Okay, there are no guns."
Cantor tried to put the visitors at ease, saying "We're all friends here."
Corrected Barney, "We've just met." Cantor assured them that the
strategic alliance with Great-West was going through. Although
Devos said little, his presence was meant to buttress that view. "You've
been able to get some props from Great-West," Barney said. "But
what steps are the company going to take to change this from a going-
down-the-hole situation to going-up-the ladder?"

Replied Cantor, "We'll sell more insurance." Villani chimed in
supportively to say that Equinox had already paid out $500,000 in
commissions for new Confed business sold in 1994. The brokers'
group was dubious about such a strategy. "I do that [much business]
myself," Bullock scoffed.

Bullock had heard rumours that the federal government had
already appointed a liquidator, but he felt uncomfortable asking about
that with Great-West present.* As further assurance, however, Cantor
said he'd be agreeable to meeting with Bullock later in the month,
along with John Thompson, OSFI's deputy superintendent, insurance.
The meeting was set, but eventually cancelled.

By mid-July, as Great-West totalled up what it had uncovered
about Confed, it was clear to Orest Dackow that the year-end 1993
balance sheet was a joke. Depending on what scenario was used for
real-estate values in the future, Great-West had found enough losses to
eliminate all the surplus, leaving Confed in a deep hole.

The Michigan notes were now becoming a critical issue. It was no
longer a left-pocket, right-pocket thing. "In analysing a company's
financial condition, attention must be paid not only to the quantum
of capital and surplus *but also its location* [emphasis added]," concluded
Dackow. "In this context, location has two important attributes. First
is the identity and the geographic location of which regulator has
control over which assets in the event of the financial difficulty of the
company. Second, the position, within the corporate structure, of the

---

* The rumours were accurate. Peat Marwick Thorne Inc., the same firm that
handled Sovereign Life, had been on a standby retainer since March.

assets within each regulatory jurisdiction. It is not enough to have the appropriate quantum of assets located by regulatory jurisdiction. It is also necessary to ensure that the properly allocated assets are within the control of the regulator of the jurisdiction."

"There was one thing that spooked the people in Denver – and those were those damned notes," says Michael Mackenzie.

As the end of July approached, Great-West was coming to the conclusion that more capital was required than had been envisaged at the time of signing the letter of intent in April. "At what point do you say, 'Ouch, we're going to need someone else to join us in this venture,'" says Dackow. Dackow informed Cantor that Great-West would not be closing the deal.

Great-West comes under the corporate umbrella of Paul Desmarais, chairman and CEO of Power Corp., a firm and a family with which both Prime Minister Jean Chrétien and Finance Minister Paul Martin have connections. Martin had been a vice-president at Power; Chrétien's daughter is married to Desmarais's son.

As a result, staff to both Martin and Chrétien claim that they were kept away from daily negotiations during the time that the Great-West strategic alliance with Confed seemed possible, in order to avoid any appearance of a conflict of interest. Doug Peters, secretary of state for international financial institutions, says he consulted neither Martin nor Chrétien, choosing instead to sound out other ministers for views. In the end, however, that antiseptic stance may have worked against the deal. Although everyone in Ottawa wanted a going-concern solution, no one ever picked up the phone, called Desmarais, and urged that Great-West push ahead. "Everybody knew the phone numbers, but government wasn't interventionist as they have been in the past with financial-services problems," said one Ottawa insider. Another opportunity for a timely bit of assistance was missed.

Paul Cantor was at the precipice again. Although Dackow could have just bolted and gone back to Denver, he didn't. Instead, he had another idea: Why not ask the five industry CEOs who had already been meeting with Di Giacomo about COLI to see if they'd be part of a multilateral approach? Cantor, happy to grab any solution that might save his company, agreed.

"I never did understand why a strong attempt to form a consortium wasn't made early on," says Adam Zimmerman. "I think it was believed that: (a) it would disrupt the market considerably, because the level of stress would be either more generally known or thought to be higher than it was; and (b) that it was unlikely that other companies would run to rescue a competitor. But I always saw it as being the insurance industry saving itself."

But would the industry have the savvy to act? Or the time?

CHAPTER 11

❧

The Gang That Couldn't Think Straight

"No problem is so big that you can't run away from it."

– Snoopy

S ecrecy was paramount July 23 when the high-powered industry group met with hopes of saving Confed after the alliance
with Great-West foundered. The timing and the setting –
Saturday in Great-West's group-insurance offices in the Merrill Lynch
tower on Toronto's King Street – were both selected to avoid curious
staff and nosey journalists. The eleven participants needn't have
worried. As the last-ditch rescue operation gathered more players and
became one continuous meeting at several Toronto and Ottawa
venues over the next three weeks, no outsider ever became suspicious.

Attendees that first day represented the seven largest life-insur-
ance companies in Canada, and $170 billion in assets. They included
Orest Dackow, Ray McFeetors, and Bill McCallum, CEOs from
various segments of Great-West, and Paul Cantor and Michael
White from Confed. Also there were the five insurance-company
CEOs who'd been meeting since mid-June with Tom Di Giacomo:

John McNeil from Sun, Bob Astley from Mutual Life, David Nield from Canada Life, Gordon Cunningham from London Life, and Dominic D'Alessandro from Manulife.

The five CEOs had been going down one track, attempting to reinsure Confed's U.S.-based corporate-owned life insurance; now they were being shown the entire swamp. With Di Giacomo acting as chairman, Dackow took the floor shortly after 3 P.M. His presentation lasted ninety minutes and included several possible outcomes, based upon various future values of real estate and other assets. The worst-case scenario, called "scenario one" by Dackow, predicted that Confed's unrealized losses could go as high as $1.7 billion.

As a result, Great-West had concluded that the $225-million injection by Great-West, envisaged by the letter of intent, was not enough. Dackow said that Confed needed $300 million in capital, an amount that was too much for one firm to bear. He proposed that Great-West would contribute the $75 million, with the remaining $225 million coming from the industry as a show of force and faith in one of its own. He proposed that the six companies, led by Great-West, would take over the $1 billion COLI business.

Dackow proposed that the management agreement promised by the letter of intent would continue and that Great-West buy group life and health for $50 million. Because Great-West had spent $25 million during the six months of negotiation and due diligence, Dackow said, his company deserved some reward. They wanted Great-West to be "sponsor," that is, act as head of the management structure that eventually would be created. As a sop to the others, he suggested that Manulife would get an option to bid on the United States individual life and the pension business in Canada.

Dackow's presentation was at once a surprise and a setback. As it became clear to the five newly recruited CEOs that they were being asked to expand their role from one obscure aspect of the deal to full-blown participation, they peppered Dackow with questions. They didn't like the idea of Great-West as "sponsor," a role like the lead bank in a loan syndication. As sponsor, Great-West would collect fees from the other participants. Everyone's hackles were up. As far as they were concerned, Great-West had pushed Confed to the wall, and now wanted help, fees, *and* the crown jewels.

The CEOs who were now being asked to form the rescue party were taken aback by the size of the $1.7-billion loss under Great-West's "scenario one." Everyone evaluates insurance companies differently, and since Dackow was not prepared to turn over his work papers, they couldn't know if they'd agree with Great-West's calculations or the assumptions on which they were based. Nor did the five executives much like being asked to climb aboard at this late date. Both Astley and McNeil were angered by Great-West's proposal and told Dackow so in no uncertain terms. As far as Cunningham and D'Alessandro were concerned, Great-West just wanted to make a sweet deal even sweeter by attempting to buy Confed with financial assistance from the other firms.

Reaction towards Great-West ranged from negative to outright hostile. "This is a pretty powerful group," said one participant. "Trying to keep it under control was a yeoman's task." Various solutions were discussed, but hanging in the air was one nagging question, recalled by a participant, "You've taken eighty-five days to put this together and you're asking us to do an industry deal within ten days or two weeks?" The CEOs felt painted into a corner, forced to invent a structure that didn't exist in order to save a company that appeared beyond hope, based on numbers about which they were dubious, presented by someone with little credibility. Great-West told the group that it had just decided on Thursday, two days earlier, it would not go ahead. "That's garbage," snapped McNeil.

Cunningham offered a counter-proposal. If Great-West had now concluded that $300 million in capital was necessary, he said that Great-West should contribute $200 million; the other five firms would share the remaining $100 million. Great-West retired from the meeting to call Robert Gratton in Montreal to get his reaction.

The CEOs left behind were not pleased to be negotiating with a phantom. After a few minutes of collective thumb-twiddling, D'Alessandro, who had an office in Toronto but had not moved from Montreal, said, "Screw this. I'm going home to Montreal." Cunningham also decided to bail out; since Toronto's Pearson airport was on his way home to London, Ontario, he offered to drop D'Alessandro on the way. Astley also departed, leaving a rump group of Di Giacomo, McNeil, and Nield.

When the Great-West trio returned, McNeil threw an entirely different proposal out for consideration, which took into account their respective corporate sizes. On a single sheet of yellow lined paper, he had devised a formula that saw Great-West contributing $50 million; the other five firms would split the $250 million. Sun and Manulife would each come in for $60 million, Mutual would contribute $45 million, Canada and London, $42.5 million each. If that arrangement didn't fly, McNeil's fallback suggestion was that the six simply split the $300 million evenly.

There was consent on one matter. "We all agreed we had a problem," said a participant. "Not just for the industry, but for Canada." Without all participants present, however, no progress could be made on the monetary participation. They decided to meet again the following day.

❖

Sunday morning, it was Orest Dackow's turn to kvetch. He telephoned McNeil and said, "The group is not sufficiently appreciative of Great-West's role since April in keeping Confed alive." The tendentious atmosphere continued when the group reassembled that afternoon at the Office of the Superintendent of Financial Institutions (OSFI) in the Standard Life tower, one block east on King Street from Saturday's meeting place. The industry representatives who had attended the day before were joined in the Upper Canada Room by OSFI deputy superintendent John Thompson and acting superintendent Suzanne Labarge. "This is something that needs a private-sector solution," said Thompson. Without missing a beat, McNeil said, "If this is a private-sector problem, why are you here?"

Labarge was at a serious disadvantage. Insurance was not her area of expertise, nor had she participated in the April talks leading to the letter of intent. So it was left to Thompson to do most of the talking for OSFI.

From the Department of Finance came David Dodge (who cancelled a two-week cottage holiday to get involved), Nick Le Pan, and Sheryl Kennedy, general manager of the financial sector, policy branch.* Ottawa was not pleased to be back in the same soup. It had "churched" a deal in April that was proving inadequate three months later.

A large abstract painting hanging on one of the boardroom's walls – a stark oil-and-enamel on plywood by Ronald Moppett called "Prairie Winter" – symbolized the chill in the room. The small colour photos by Randy Bradley on the opposite wall showed the necessary direction: a saw horse, winch, and construction site. No one, however, was yet building a structure or writing a cheque. Such a surprise investment was not in anyone's corporate plans, and each CEO would need to consult his respective board of directors.

Dackow reprised his numbers. The industry CEOs had concluded that they were willing to consider a capital injection, but not without a commitment that they would get something from the government in return, such as special tax treatment. They were no happier about being dragged in than they had been the day before. McNeil, an outspoken character, was openly derisive of Confed's predicament, and he played reluctant hero. "I'm here to help," he said, "but if you guys hadn't screwed it up, we wouldn't be here." Dodge indicated that Ottawa might be prepared to consider various tax concessions and some sort of consumer-protection agency similar to the CDIC, which, unlike CompCorp, had ready access to government funds rather than just money from the life-insurance sector.

There were so many permutations and combinations discussed that the result was confusion. "There were a lot of numbers put out on the table that day," says Labarge. "I don't think anybody walked away from the meeting with a clear understanding of what the numbers were, what they meant, or what underlay them." The main cause for their quandary was the difference in value between a "going-concern" situation as opposed to a company in liquidation. In a going concern,

---

* Doug Peters, who was holidaying at Clear Lake, Manitoba, in Riding Mountain National Park, was briefed daily by phone.

value can be computed far out into the future, because the company expects to be around. In a liquidation, assets sometimes get dumped, because cash is needed and there's no chance to wait until values rise again. Bargaining power is also reduced; potential buyers know they can squeeze sellers. Buyers will always put lower values on an asset than the value the seller has assigned to that asset.

The discussion about setting up a Crown corporation like the CDIC reopened old wounds that had barely healed. The industry had been badly divided about the need for such a back stop, but had been forced by government to establish a private-sector fund in 1990. In less than two years, CompCorp had been wrestling with its first failure, Les Coopérants.

In December 1992, there had been another problem when Sovereign Life Insurance Co., of Calgary, was seized by the regulators. This time, the solution was cleaner. CompCorp stayed away from the tar baby, and Standard Life purchased the company, problems and all. To date, the losses covered by the industry run to $80 million for Sovereign and $200 million for Les Coopérants.

Throughout 1993 and 1994, the industry and Ottawa dickered about possible changes to CompCorp. Confed's situation in that summer of 1994 shoved the industry's face in their own failure. Life-insurance officials began saying that maybe Ottawa should take over CompCorp and create another Crown corporation, something that came to be known as the CDIC-II.

Ottawa was not enthusiastic about creating such a drain on fiscal resources – and there were very good reasons for government reluctance. From 1923, when the Home Bank failed, until 1967, when the CDIC was formed, no other bank had gone under. Since 1967, three dozen deposit-taking institutions have either been liquidated or absorbed by others in the industry. The cost to the CDIC and ulti-mately the taxpayer – even after asset recoveries – has been about $3.5 billion. Given the deficit-reduction realities of governments in the nineties, there was little support in Ottawa for another Crown-corporation cash cow like the CDIC.

Beginning with the first session on Saturday, the rescue party met daily for ten days running. Sustenance was sandwiches and coffee, although OSFI did organize one hot pasta dinner. At the end of that long bargaining session, when consensus had been reached on some matters, Di Giacomo – whose wit leavened many tense moments – quipped, "It's only because Italian food was served tonight that we were able to reach a conclusion." Although each CEO had power in his own right, one participant joked that real control was in the hands of those OSFI staffers who had the magnetic-stripe cards necessary for access to the washrooms. At least two of the cards given out were never returned.

Debate focused on three main areas: how much capital was required; the legal structure of the coalition; and how Ottawa might help. Discussions were barely under way when Great-West upped the ante, saying that the $300-million figure it had cited at first might not be enough. Confed could need a $450-million capital injection. Once that number had been digested, debate ensued about how it might be shared.

Cunningham of London Life, whose board had agreed to contribute up to $100 million into a deal, proposed that any capital injected into Confed should be credited against future assessments by a CDIC-II – if one were created and if Confed ended up failing anyway. His position was popular with the other CEOs, who saw themselves in double jeopardy. They liked the idea of what came to be called a "roll-up," an investment now that would reduce later exposure.

There were several thorny tax issues. Key was the federal government's treatment of any preferred shares purchased by the coalition to inject capital. Under tax rules, if an issuer pays no tax (and Confed would likely fall into that category), dividends on shares are taxable. That meant that the industry coalition might have, say, a stated 9-per-cent return on the shares, but something like 6 per cent after taxes were paid. The CEOs argued they'd be taking both an equity risk and suffer an earnings drag. They wanted an exemption.

Finance agreed to a "mix-and-match" solution that involved some tax breaks and a CDIC-II with "roll-up," but it wasn't prepared to cede everything. Dodge insisted that Ottawa would not participate in a bailout. The industry, he said, must have real money at risk. From Montreal, Power Corp.'s Gratton tossed in another possibility. He would try to organize the debtholders in Europe, those investors who, a year earlier, had bought CTSL bonds worth about $300 million. Gratton was certain that he could convince them to participate in an arrangement that saw them being repaid less than they were owed as a way of helping reduce Confed's liabilities. The other members of the rescue party were dubious, but agreed to let him try. Nothing came of his efforts.

By Wednesday, however, a deal seemed possible. Promises of money seemed to be coming together, and Ottawa had made certain undertakings. Not everyone, however, was onside. Astley was a constant critic. At one point, he turned to McNeil and said, "Why in hell are you so keen to save this thing?" Because, said McNeil, "The whole mystique of Canadian companies in foreign markets will be shattered for all time." Astley, whose firm did little business outside Canada, remained unconvinced.

Away from the bargaining table, few observers were aware how precarious the Confed situation had become. On Friday, July 29, a Great-West spokesperson announced that the end-of-the-month closing date on the strategic alliance would not be met, but said, "discussions are continuing . . . [the delay reflects] the scope of things." The consortium was not mentioned. OSFI said it would seize Confed at the beginning of the following week.

The participants decided they would take one last shot at trying to stitch together an approach everyone could live with. They met on August 1, the civic-holiday Monday, in a boardroom at the Toronto law firm of Tory Tory DesLauriers & Binnington, where the firm's senior partner, Jim Baillie, had been drafting the documents that might be required. Most players were on hand. Others – including Astley of Mutual, D'Alessandro of Manulife, and Nick Le Pan, assistant deputy minister at Finance – participated by phone. CompCorp's Al Morson and CLHIA president Mark Daniels joined the rescue party for the first time.

The group had agreed by then that it might inject $450 million into Confed, but each member still had very specific conditions for participation – in addition to hopes for Ottawa's help. At one point, Dackow specifically asked, "Will the government do everything necessary to make sure Confed doesn't fail?" Replied Le Pan, "No." Some among the attendees were surprised, but continued to push Ottawa for a decision on the preferreds and the CDIC-II.

Hanging over the group was the knowledge that Great-West would have to make a public announcement that week, saying that the strategic alliance was not going ahead and that talks had begun with the consortium. Because Great-West is a stock company, and such information could have a material impact, the Ontario Securities Commission rules required such disclosure. The announcement was even a little overdue.

What had started as a Great-West alliance with Confed, then become an industry approach led by Great-West, had now become an industry deal in which Great-West was no longer seen as a lead company. The atmosphere had become superheated. "Every assessment Great-West made came back more negative than the previous," says Dodge. "The other CEOs started to get suspicious."

Dackow was now saying that $450 million might not be enough and suggested that maybe the deal needed $600 million now, with a further $300 million at some later, unspecified, time. "There was a real question of whether the $600 [million] was the right number. Nobody really had confidence that that necessarily was what it was," says Daniels. "These numbers weren't all that hard. They could have been hard in some people's minds, but they surely weren't in others. These guys had no opportunity to put their own actuarial staff to work. Even at $450 million, you're talking shares of $75 million to $100 million. That's a huge amount of money that companies were being asked to put up on the basis of no analysis at all."

There was also the infamous trust in Michigan. "There were elements of the transaction that certain people didn't like. This sort of issue, which country is the money staying in, was certainly one of them," says OSFI's John Thompson.

"The business needed the liquidity. If they put in $400 million for liquidity to keep the business running, they don't want any of that liquidating the [Michigan] trust," says David Murray of Deloitte & Touche. "Money going into the trust doesn't do anything for [Confed]. The business is still just as cash dry. It's like a bank giving you loan of $100, but saying you have to keep $50 on deposit. How much did they really loan you?" In the circumstances, the consortium couldn't help but be wary. "If they're being told the company needs $600 million and, when you put in $600 [million], the company sees $450 [million] of it, that's the same as saying 'This ain't going to work.'"

The rescue party was ready to give up and let Confed go bust, but Cantor pleaded for more time. He said that the federal cabinet was meeting the following day and might offer some help. He also said that he had a merchant-banking solution that he wanted to explore. Moreover, Michigan's David Dykhouse had visited Toronto the previous Wednesday for an update and had phoned Cantor on Friday to say he'd try to round up $150 million from American firms, enough, when combined with $450 million from the Canadian CEOs, to total the $600 million needed. For Dykhouse and the American industry, motivation for involvement was simple. Support for a solution now would be less costly than dealing with insolvency later. According to Dykhouse, American losses could hit US$700 million if Confed went under. "There was," said one participant, "still a glimmer of hope."

<hr />

On August 4, Great-West could stay silent no longer. Under the letter of intent, a definitive agreement with Confed was supposed to have been signed on July 31. The deadline had passed, so a press release was issued saying that during Confed's "discussions with Great-West, it became apparent that more capital was needed than was available under the letter of intent. As a result, negotiations were expanded to include other companies."

The announcement surprised even the rating agencies, which realized they hadn't been as close to the situation as they'd believed. Standard & Poor's knocked Confed down from A+ to BBB+. A. M. Best downgraded Confed from A− to B++; Duff & Phelps followed, dropping its rating down from AA− to A−1, and said it was keeping Confed on a ratings watch. Dominion Bond Rating Service, which had downgraded Confed to BBB− after the letter of intent, held off doing any more damage. Instead, the Canadian firm suspended its rating, saying it would wait until there was enough information to make a judgement.

As a result, Confed could no longer issue commercial paper or draw on credit lines in order to fund cash required to pay any cash-surrender values requested or repay maturing commercial paper or other borrowings. "It's in the best economic interest of the industry to go forward and make the capital infusion," said Kevin Cuervost, vice-president, Duff & Phelps. "If they don't, what we may be seeing is the next stop before the regulators."

The next stop was not far off. Before this, deadlines could be dictated in a boardroom. Now, marketplace restlessness would decide how much time remained. "What they did was sort of drop the ratings of Confederation Life down the elevator shaft," says John McNeil. "I will not say that is what brought down Confederation, but it was not helpful." Cantor did not agree. "When dealing in the retail market, media exposure is the most critical issue. Ratings don't mean much."

The first session with the American group was held the same day, August 4. Some powerful names were involved: Prudential Insurance Co. of America, Metropolitan Life Insurance Co., New York Life Insurance Co., Equitable Life Assurance Society, Northwestern Mutual Life Insurance Co., John Hancock Mutual Life Insurance Co., Lincoln National Life Insurance Co., and UNUM Life Insurance Co. Members of the Canadian rescue party briefed them by phone, and the Americans agreed to visit Toronto as early as the next day to assess matters firsthand.

But when the Canadians tried to round up Great-West for such a meeting, they made a startling discovery. The three-man team of Dackow, McFeetors, and McCallum had decamped for their respective homes in Denver and Winnipeg. When informed that some powerhouse American companies might join the rescue party, Dackow said that Great-West would need time to prepare. He suggested that everybody gather in Denver the following Wednesday, six days hence. Dykhouse and Labarge instructed Dackow that the next meeting would be on Monday, in Toronto. Michael White began to talk yearningly about what he called a *Home Alone* solution, one that – by his tongue-in-cheek definition – would not involve Great-West.

The delays meant that Cantor was beginning to fret about a run on Confed. Insurance policyholders can apply for policy surrenders, but payout takes three months. By contrast, annuity holders and group and pension clients can switch carriers quickly; holders of commercial paper can go elsewhere as soon as their notes come due. The resulting demand on liquidity not only squeezes corporate cash but also causes unfairness. Sophisticated institutional investors can ask for their money, and those funds immediately flow out and are no longer available to policyholders. While there was no run yet, Cantor claims his monitoring showed pent-up demand building. Cantor and Zimmerman took one last stab to convince Ottawa that help was needed. On August 6, the two executives faxed Finance Minister Paul Martin a two-page letter outlining a $600-million plan "which will lead to the preservation of policyholder and creditor value through the orderly down sizing of the company."

Cantor noted that the Canadian companies were prepared to commit up to $450 million and American companies might add $150 million. The letter asked for a $150-million guarantee of a bridge loan for three months until the American financing was in place.

Martin dismissed the request out of hand the following day. "It is my clear view that it would not be appropriate for the government of Canada to provide direct financial assistance," wrote Martin. "To do so would risk taxpayers money in what should be, I believe, a private sector solution." For the modest cost of a guarantee – Cantor had not asked for "direct financial assistance" – Martin had all but scuppered the deal.

On Monday afternoon, August 8, the American companies arrived for briefings at the CLHIA office in Toronto. The companies were all members of the American Council of Life Insurance (ACLI) insolvency committee, headed by Ian Rowland of Lincoln National. What the Americans heard that day and the next could hardly have been worse. Dackow made his "scenario one" presentation, with its $1.7 billion in unrealized losses. OSFI's Thompson told the group that losses on liquidation could reach $3 billion.

Nor did the Canadian CEOs present a cohesive and confident force. They seemed frazzled by the number of issues involved. Nield of Canada Life and Astley of Mutual Life were particularly concerned with Ottawa's reluctance to offer tax considerations for the capital injection and a CDIC-II to protect policyholders. According to Astley, discussions never got to the point where there was enough of a package for a hands-up vote. "There was never any deal. The issues on the table were so complex. The problem was that there was no mechanism."

In fact, the problem was systemic. The CEOs simply had no experience in deal-making at this level. Unlike the banks, which operate together as part of the payments system, the insurance-industry CEOs have no regular contact other than at annual association gabfests and at various committees where legislative positions are debated. "The banks are lucky because there is a duality," says Robin Korthals, former president of the Toronto–Dominion Bank. "The banks compete at the counter, but they cooperate out back. The payments system means they deal with each other daily." A cheque deposited at one bank but drawn on another needs to go through the clearing system of which all banks are members. Insurance companies are not members; they put their cheques into the system just like any other consumer.

Moreover, the banks cooperate on fraud problems, because each has a vested interest in hearing about bunco artists uncovered by a competitor and in learning from another institution's experience. "Royal's crook today is yours tomorrow," says Korthals. "The insurance industry was crazy not to look after one of their brothers."*

Cantor's banking background was helpful, but his lack of experience in insurance worked against him and a deal. "Whether it was necessary to put the company into liquidation will always have second-guessers," says Confed's Roger Cunningham, "but not being an insurance man didn't give Cantor an inside advantage to try to successfully strike a deal with another insurance company."

---

* Korthals became chairman of North American Life in 1995, and, within six months, the firm merged with Manulife. "By working out North American before people lost confidence, it cost a lot less than Confed," he says.

Nor did anyone else offer real leadership. The likely leader, John McNeil of Sun, had the intellectual horsepower, and he had also just completed his year as chairman of the CLHIA, so had some residual clout from that role. But McNeil was not yet fully healthy following surgery earlier in the year and was heading for a final, corrective procedure in mid-August. McNeil freely admits that it was spring 1995 before he was feeling his old self again. At the time the consortium was struggling with the issue of Confed, McNeil was not yet operating at full throttle, although he did make every effort to keep loose cannons like Bob Astley in line.

While the American companies were considering their possible involvement, twelve of Confed's general agents in the United States spontaneously issued a signed letter in support of Confed, urging clients not to surrender policies or borrow against them. It read, in part: "We believe there continues to be good reason to be optimistic that our clients will be protected in this transaction."

Even at this crucial stage, Great-West seemed to be playing spoiler. Great-West had been leery throughout the negotiations about allowing the other companies to look at its work papers, particularly the American firms. Great-West had taken a view of Confed's health as a result of its due diligence, but it insisted this was just a view, and the firm didn't want to be held responsible later if that view turned out to be wrong. As a result, some members of the Canadian consortium who wanted to see the work papers, did. Potential American participants did not, because they would not agree to sign hold-harmless agreements that took Great-West off the hook.

But Great-West wasn't alone in its truculence. Ottawa's promised tax concessions evaporated. Officials refused to give written assurances that would alleviate the companies' double-jeopardy concerns. David Nield of Canada Life, in particular, was dubious about Ottawa. He cited what happened in the case of CCB and Northland banks. After the government convinced the banking industry to contribute $60 million, it still pulled the plug.

For its part, the government says it couldn't seem to get a handle on how much capital was needed to save Confed. "One of the frustrating things at the end was that the amount required seemed to escalate," says David Dodge. "Every assessment that Great-West made came back more negative than the previous one. We had to rely on Great-West at that point, and the other guys began to get suspicious that Great-West was just pushing them."

Finally, there were the contentious IOUs in the Michigan trust. "A promissory note is a promise to pay from somebody else," says Suzanne Labarge. "That somebody else presumably had the assets to back that promissory note. So the question is, are the assets there, what are they worth, who else shares. When you get to the situation you're at, the question is, what's the value of the note?"

The consortium was collapsing. "Everybody in the end, particularly Great-West, but everybody basically, came to the conclusion that the risks in putting up the dough – or, from our side, the risk of giving special deals – were so high that we couldn't do a deal," says Dodge. "Every time you looked at it, you had to put in more money from the company side, more support from the government side. It was always more, more, more. That made it very hard for everybody."

Mutual's Bob Astley was the first to call it quits. In a conference call early in the afternoon of August 9, he told the other members of the rescue party that he would be phoning Labarge at 5 P.M. to tell her that Mutual would not participate in any support package. Gordon Cunningham of London Life tried to convince Astley to stay, telling him that he was making a tactical error. John McNeil also tried to get Astley to remain aboard, advising him to "shut up and sit tight and that this whole thing will collapse of its own weight."

Astley would hear none of it and called Labarge to inform her that Mutual was pulling out. "When the industry walked away from the discussions, effectively the options available to the company, its manoeuvring room, had substantially disappeared," says OSFI's Thompson. McNeil denies that the industry "walked away." He says, "I think it's fair to say that we came up with $600 million, if the government had come through. They put all the tax deals on the table, then they took them off one at a time."

"They weren't willing to say that, with that [$600 million], it was a viable operation," says Doug Peters, secretary of state for international financial institutions. "The Canadian government and Department of

Finance people were far more concerned with the reputation of
Canadian insurance companies than were the Canadian insurance
companies. If they had been concerned with their reputation, they
would have made sure that Confed did not fail, and they would have
taken a much more active interest in developing a solution.

"There had to be some sort of private-sector agreement that it is
viable. You cannot simply go out and throw taxpayers' money at a
financial institution just because it's big," Peters says. "Companies do
go broke. Just because they're an insurance company doesn't mean
that they're 'too big to fail' or that they're not going to fail."

Victor Palmieri agrees that the unwillingness of the Canadian CEOs
to put up the money caused the deal to founder. Once the American
firms saw that the Canadian companies weren't in, neither were they.
"I mean, it wasn't much money. On MBL, the ACLI group came in for
$2 billion U.S.," he says. "This was only $150 million Canadian."

Lack of leadership in Canada was also a problem, says Palmieri,
who has worked on most of the major U.S. life-insurance rehabilita-
tions. "There was no father figure, there was nobody dedicated to
the preservation of the company. The minute they got the sense the
Canadians weren't bound and determined to save the company,
[the U.S. companies] could care less," he says. "They didn't need the
competition in the United States anyway."

At Confed, the main participants had no energy left to try and find
any other solution. "Cantor and Mike [White] were burnt out by that
time, so they couldn't supply the leadership," says Palmieri. "They
were part of the problem, so to speak."

"This is one of the great tragedies of Canadian corporate history,"
says Paul Cantor. "Everybody lost their zeal to find a collective solution. They all went home to their collective camps to preserve whatever they had."

Cantor decided he had to do the same. Although there had been no
"run" on assets yet, the liquidity committee that had been monitoring
the situation at Confed for weeks concluded that once word spread
that the industry consortium had failed to find a solution, the run
would begin. According to one internal estimate announced later,

Confed would have needed as much as $3 billion over the next ninety days to pay those making demands.

"Liquidity is always the problem," says Palmieri. "There is almost never a *real* liquidity problem. The problem is a *perceived* liquidity problem. In both cases, the minute that you have a perceived liquidity crunch, where the market suddenly recognizes that you're over-concentrated in illiquid investments on the asset side and over-concentrated on highly liquid liabilities on the liability side, GICs and commercial paper, then, when that big-ticket money starts to move, the authorities have no choice, because they cannot allow the smaller investors to be left holding the deficit bag. They have to move. If there is a potential liquidity crunch, you have to move."

Once OFSI acting superintendent Suzanne Labarge heard from Astley, she polled the other participants by phone. She discovered little headway in any of the key areas. First, no capital had been committed, either by Canadian or American companies. Second, no management structure had been devised. Third, there was no consensus that a viable deal could be accomplished. She called Cantor and asked to see him the next day, August 10.

Cantor had already called a last, desperate gathering for that same morning to update three dozen key constituents, including the heads of major insurance-consulting firms William Mercer Ltd., Alexander Consulting Group, and Sedgwick Noble Lowndes. He reported on the impasse, outlined the arrangement involving the preferred shares, and expressed concern that the necessary tax exemption wouldn't be forthcoming. Cantor then asked that everyone write to the minister of finance, urging that the regulators give the coalition more time to find an industry solution.

The write-in campaign was launched too late. Cantor's next visitors were OSFI's Labarge and Thompson, telling Cantor there would be no rescue by the industry coalition. Labarge told Cantor, "Unless you can convince us otherwise, we think time's up." Cantor asked for twenty-four hours. The request for a stay of execution didn't surprise OSFI. After all, how often had Cantor said, "We were close to death, but something always came up."

Cantor agreed to schedule a board meeting for the following day so OSFI could present its views, and at this meeting Labarge presented OSFI's case and told the board it was time to invoke the Winding-Up Act. Labarge next met with the board of Confederation Trust; that firm had to be seized as well, since its money came from its parent, Confederation Life.

After the regulators withdrew, Cantor told the directors that he agreed with the assessment. Not only did Cantor not have a deal, but there was less likelihood of a deal now than there had been a week earlier. Liquidity pressure would soon build, he said, once word spread. "There wasn't a run, but there was the potential for a run," says Cantor. "We had pent-up demand, and, had we responded to it, it would have been unfair to policyholders who did not submit applications for surrender at an early date. Had we responded to a run, we would have had sufficient liquidity for a period of time, but I don't think there's a financial institution in the world that can withstand a concerted run in the absence of either government intervention or industry support. It was inappropriate to respond to the early portion of a run, even if we could have supported it, because I don't see how we could have stopped it."

A resolution for the board's approval had already been drafted. The board waived its right under the act to make representations to the minister or stave off execution by demanding four days' notice. The board passed the resolution, signed by Adam Zimmerman and Cantor, calling for the minister to direct OSFI to take control of the company.

Labarge sent Doug Peters a four-page memo, declaring, in the grand words required by law, "There exists a state of affairs that is materially prejudicial to the interests of the policyholders and creditors of Confed." In her estimation, Confed had reached the critical point set out in subsection 680(1) of the Insurance Companies Act: assets were insufficient to protect policyholders and the company would not be able to pay liabilities as they came due.

Wrote Labarge, "I believe that the public disclosure of Confed's failure to secure an agreement for additional capital support will trigger significant surrender activity and make it almost impossible for the company to raise funds in the capital markets to finance its operations and to meet its obligations as they come due."

She recommended that, pursuant to subsection 680(2), she be directed to take control of the company, and that the attorney general apply to the court for an order under the Winding-Up Act. Confed Trust would be closed pursuant to section 511 of the Loan and Trust Companies Act.

Once her letter and the board resolution had been faxed to Ottawa, Peters faxed a one-paragraph reply to Labarge the same day. The last line read, "Accordingly, I hereby direct you, pursuant to paragraph 680(2)(c) of the Insurance Companies Act, to take control of Confederation Life Insurance Company."

On the evening of August 11, Robert Sanderson, president of Peat Marwick Thorne Inc., and Al Morson, president of CompCorp, met at OSFI's Toronto offices. Legal documents began to arrive from Ottawa via fax. A flurry of agreements were signed; one declared that Peat Marwick would be the agent for Confed, another appointed Price Waterhouse to run Confederation Trust, a sixteen-pager triggered CompCorp's participation, and a fourth document was dispatched to other financial institutions ordering accounts to be frozen.

Senior executives at both accounting firms, Peat Marwick and Price Waterhouse, arrived at One Mount Pleasant Place at 10:40 P.M. The liquidators had identified specific members of Confed management in advance, so had set up a pairing — another "buddy" system. Peat Marwick attached a partner to each of the key areas, fifteen of them in all, including cash management, investment, real estate, and policyholder issues. "It was a very somber, quiet evening," says Sanderson. "We all realized there was a tremendous amount of work ahead of us, but there was also a sadness that it had come to this, that a venerable institution like Confederation Life was in its last steps."

The small SWAT team focused mainly on getting control of the computer, because the liquidator wanted to make sure that the fifteen thousand cheques issued daily by Confed, for everything from dental claims to death benefits, continued to flow. If ever they got a few days behind, they'd never catch up. "It was important for us to demonstrate early on that it was business as usual, or as close to usual as could be expected," says Sanderson.

There was one cheque, however, that did not go through. When Mike Regester was fired in 1993, he chose to have his pension and severance settlement delayed for income-tax reasons. The cheque for $435,000 was sitting ready and waiting to be picked up on August 12, but he wasn't able to cash it; he'd waited one day too long. The liquidator would not honour it because, under rules that apply to a company in liquidation, no severance pay could be paid to someone who had left more than six months earlier; Regester's official departure date had been May 1993. If the cheque had been available the day before, and he'd been able to get it certified, he would have been home free.*

A toll-free number was established by noon the following day for panicky policyholders. Peat Marwick ran the system until Confed staff who dealt with policyholder questions could be trained to talk knowledgeably about topics like insolvency, how things would unfold, and CompCorp rules. The CLHIA's "help lines" at the industry association's information centre were swamped. Usually, the centre receives a total of about 250 calls a day on all topics. In the days immediately following the announcement, that daily number shot up to 1,600. In all, the centre fielded 10,000 calls about Confed. Hundreds of other worried policyholders with coverage at other firms phoned to ask about their own situation.

In the early weeks, Peat Marwick staff assigned to the liquidation totalled eighty-five. Thirty-five of them were immediately equipped with cellular phones, a toy some of them had never had before. Within days, a rule was invoked. All cell phones had to be turned off during management meetings. Incoming calls were causing too many interruptions. Twelve months later, the bill for the liquidator's services (paid for by the insurance industry) would reach $15 million, and it is still climbing.

---

* By contrast, Roger Cunningham's timing was impeccable. The head of human resources departed August 4, after thirty-one years with Confed, his severance pay safely stashed in his pocket.

In the United Kingdom, with the consent of the Department of Trade and Industry and the Bank of England, Peat Marwick took over Confed's United Kingdom operations and subsidiaries. In Michigan, by ex-parte order of seizure, David Dykhouse was appointed domiciliary conservator of Confederation Life in the United States. He was thereby authorized to take possession, control, and administration of all the assets and operations of Confed in the United States, including trusteed assets. On August 12, Dykhouse appeared in circuit court of Ingham County in Michigan and was appointed rehabilitator of the estate, now known as Confederation Life Insurance Co. (United States) in rehabilitation. Victor Palmieri, who had been advising Michigan for four months, was appointed deputy rehabilitator.

In Atlanta, Georgia, state insurance commissioner Tim Ryles, with the blessing of Fulton County Superior Court, seized control of Confederation Life Insurance & Annuity Co. (CLIA), Confed's Georgia subsidiary.

Bureaucrats began covering their asses. William O'Connell, director of the examinations division for the Office of Commissioner of Insurance in Georgia, claimed he had ordered an examination of Confed in October 1993, based on 1992 financials. He said he uncovered assets that were not admissible in the mortgage-loan portfolio and thus declared that total capital and surplus was deficient by US$54.3 million. "[T]he non-admissibility of the mortgage loan assets renders the company insolvent," said O'Connell in an affidavit dated August 19, 1994. The same document also states, "The examination report is not yet finished." So much for *that* advance warning.

On August 15, by order of Mr. Justice Lloyd Houlden of the Ontario court, general division, Peat Marwick was appointed agent, Sanderson the sole director, and Confed began operating under the Winding-Up Act.

After 123 years, the Confederation Life Insurance Company was no more. The institution launched in 1871 by John Kay Macdonald had suffered an ignominious death. Greed, stupidity, and sloth were the culprits.

———◆•◆◆•◆———

CHAPTER 12

Vulture Funds and
Shark Attacks

"Quiet calm deliberation untangles every knot."

– *The Gondoliers*, Gilbert and Sullivan

Finding a victim to blame took no time at all: Great-West Life in general and Orest Dackow in particular. Adam Zimmerman became the self-appointed assassin. "They're very risk-averse. They're known to be very good buyers; if not bottom-fishers, they're certainly bargain hunters," he said, only days after the seizure. "You could develop two theories. One that it was a perfectly straightforward but laboured and difficult investigatory procedure that [Great-West] went through, [and] because – in quotes – 'because there was so much trouble' – it took them a very long time. You could also say that they were contriving to take the company to the wall and get it at the lowest possible price."

Great-West Lifeco CEO Orest Dackow bristles at the bad-faith label. "We felt some sort of responsibility to see whether or not something could be done to save one of the major insurance companies in the country. But that had to be done in a way that made sense to those people participating," he said. "Our efforts in that direction, in retrospect, were misunderstood. We might have been better served in terms of our public image if we had simply walked on the twenty-third [of July]."

Most outside observers were caught off guard. "This is like the Reichmann situation; nobody thought it could happen," said Dan McCaw, president of William M. Mercer Ltd., Toronto-based actuarial consultants. "That attitude is certainly going to change on a go-forward basis. A lot of people are looking back and wishing they'd pulled the plug [on their own policies] sooner."

Manny Nowacki of A. M. Best now admits that his rating agency would also act differently if presented with the same situation today. "We certainly wouldn't put as much faith in what Great-West Life told us."

"We had assurances from the president's office on down that the deal would be done," said Mark Puccia, director of insurance ratings services at Standard & Poor's. "We were surprised by the magnitude of the problem. Right into July, Great-West assured us of their intent to do the deal." Since the Confed collapse, all of the American agencies now pay much closer attention to Canada. They also became tougher to please. Most Canadian companies were downgraded shortly after Confed went into liquidation. Moody's, for example, downgraded US$1.5 billion worth of GICs issued by Crown to junk-grade levels.

Confederation Trust, a major cause of death, had $605 million in assets when seized. Burial was relatively straightforward. Within a year, Price Waterhouse found buyers for the $200-million residential portfolio, a $70-million group-mortgage-benefit portfolio, and a $100-million commercial-mortgage portfolio. North American Life took the estate trust business, and National Bank took on the deposits. Total loss will likely be less than $5 million.

Confederation Treasury Service Ltd. was another story. CTSL has assets of $625 million and liabilities of $1.6 billion (including the $843 million claimed by the Michigan trust), so the battle goes on among creditors, since there aren't enough assets to go around. While Confed stuck to its April 1994 agreement and removed no additional funds from the trust, there was activity right up to the bitter end, as items came due and had to be rolled over or consolidated. On July 29, 1994, for example, there was a $100-million promissory note signed by Bill Alexander and Bob Walsh, as president and vice-president respectively of CTSL. On August 11, the day of the seizure, Alexander and Walsh authorized two final notes: one for $274,531,929.69 and another for $100,011,979.17 – more than half the assets of CTSL, all pulled together into two convenient IOUs.

For the 4,400 Confed employees around the word, of which 1,800 worked in Canada, prospects were bleak. These were not high-rollers; most were in low-paying administrative positions. In the realty department, for example, there were 301 employees. Average annual salary was $26,000.

Donald Woolridge, who retired in 1991 as vice-president, corporate information services, after forty years with Confed, formed the Former Confederation Employees' Association in the autumn. By January 1995, the group had more than 1,800 members. "The business of their company was selling security, and all of them believed it," says Susan Rowland, a lawyer with the Toronto firm of Koskie Minsky, who represents the association. "The biggest emotional shock to them was to find out that what was their bedrock is no longer, [that] there is no security in the world. It was paternalism at its best and its worst. They relied on the company. It never occurred to them that the fourth-largest insurance company in the country could go bankrupt."

For a time, benefits such as major medical, dental, and life insurance were continued for seven hundred retirees, but they were eventually ended by court order in August 1995. Supplementary pensions of thirty-one senior officers were also ended, and their incomes were slashed immediately by as much as 70 per cent.

"When employees work for a great number of years, when they go out with an array of benefits, *that* is their financial plan. To have it disappear, it's certainly very disconcerting to say the least," says Rowland. So disconcerting for Woolridge, in fact, that one month after the court's ruling, he suffered a heart attack from which he was still slowly recovering the following year.

The clawback also affected Jack Rhind and Pat Burns. In 1981, they had decided to defer some of their future compensation until after retirement. In Rhind's case, the amount owing at December 31, 1993, including interest, was $707,142.76. Burns was due just under $500,000. They sued, but lost, and will not receive a cent.*

For others, the loss goes beyond money. "I wake up every morning and I still don't believe it," says Dave Hare, former group vice-president in Atlanta. "We all thought it was as solid as the rock of Gibraltar. When you work for a big company, you give something up. All my life I kept saying maybe I should go and do something entrepreneurial. But you don't. There's a certain comfort."

Some might say, "Well, welcome to the real world." People get fired daily; private-sector companies go bankrupt with fearsome regularity. From the start of the recession in 1990 to the time of Confed's seizure, 139 financial institutions went out of business in Canada – and that number does not include those firms that merged with others and therefore disappeared.

The stunned attitude of Confed employees after the seizure says much about the firm's corporate culture – "Nothing bad can happen to us, we're Confed, we're too big too fail." In such a shop, no one ever had to run scared and actually do something to set things right until it was far too late to act, not Pat Burns, not Paul Cantor.

Some outcomes seem particularly unfair. For example, two Confed employees on long-term disability had their monthly disability income cut to the maximum allowed by CompCorp ($2,000 a month), despite the fact that the program established by Confed had been totally funded by employee contributions and there was a surplus in the account. One of them, Bill Caverley, who has Parkinson's disease, saw his monthly income reduced by more than half – from $4,185.57 to $2,000. Mabel Wornell of St. John's, Newfoundland, the widow of a former Confed employee, had been living on investments and government pensions totalling $2,000 a month. Without the major medical plan, the eighty-nine-year-old,

---

* The court did, however, award each man $8,492.59 to cover legals in bringing the action.

who had been classified as legally blind, now has to pay for her prescription drugs. Confed had been covering 80 per cent of the $1,000 annual bill.

Paul Worthen of Fredericton, New Brunswick, who had retired in 1989 after thirty-three years with Confed, had a similar problem. Drugs worth $2,000 for cancer treatment during the previous twelve months had been paid for under the Confed medical plan. Costs to find new insurance were prohibitive. So, too, with Carol Angela Westcott of St. John's, whose drug bills in 1994 totalled $1,950.

Companies carrying large insurance policies for executives, in which the death benefits were over the CompCorp limits of $200,000, were also out of luck. Typical was Grant Forest Products, which had a policy with a death benefit of $11 million and an annual premium of $70,700. To go out and replace that policy at another firm (assuming the beneficiary could pass the physical) would mean a new annual premium of $204,565. Moreover, even with that increased premium, the guaranteed cash value in 2014 – money intended for estate-planning purposes – would be $3.3 million, much less than the $4.1 million available six years earlier in 2008 under the Confed policy.

Seizure also threw into doubt US$2 billion in GICs and US$1.3 billion in structured settlements in the United States. Confed had sold 6,250 of the latter, purchased by individuals using court settlements or severance lump-sum payments. Confed then sent out monthly cheques. Typical is the case of Milagro Partner, a six-year-old living in San Francisco, who has innumerable birth defects resulting from radiation and chemotherapy treatments that had been given to his mother for breast cancer. At the time, she was pregnant, did not know it, and doctors failed to test her. A US$1,755 monthly annuity from Confed helps pay for full-time care of the boy, who is a dwarf with facial deformities and limited mental capacity.

All Canadian life-insurance policyholders are protected to a ceiling of $200,000 by CompCorp. For those with policies beyond the limits, losses could hit $175 million. In the United States, policyholders are covered, usually up to US$300,000 by guaranty associations in each state. Losses over and above those limits could reach $800 million.

Some institutional investors in CTSL lost huge amounts, for a total of $157 million. The biggest loser, by far, is the Province of Ontario – $100 million of taxpayer money. During the eighties, Ontario had been among the most aggressive jurisdictions when it came to doing bond deals, then converting some obligations into swaps. When the knife came down on Confed, Ontario was caught – even though its own financial-services regulators had been the most diligent about irregularities at Confederation Trust four years earlier.

About twenty thousand Bell Canada employees had the $450 million in their RSP plans frozen for nearly two years. The collapse also reached into the State of Michigan pension fund, covering fifty thousand current and former employees. The fund had foolishly invested US$98.5 million in Confed GICs, mostly in 1991.

For Pat Burns, along with the money lost, there was humiliation. On November 12, 1994, the *Toronto Star* launched a three-part series investigating the collapse. A picture of Burns ran on page one. "RECKLESSNESS IN TOP MANAGEMENT," blared the headline. "ROAD TO RUIN," screamed another headline inside. That Saturday morning, Burns was spotted at the Donalda Club in the informal dining area, where members can grab a sandwich after a workout or a curling game. As a courtesy to members, the club supplies a few daily papers to read while they relax. Burns gathered up all available copies of the *Star*, headed into the locker room, and was seen returning empty handed a few minutes later, as if the futile gesture of ditching those few copies among the seven hundred thousand printed that day would somehow stop the story from spreading.

———

Confed did not need to fail. Some members of the industry consortium saw the exercise not as a chance to prevent their industry from suffering a crisis of confidence, but as an opportunity to fire the final torpedo into a competitor. For a bunch of guys who think long term, the vision of some of them did not stretch much beyond lunch.

"We were willing to put up a very large sum of money. The estimate at the end was that it was not enough," says John McNeil of Sun

Life. "That was a view I did not entirely share. Personally, I thought it might have worked. However, we ran out of time. We could not raise enough dough to do the trick. We were not far off [$600 million]. That is big bucks." McNeil believes that if Cantor had sent out his distress call earlier, the industry might have been able to help.

As for Ottawa, no one there felt any real reason to save this particular insurance company. If the financial-services sector is run by a few fit firms, that's just fine with bureaucrats and parliamentarians alike. They can publicly castigate the big firms about poor service to consumers, but never actually have to do much.

Because there was no leadership from Ottawa, the industry, or Confed, a malaise set in that meant: If nothing is achieved for long enough, there comes a point where there's nothing left to do but pull the plug. And that's exactly what happened on August 11, there was no one in whose best interest it was to carry on, to persevere until there was success.

Paul Cantor maintains that runs start when policyholders request early surrenders or policy loans. Such activity would force liquidation of assets at discounted values and, as a result, would mean that soon there might not be enough cash available for other policyholders. In such circumstances, the company is insolvent. While what he says is true, the process is slow. Insurance companies don't process such requests on an overnight basis. Weeks, even months, can pass before the cheque is in the mail.

At any rate, members of the Confed liquidity committee that met daily say there was no change in the situation in August. There was no liquidity crisis, no "run on the bank," and no particular reason to pull the plug on August 11 as opposed to September 11 or a week next Tuesday.

In fact, if those trying to craft a deal had waited a mere two more weeks, the whole messy, expensive, confidence-shaking seizure might not have been necessary. Here's why: On August 10, the day before liquidation, Newcourt Credit made three wire transfers to two CTSL accounts at the CIBC. The total was $218 million, money owed by the former leasing arm but not due for years, a debt that had been ordered paid by the letter of intent signed in April. In 1995, Newcourt paid a further $107.2 million (and still owes $67.2 million). All the funds steered Newcourt's way by Bill Douglas had finally came home, so there was no shortage of pin money.

Before the end of August 1994, deals were struck to sell three major divisions of Confed. United States group insurance went to Great-West, Canadian group to Manulife, the British division to Sun Life. The latter deal alone was worth $430 million. Such disposals show active interest in the constituent parts of Confed by competitors. Just how genuine was the rescue effort when liquidation meant cheaper pickings?

When required, Great-West could complete deals quickly. The same company that dallied through eight long months of due diligence only to back off in a lather at the last minute nabbed Confed's group life and health insurance in the United States. Great-West was able to organize a one-inch-thick business-purchase memorandum of agreement that was signed on August 16 – less than a week after seizure – by the United States rehabilitators and two senior vice-presidents at Great-West, James D. Motz and D. C. Lennox. Included was a twenty-six-page client list, from the American Heart Association running through Larry's Cartage all the way to Webb Furniture.

Even so, Great-West pined most for the prize Manulife won – Confed's Canadian group life and health. The division generated about $1 billion in annual premiums from 750 policyholders – most of them large corporations. "Manulife's purchase of the Canadian group was the most valuable, single business," says Dackow. "In terms of relative market share, that was the best block of business to be had." The choice of Manulife as the buyer was popular with Confed staff. When the announcement was made at a Confed employees' meeting, several hundred people spontaneously cheered and applauded the news. Their own future might be uncertain, but at least those louts from Great-West didn't get all that they wanted.

Neither did Paul Cantor. In the end, he didn't save Confed, and he could have. After nearly two years of working towards a slimmed-down company that might have survived, Cantor was only two weeks away from success when he gave up the fight, choosing not to battle OSFI's call for liquidation. His hero's crown is tin, not silver.

Lawsuits quickly followed. Class actions have been filed in New York, New Jersey, and Georgia by policyholders who felt they'd been hood-winked by agents into buying death benefits from a life company at death's door. DuPont Canada Inc. has sued investment dealer Wood Gundy Inc. to recover $10 million that DuPont says it lost on com-mercial paper purchased from Confed in May 1994.

Fidelity Management Trust Co., a subsidiary of Fidelity Invest-ments, of Boston, was sued in California for recommending Confed GICs in 1991 as investments in a pension plan run by California Casu-alty Management Co. Confed had about 1 per cent of the entire GIC market in the United States and had issued about US$2.2 billion in GICs to various retirement-plan managers, including Fidelity, Vanguard, and T. Rowe Price.

The most potentially devastating suit was launched on June 28, 1995, when Michigan insurance commissioner D. Joseph Olson sued Harris Trust and Savings Bank of Chicago, Ernst & Young, and twenty-seven former directors and officers of Confed. The suit charges breach of trust, negligence, common-law fraud, breach of fiduciary duty, professional malpractice, and breach of contract. Based on the missing US$620 million, the suit claimed triple damages, or more than US$1.8 billion. Everyone named was sued jointly and severally, which means that each is liable for the full amount. Confed directors and officers have $50 million in liability coverage.

Ernst & Young is named in the lawsuit, because lawyers know that auditors have deep pockets. In 1992, Ernst & Young paid US$400 million to settle lawsuits in the United States that flowed from the firm's role as auditor for a number of the failed savings-and-loans institutions. Auditors involved with Northland Bank and the Cana-dian Commercial Bank also participated in settlements with creditors totalling $125.6 million.

In response, lawyers for directors and officers have been arguing that Michigan has no jurisdiction. "Many have never been to Michigan for even the briefest of visits and have never transacted any business whatsoever in Michigan. A number have never had any contact with Michigan whatsoever," argue the defendants' court filings. Officers and directors are represented by the Atlanta-based law firm of Bondurant Mixson & Elmore and the Detroit firm of Honigman Miller Schwartz and Cohn, who argue that none of their clients had any role in preparing statutory filings with Michigan. "[T]he great majority of them – all but Defendants Burns, Cantor, Edwards, Rosenfelder, and Rosiak – had no role in preparing, reviewing, approving, or transmitting the documents, and many did not know of their existence prior to this litigation."

Directors and officers have filed affidavits saying how little they knew. Director Daryl McLean notes that her time in Michigan was limited to driving through the state en route to Florida on Interstate 75 the previous year. Others maintain that they never visited the state, nor even made a business telephone call to anyone who lives there. Pat Burns also makes much of the fact that his presence in Michigan was limited to business travel some time back in the misty past prior to 1975. As for the required signing of the 1991 annual statement for filing with the appropriate authorities, well, he apparently didn't give it much thought. "Although I was required as president to sign the statement, I had no reason beyond my usual due-diligence practices to check behind the employees who performed those job functions." Moreover, he denied any knowledge of the arrangements that established the cash transfers from the trust or the fact that CT3L IOUs were lodged there. "I was not aware that CTSL notes had been lodged in the United States trust account until after the rehabilitation was commenced, when I read press accounts." Burns pointed out that Atlanta housed "voluminous" files and submitted a photo of the exterior of the Atlanta office building so the court could see the possibility for itself.

Equally interesting is what one affidavit leaves out. While other officers and directors specifically deny in their affidavits knowing about such specifics involving CTSL as the Benton–Rae memo, the setoff agreement, or the Alexander–Curtis memo, Bill Douglas's affidavit makes no such claim. All the affidavits were prepared by the same law firm, Bondurant, Mixson & Elmore in Atlanta, and that paragraph is so common among the other affidavits that it reads like boiler-plate. The CTSL paragraph does not appear in the Douglas affidavit. The paragraphs in all the affidavits are numbered, and the Douglas affidavit actually skips a number, going from paragraph fourteen to paragraph sixteen. Douglas says he did not ask that any paragraph be stricken before he signed. The law firm says it must have been a typo. Just another irony in the fire.

The plaintiffs appear to be in no hurry. "That side won't be ready to try its case until it can prove damages," says Jeff Bramlett of Bondurant. "The extent of damages is not going to be settled until rehabilitation is far closer to completion than it is. If we went to court tomorrow, and they had to put up their case, they couldn't say what harm there's been to United States policyholders. From that standpoint, I guess I'm ready to go to trial. I know they can't win."

By contrast, the fight about CTSL's assets has already gone several knock-down rounds. On October 26, 1995, forty people representing creditors of Confederation Treasury Services Ltd. (CTSL) squeeze into a small meeting room at the Metropolitan Toronto Convention Centre. The floor is a jumble of cables. A sixty-inch television screen shows a similar scene at the International Management Centre, in London's Finsbury Square, where more creditors are gawking at a similar screen showing the room in Toronto.

But this is no scene from a modern-day *Alice Through the Looking Glass*. The video screens in the respective cities show creditors milling about and looking for all the world like piranhas in fish tanks fighting over scraps of a carcass jettisoned from a doomed vessel. On this day in October 1995, those with claims totalling some $1.6 billion against CTSL have gathered to hear a presentation on how they might share assets of between $600 million and $650 million.

Accounting firm Deloitte & Touche Inc. has been acting as what's known as a "monitor" since CTSL was placed under the Companies' Creditors Arrangement Act (CCAA) more than fourteen months earlier, when Confed was seized. CTSL was the arm of Confed that issued bonds, swaps, options, and other derivative deals with institutions – all of whom, not surprisingly, want to get the money back that they had invested in what they thought was an ongoing market through CTSL.

Deloitte has been overseeing the affairs of CTSL and has hammered out a proposal that nobody likes: creditors will receive forty-eight cents for every dollar they're owed. This division of loot, according to the advance billing, is the last chance. CTSL came perilously close to being declared bankrupt earlier in the year, but Mr. Justice Lloyd Houlden told the parties in August to take one more shot at reaching a consensus before he petitioned CTSL into bankruptcy, a process that will add many more months and eat up more of the assets through legal and other costs associated with fighting over the available funds.

Dominating the audience are attorneys from Toronto and New York, as well as managers from the vulture funds that have bought up about half of the $319 million in bonds issued by CTSL. Little people need not apply. A lawyer, charging a typical fee of $300 an hour, who attends the five-hour session (plus the ninety minutes it takes to count the vote) will bill $1,950 for professional services rendered – whether he or she utters a word. Add to that the 219 attendees in London. Because attendees were told which meeting to attend (bondholders to London, derivative and general creditors to Toronto), there will also be expenses charged.

Corey Simpson of the Ontario Financing Authority journeyed to London to represent her client, the Province of Ontario, and submitted expenses, for air travel, taxis, accommodation, and meals, of $4,367.73. Her Toronto office is a twenty-minute walk, or $4 return via subway, from the Toronto meeting location. Total administrative costs for this one meeting, separate from professional fees, were $357,571.

Outside the meeting room, officers of R-M Trust Co., who are serving as independent scrutineers of the vote*, corroborate identities of the attendees, then issue credentials in plastic pin-on lapel badges,

---

* Hambros Bank Ltd. handled the London end.

as if this were a cocktail reception to promote some city's economic-development program. In place of the usual cheery greeting "Hello, my name is . . .," the badges carry the signature of the wearer. Blue means voting creditors, white for advisers, green for meeting officials.

Two security guards patrol the doorway to keep out ne'er-do-wells who can not attend, namely journalists, as opposed to those ne'er-do-wells who can enter, namely vultures of a different sort. Next door to the CTSL meeting room, the Canadian Health Food Association draws a fresher-faced crowd. A table laden with pots of coffee, jugs of orange juice, muffins, and Danish pastries supplied for the creditor supplicants goes largely untouched – almost as if the happy healthies had issued a cholesterol warning. Or maybe the vultures attending this meeting prefer the carrion of a corporate carcass to the tasty snacks provided.

The parties fall into four categories. The first is private and institutional investors who hold notes issued in Europe by CTSL for $319 million. The second group includes "swap" creditors, owed $161 million, including the Province of Ontario, on the hook for $100 million. The third is investors holding commercial paper issued in Europe by a CTSL subsidiary, Confederation Treasury Services (United Kingdom) plc, owed $57 million. Finally, there are other noteholders of private placements and various trade creditors owed $10 million. With available assets of about $600 million, they all would be in excellent shape were it not for the claim by the American liquidator for cash to replace the $843 million worth of IOUs in the Michigan trust account.

Among those who have a vested interest in delay are the vulture funds that try to make money on the corporate difficulties suffered by others. In the weeks following seizure, the markets were so pessimistic about Confed's prospects in liquidation that bonds issued by Confed fell in value to thirty cents on the dollar; by the time of this meeting, value had improved to almost fifty cents on the dollar, a hefty increase of 67 per cent in just over a year.

At 10:10 A.M., the meeting is gavelled to order in London by David Murray, senior vice-president of Deloitte & Touche. His visage appears on screen; his voice emanates from the speakers. Now that Toronto is connected, first things first. "Turn off all your portable cell phones while you are here in the meeting room," he announces. Welcome to the nineties.

Murray spends the next sixty minutes outlining what's called "the monitor's plan," which would make $265 million available to assembled creditors, with the remaining $335 million of the $600 million in available assets split between the Canadian liquidator and American rehabilitator under whatever agreement they eventually devise between themselves. "We struggled to get a dollar amount that was equally repugnant to all creditors," Murray says.

With the numbers now officially released, Murray describes the plan as "a bird in the hand," and issues a warning. "If the amount is not acceptable to creditors now, there is no likelihood of any agreement in the near future." He points out that, if the creditors vote down the deal, the resulting bankruptcy proceedings could take "a considerable period of time." He then offers another metaphor. "If you want cash now, vote yes. If you want to roll the dice, vote no."

The monitor, he claims, takes no sides. "We are not," he tells those assembled, "advocating any position." Having pointed out the vagaries of time that may be required, he notes the unpredictability of bankruptcy proceedings, namely that creditors could end up receiving anywhere between forty and sixty-five cents. Bankruptcy will also whittle away another three cents of every dollar available, because of legals and other procedural costs (a consideration that may play well with those in the room, since they are standing at that very same fee trough). Moreover, a specific amount of money today is worth more than the same dollar figure next week, because inflation takes its toll along the way. As a result, "it has to be a bigger share than the pot [now] provides just to break even on a present value basis. You might do a little better or a little worse." The final plea from the monitor: "Take liquidity or stay for the long haul."

This is what has become of just one part of Confed, as creditors pick over the carcass. David Murray spends a few minutes reviewing his efforts of the past year. The first six months were passed getting organized, then letting noteholders and the American rehabilitator try to sort out their differences. By May 1995, there was no progress towards a compromise.

In June, Deloitte floated a plan. Because no one liked it, representatives of all parties were brought together by Mr. Justice Lloyd Houlden in his chambers. That brokering also failed. Deloitte then thought that, perhaps, if each creditor could hear the other's arguments in detail, more progress could be made. So, on July 6, they convened what became known as the "Day of the Duelling Lawyers." Again, there was no breakthrough.

On July 14, Houlden announced he would put CTSL in bankruptcy, but several creditors asked for a reprieve. A hearing on July 24 found several plans circulating, including Deloitte as monitor. On August 3, that plan was filed with the court for the vote this day in October.

Murray notes that the creditors' committee has spent $1 million on forensic advice and more than $1 million on legal advice in three countries, and still has not achieved a consensus. "Creditors should conclude that there is substantial risk in pursuing a litigious course and it may be that creditors would be well served to take that bird in hand."

"If you want a realistic distribution, then it is a good deal," says Murray, and returns to his earlier metaphor. "If you want cash now, it is a very good deal. But if you want to roll the dice and risk less money later for a shot at more money later, then vote no, and let the bankruptcy proceedings begin."

The first question from the floor makes it clear that Murray might as well have been trying to force cod-liver-oil pills down the throats of sick cats. A bondholder, Michael Leffell of M. H. Davidson & Co., points out that CTSL had borrowed money from him and still owes it. That's different from the rehabilitators in the United States who, on the other hand, do not have such a direct claim. Asks Leffell, "How can you justify paying over several hundred million dollars to him without his having justified his claim? Maybe my grandmother should come up and say, 'You know, you owe me some money.' You have got to justify it.

There has got to be a logically rational explanation for what the claim is. And if they have not articulated it, then why do they get it?"

Next up to the microphone is Chaim Fortgang of the New York law firm of Wachtell Lipton Rosen & Katz, representing the arm's-length creditors committee.*

Fortgang is a truly legendary figure in a field of self-described legends, all of whom are masters of the performing legal arts. Called "the junk-yard dog," Fortgang, who charges US$575 an hour, is said to have once punctuated his comments during a conference call with other counsel by placing his phone against his rear end and breaking wind. Mr. Justice James Farley of the Ontario court, general division, took on Fortgang during one fabled meeting prior to a CTSL court proceeding. The session was lively, and several people were castigating others for being the cause of delays. The monitor, David Murray, was coming under particular attack over his proposals for a solution.

Several times, Fortgang launched a diatribe by saying, "Without pointing a finger," when, in fact, he was. Finally, Farley stopped Fortgang in midstream and said, "If you start another sentence saying, 'Without pointing a finger,' I'll cut your fingers off." It was a particularly emotive comment for Farley, considering that he himself has lost a finger.

At the creditors' meeting, Fortgang presses Murray on the fact that his firm had not even consulted United States counsel about American law that might be involved in paying the rehabilitator. Les Wittlin, of the law firm Gowling Strathy & Henderson, who is acting as secretary of the meeting, is soon drawn into what quickly becomes a testy exchange, in which the two could barely agree that if $265 million of the available money went to one group of creditors, then $335 million went to the other.

---

* Fortgang's firm billed a total of C$685,392.09 for fees and disbursements from April 1 to October 31, 1995. Others were even busier. The Toronto firm of Gowling Strathy & Henderson billed $2 million in the twelve months ending September 30, 1995. Price Waterhouse, the liquidator handling Confederation Trust, billed $3.4 million for the same period.

"Answer the question," demands Fortgang. "I am asking you a question. Is that not tautological? If you subtract one number from another you get a number?

"Your advice to creditors is, if your engine fails, go kick in your windshield," snapped Wittlin.

Other questioners focus on how Deloitte came up with the forty-eight cents. Now it is David Murray's turn to express his frustration. "We begged and pleaded for some guidance from each of the stakeholders, and none of them gave us any kind of response. There was no number that any of the stakeholders could agree on."

The creditors are not appeased. In what must amount to the longest sentence – 139 words – uttered at the meeting, David Randall of Parnassus Enterprises puts his case as a creditor this way: "I would like to ask Mr. Murray whether he does not agree that it is highly presumptuous of him (and indeed cynical of him) to suggest that this Alice in Wonderland situation should be accepted by intelligent people whereby those who have invested their savings in a company in good faith should accept a situation where somebody in an arbitrary way behind closed doors, after secret deliberations (of which we have no information whatever), decides that there is some form of consensus that investors might accept the carrot of some arbitrary figure of less than half their investment at origin in exchange for shutting up and accepting the situation and asking no further questions and not taking the risk to proceed further to find out more information that might put them in a better position to assess their rights."

For all its length, however, the question does capture the essence of the dilemma. Why should a creditor take a bird in the hand when there might be two in the bush? What lawyer, in good faith, could ever advise a client to take forty-eight cents when there might be more?

The momentum is running against him like the tide relentlessly moving higher on the beach; David Murray's hopeful sand-castle arguments do not last. When the vote results are announced later that afternoon, the creditors have rejected the deal by a wide margin. Both groups, about eighty bondholders and four hundred other smaller creditors, have decided to roll the dice.

Not only does the plan fail, but creditors decide to remove Deloitte & Touche from having any further involvement. More than a year has elapsed since Confed went bust; CTSL creditors are no nearer to a solution. Lawsuits are only at the early stages in a liquidation that could take decades. Maybe this is what is meant by eternal life.

CHAPTER 13

────◆◆◆────

Reforming the Future

"If life had a second edition, how I would correct the proofs."

– letter to a friend from poet John Clare, 1793–1864

Jack Rhind is sitting in the living room of the house where he's lived for forty years, across the park from the church where he went to Boy Scouts. He should be a contented and fulfilled man, with a respected and respectable corporate life behind him.

He is no such thing. When he ventures out of doors, he gets odd looks and startled reactions, as if he carried some disease. He does. It is called failure.

The simplest question, "How does it feel?" sets off a five-minute monologue. "That's a pretty good question," he says, then pauses for a few seconds while he opens and closes his left hand, making and unmaking a fist. He repeats the question, "Well, how does it feel?" then pauses again to collect his thoughts.

Finally, he begins. "I'm very saddened, very saddened. I am saddened to see teams of people broken up that were so effective. The United Kingdom operation is lost . . . but there were other great teams that are now disintegrated. I'm sad to see something that had been built up just torn down. I'm sad to see the personal losses – the loss of jobs, the loss of security – for so many people that are younger. I'm not thinking of myself, I'm thinking of the people in their mid-fifties and early fifties who had good jobs and are now out trying to compete in this very difficult market for middle-management jobs. I'm thinking of the people who have lost a lot of benefits."

The words pour out uninterrupted, a release of pent-up thoughts. "I'm thinking of the unfortunate circumstances that seemed to be stacked against the company. I'm thinking about how in other eras this would never have been allowed to have happened. I'm thinking of how banks in other eras have been in trouble, how this industry was in terrible trouble in the thirties, the Sun Life and all the companies, and how the federal department was able to sustain the companies

"The things that happened then, say, to Sun Life; they were in such serious trouble when they had 50 per cent of their assets in equities in 1930 and their surplus went from $60 million to $6 million in one year and was falling. Sun Life was going to go under. The federal government gave them authorized values. They met with all the other insurance-company heads and gave the whole industry – which was getting into trouble – authorized values. And, of course, as day follows night, in time the values came back and far surpassed those [authorized] values, and Sun Life went on to be a very strong company.

"Real-estate values come back, and many of them in the States have already. I'm saddened to see how assets, when you have a liquidation, forced sale, what happens to values. I'm saddened to see that the public image and confidence in the industry is unnecessarily shaken.

"I've suffered a major setback, as far as I'm concerned. I'm seventy-five years old; I've been fortunate all my life. Everybody has some setbacks at some times, so I'm reasonably philosophical about it. I'm still living in a lot more comfort than a lot of people, so I've just put it out of my mind." His deferred compensation and supplementary pension are gone, a loss of $4,000 a month that would have continued until he died and been paid to his wife if she survived him. "That was money that I had taken from my salary and squirrelled away. I thought I was squirrelling money away for my retirement, like putting it in the bank."

As for his reputation, "I couldn't tell you. Who knows what their reputation is? I've had a lot of people come up to me and say nice, consoling things. People do that, but who knows what people are actually saying." Rhind then affects another voice, as if speaking the part of the Greek chorus in the tragedy: "He was there, he knew what was going on."

"I'm bound to be seen to carry some of the baggage. I suppose people always find ways of excusing themselves, but, certainly, at least for my own peace of mind, I don't have any doubts as to whether I made any very bad decisions or did something that was bad for the policyholders."

Policyholders. Rhind almost seems startled when he utters the word. It hangs suspended in the silence like a nagging conscience. Say, isn't that what a mutual insurance company is supposed to be all about? Aren't policyholders supposed to be more than just the bread and butter? Aren't policyholders the ones who actually own the company and get to call the shots? In the religion that is called mutual life insurance, don't they come first?

Policyholders. Rhind has them very much in mind now. "A glaring thing that I didn't say was the hundreds of thousands of policyholders. That's what I should have said first. I'm personally aware of policy-holders who are suffering either from uncertainty or a deferrence of their benefits. Apart from the image of the industry, the direct suffer-ing of people is a sad thing. The directors' first responsibility, the absolute concern, is existing policyholders.

In the religion that is life insurance, the first shall be last.

The modern era for financial services in Canada is marked by three important dates. The first is July 1981, when the first Japanese bank, the Bank of Tokyo, arrived. Today, there are fifty-two subsidiaries of foreign banks operating in Canada, with $65 billion in assets.

Even with the influx, the four pillars of Canadian finance – banks, insurance, securities, and trust companies – stayed intact and separate for the next half a dozen years. Foreign banks were restricted in how much business they could do. In that era, the insurance industry still felt some protection from Ottawa. "There seems to be reservation about the development of more power in the banks," said Jack Rhind in 1983. As chairman of the industry task force on legislative review, Rhind was either whistling past the graveyard or was not aware of the real feeling in Ottawa as momentum built towards changes that meant that the banks would become more powerful.

The second important date was 1987, when ownership of Canadian securities dealers and brokerage houses was opened up to anyone, including foreign firms and other Canadian financial institutions.

While the effect was supposed to strengthen the capital base of such companies, the practical result was that the banks bought the major brokerage firms. The Royal bought Dominion Securities, CIBC acquired Wood Gundy, Bank of Nova Scotia got McLeod Young Weir, and Bank of Montreal bought Nesbitt Thomson. Only the Toronto–Dominion decided to build, not buy, an investment firm. Today, about 150 brokerage firms remain in Canada, but the seven bank-owned firms have two-thirds of the industry revenue.

In 1992, legislation altered for the third time, as further barriers were dropped. Banks, trust companies, and brokerage firms could buy or launch insurance subsidiaries; mutual companies could convert to joint-stock companies; and restrictions on foreign ownership were slowly lifted. Banks were now able to cross-market in other areas. They could use their branches and customer lists to sell mutual funds, trust and estate services, but not life insurance.

The power of the banks grew. Quipped Doug Peters, Ottawa's junior minister of finance and himself a former Toronto–Dominion bank economist, "They are not quite in the same class as the Montreal bike gangs, but . . ." Royal Trust was taken over by Royal Bank, Central Guaranty Trust by Toronto–Dominion Bank, and First City Trust by North American Life (which in turn merged with Manulife in 1995.) The banks' share of assets of trust companies was zero in 1984 and reached 45 per cent by 1994.

As a result, the banks spill more than the insurance companies drink. With more than $800 billion in assets, banks are four times the size of the insurance industry's $200-billion total. Moreover, the bank camel has been squeezing into the insurance tent for a long time. For thirty years, banks have been selling creditor life insurance to customers taking out loans or mortgages. Canadians have purchased 3.7 million insurance policies from banks, for coverage of $107.3 billion.

The Royal Bank has acquired Voyageur Insurance and Westbury Life, the CIBC bought Principal Insurance, a group insurer of home and auto, National Bank acquired Canassurance Life from Quebec Blue Cross, the Desjardins group took over Laurentian Group and AEterna Life. In Quebec, consumers can buy insurance through *caisses populaires* and pay premiums that are about two-thirds less than those charged by the life-insurance companies. Several banks have also incorporated their own life-insurance companies or acquired a charter in order to market insurance directly. They include: CIBC (offering life and auto insurance by phone) and TD (direct mail and telephone sales of life insurance); Hong Kong Bank, National Bank, and the Bank of Nova Scotia all offer some insurance services.

Banks cannot, however, market life insurance directly through their branches. Banks had been hoping to gain that power in 1997, when the legislation is next scheduled for revision, but a surprise announcement by Ottawa in 1996 said there would be no change from the status quo. While insurance agents were credited with conducting a successful lobbying campaign, there was something else at work. Ottawa, a sorry participant in the Confed débâcle, had thrown the insurance industry a bone.

In this area, however, Canadian banks are out of step. Banks are coming to dominate the global insurance industry. In the United States in 1985, banks had 30 per cent of a $75-billion life-insurance market, while life-insurance agents had 62 per cent. Today, banks command 56 per cent of the market; the agents' share has slipped to 36 per cent. In Britain and most other European countries, banks sell insurance. Crédit Agricole, the largest bank in France, has thirteen hundred life-insurance sales representatives. Canada and South Korea are the only two industrialized countries where banks are prohibited from selling life insurance.

For now, Canadian insurance companies have a reprieve, but will they be able to take advantage of it? "Canada's life- and health-insurance companies could prove to be victims of their long and successful histories," says John Palmer, an accountant from KPMG Peat Marwick who was appointed superintendent on August 12, the day after Confed was seized. "I worry that they may be so wedded to existing ways of doing things that they prove more resistant to change than other financial institutions."

Particularly egregious are the networks of brokers and agents who sell insurance products. Says Palmer, "[T]he system of distribution of which they are a part is expensive, and some of the functions they provide, particularly with respect to similar products, can be provided electronically, or with less manual intervention than is needed by the existing system."

But more harmful for the industry than the distribution system is the behaviour of participants in the Confed debacle. Directors maintain that they did all they could. "The board only knows what management tells them," complains André Monast, senior partner at the Quebec City law firm of Desjardins Ducharme Stein & Monast, and a Confed director for thirty years. "With hindsight, it's easy to say that people could see the real-estate market crumbling. The question is, should every director have a better crystal ball than the one we had?"

Competitors blame management. "There's not enough bad luck in this world that can kill an insurance company," says Bill Black, CEO of Maritime Life Assurance Co., of Halifax. "It's stupidity and bad management. They didn't wake up every day and say, 'How do I manage my risk?' They had bad management for years. A life company is a complex place, and if there isn't somebody going around and tying everything together, you're in trouble."

Front-line troops – the agents who sell policies – should also shoulder some of the blame. Victor Palmieri admonished members of the Association of American Life Underwriters in a March 1995 speech for not asking tougher questions of Confed management. "Why is the agent always the last to know?" he asked them. Demand meetings with senior management and "ask the hard questions," he said.

Palmieri pointed out that 25-per-cent annual growth should have tipped them off that something was badly awry. For him, 15 per cent annually is plenty fast enough.

"If you sense that management is on a game of its own, that's all you have to know," said Palmieri. "You don't have to look at the financial statements. All you have to know is you've got the typical autocratic leader selling you his vision of the future, and there is no tomorrow. That was the time to bail out. There is a management that has really lost its grasp of reality."

Palmieri reminded the agents of the way letters were often sent out by managers who were travelling. A secretary would type up the letter, then add, at the bottom, "dictated but not read." "Believe me, when you find a company that's dictated but not lead, that's when you bail out."

Yet officers and directors persist in maintaining that management can control information. "It's pretty difficult for an outside director to pierce the armour of management," says John Heard, who moved from an entry-level job in 1947 to become the number-two man in the firm. "It would take somebody who was almost a professional corporate director. Directors come to about eight meetings a year and spend about two hours [at each]. They're fed information by management to a degree that isn't healthy."

Adds chairman Adam Zimmerman, "If management does not want you to know something, or if an owner wants to do something that you do not think is right, you can do nothing to change that. All you can do is have the quixotic satisfaction of resigning."

Others disagree. "Everybody knew that the trust company was a fiasco," says Claude Lamoureux, president and CEO of the $40-billion Ontario Teachers' Pension Plan Board, who is an actuary and worked for Met Life for a dozen years in the United States. "Everybody in the street knew, when you couldn't get a mortgage anywhere, you went to Confed. And the board didn't know that? Give me a break."

Under the Canada Business Corporations Act, directors have a solemn duty. "Boards have to see themselves as the stewards of the corporation," says William Blundell, chairman of Manulife Financial. "Business can fail with a diligent board. Nevertheless, I would not let

the board off the hook. They are the stewards, they have the responsibility for the long-term viability of the corporation."

"Confederation Life was an accident waiting to happen," says J.
Richard Finlay, an expert in corporate governance. "The board was out
of touch and allowed the CEO to run the show. Management was out of
touch with the marketplace. There was a lot of empire-building." A
concerned Finlay sought and was granted a meeting with Jack Rhind
in the early eighties in order to urge Confed to put in place better practices. "You pick up vibrations. In the case of Confed, it was dominated
by an old-style board structure which cried out for change."

Finlay recommended that Confed split the CEO and chairman's
role and appoint a non-executive chairman to oversee the CEO. He
also urged a more activist role for the board. Nothing changed, and,
as the eighties passed, Finlay couldn't help but notice that no one
from Confed even attended conferences on the topic of governance.
"There was a sense of complacency," says Finlay, "as if they were
saying, 'The formulae we've used in the past will continue to serve
us well.'"

Finlay has a favourite quote he's been using at seminars for fifteen
years to illustrate the need for good corporate governance. The author
is none other than Jack Rhind's old mentor from National Life,
Harold R. Lawson. Lawson just happened to be a director of British
Mortgage Corp., which collapsed in the 1960s and was the direct
cause of the establishment of the CDIC.

Said Lawson, "The directors of British Mortgage did not know a
lot about what was going on. We did not realize that certain so-called
secured notes were, in fact, not secured. We did not realize that a
junior note had been called a senior note. We did not realize that
companies with different names were actually associated with each
other in one way or other. We did not realize that certain short-term
notes had not been paid off when due. Looking back, we should have
known. If only we had looked under the surface. 'If only' are possibly
the most poignant words in the English language.

"But I will say this, if you wish to profit from my adversity: If you
are asked to join a board, think twice about it. Investigate the
company before joining the board. If you join, take an interest in it.

See that there are rules and by-laws which limit the powers of management of the company, and, above all, look under the surface. Get information, pry into things, and make yourself a nuisance to management, because that is your job."

Under the Insurance Companies Act, directors have a very specific role, a duty of care. They are required to develop and monitor something called "Standards of Sound Business and Financial Practice." There is a lengthy checklist that includes liquidity management, real-estate appraisal standards, capital-management standards, and internal-control standards. Refusal to comply with the by-laws means that the CDIC could cancel deposit-insurance protection. Those areas of scrutiny were precisely the problem at Confed. Considering the outcome, directors cannot claim to have fully carried out their proscribed duties.

In the Confed debacle, there is plenty of blame to go around. But ultimately Confed was also the victim of something else. No one cared enough to save it. "There was no real strong figure to hold this thing together," says Palmieri. "There just was no real centre."

Confederation Life could have been saved if any one of a series of individuals along the way with the opportunity to do something had actually carried out his or her role. If someone, just one director, had stood up to the nonsense, if the regulator had been tougher, if the auditors had been more watchful, if Ottawa had cared about the industry, if the industry had cared about itself, or if the CDIC had bailed out Confed Trust in 1989 when the trouble was first spotted rather than let it poison the rest of the well that was the Confed group. The CDIC certainly had the time and the money. For example, when First City Trust was on its last legs, it went to North American Life Assurance in 1992, then on to Laurentian Bank as part of North American Trust Co. in 1995, at a total cost to the CDIC of $600 million.

The fallout from Confed's failure has been spectacular. "The Confed business has besmirched the reputation of Canadian companies in the United States," says John McNeil of Sun. In his farewell speech in September 1995 to the Life Office Managers Association (LOMA) annual conference in Orlando, Florida, LOMA chairman Bill

Bradford worried whether the world would ever be the same. "Even for companies – and this includes virtually every company in the industry – who had pursued very different and more conservative financial strategies than Confed, this failure has ushered in a period of scepticism about our industry," says Bradford, who was CEO of North American Life from 1988 to 1994.*

"The Canadian life-insurance industry, as we know it, has undergone permanent and fundamental changes," agrees Chester Murray, managing director of Moody's Investors Service, of New York, a rating agency. "The broad-based confidence formerly enjoyed by the Canadian life-insurance industry has been damaged."

"The industry is going to be sorry that it let Confed come to this," said Walter Schroeder, president of Dominion Bond Rating Service, of Toronto. Adds Dick Crawford, former president and CEO of Maritime Life, "With the failures of Central Guaranty Trust and Confederation Life and the crisis at Royal Trust, the myth of safety in size is dead and buried. The Canadian system of consumer-protection regulation must be totally rebuilt or the next earthquake will be devastating."

By contrast, in the United States the crisis has passed. "There was a time when this industry was very close to the edge in terms of five or six major players – Travelers, Aetna, Mutual of New York, Mutual Benefit, and New England Mutual," says Victor Palmieri. "They were in very bad shape, and runs could easily have started. In fact, it's sort of a testament to policyholder inertia they didn't run and they were able to get through the problem."

Lack of consumer confidence in the Canadian companies, combined with the industry's refusal to chart a clear course, will mean fewer players in the years to come. A decade ago, there were 160 federally registered life-insurance companies; today there are 125. Most of them are tiny. The twenty biggest account for 80 per cent of the business, the top fifty, 95 per cent.

---

* North American Life was taken over by Manulife in 1995. North American had been struggling for years. Manulife cut North American's surplus in half, a sure sign that North American had been heading the same, sorry way as Confed.

Consolidation is not only inevitable, it is also imminent. Foreign firms are selling out to Canadian firms in order to consolidate their efforts in their domestic markets. Over the next decade, many of the small firms will also withdraw from the market or otherwise disappear. There will be more failures. The fifty largest will shrink to twenty-five. Regulation will become more difficult, as companies take to the Internet as a way of dealing with their clients. How will it be possible to regulate a company that has no bricks-and-mortar, only a relationship with customers?

Each year for the last four years, OSFI has processed about two dozen applications for amalgamations, mergers, and transfers. For now, banks are restricted, but in time they will offer everything, and the only insurance companies left will be small-market niche players and a handful of big names that will look more and more like banks.

For all the havoc wreaked by Confed, there has been too little introspection, official or otherwise. The Senate Banking, Trade and Commerce Committee had been investigating financial services earlier in 1994. When Confed failed that August, committee chairman Michael Kirby decided to re-open hearings.

The scope of the hearings was far too narrow. All the players were called to testify, but, rather than seizing the opportunity that presented itself six weeks after the crash, Kirby chose not to investigate how Confed's bankruptcy came about. He struck a deal with the other committee members to stay away from any scrutiny of what occurred to bring down Confed except as it related to public policy Kirby kept tight rein on all questions. If any honourable member strayed beyond the scrutiny of general rules covering financial services and drifted into the how and why of the Confed failure a month earlier, Kirby called a halt.

Senator Jim Kelleher, for one, tried to assert himself by interrogating some witnesses closely. Kirby stepped in, and Kelleher did not pursue the matter very diligently. "I was very unhappy with the whole affair, but I went along with the committee. The chairman of the committee got away with murder. I lay down on this one," says Kelleher, one of the Progressive Conservative members whose political party then dominated the committee and the Senate.

Why did senators sit in such sober silence? Did Liberal senators remember that the prime minister himself has a connection to billionaire Paul Desmarais, ruler of Power Corp. and owner of Great-West, with a Chrétien daughter married to a Desmarais son? Even the senators of the Progressive Conservative stripe were ensnared in the tentacles. Senator John Sylvain, a member of the banking committee, and, from 1975 to 1982, president of United Provinces Insurance Co. of Montreal, is a brother-in-law to Desmarais.* Or are those tentacles just typical of Canada, a tiny place where everyone is somehow tied to everyone else?

The plain fact is that, of all the tragedies to hit Canada in the last few years, Confed is just about the only seismic event that has not been subject to government hearings or a royal commission. The actions of troops in Somalia, Red Cross tainted blood, the explosion at Westray Mines, the cancellation of the Pearson airport deal, everything else seems to merit an inquiry. Why not Confed? Possible litigation should not have mattered. Such concern didn't stop the launching of the inquiry into tainted blood headed by Mr. Justice Horace Kreever in 1993. Government estimates four years earlier were that the Treasury stood to pay $1 billion to victims and families who had suffered.

Kirby explained his action by saying that there were reluctant witnesses who were under confidentiality agreements. That should not have been a factor, either. The Senate can subpoena witnesses; sessions can be held *in camera*. Such subpoena power was used during the 1995 Pearson airport inquiry – costing $1.25 million – when sixty-five witnesses testified about a construction project, hardly the stuff of international economic confidence in an entire Canadian business sector. Nor has there been reluctance in the recent past to investigate financial failures. Two much smaller financial institutions, Canadian Commercial Bank (CCB) and Northland Bank – which between them held only 1 per cent of the country's banking assets – somehow

---

* Sylvain surprised his colleagues by resigning his Senate seat in 1996, explaining that he wanted to spend more time with his ailing wife.

merited a full judicial inquiry after their 1985 collapse. Eighty-five
witnesses appeared, including cabinet ministers, bureaucrats, and all
the CEOs of the major banks. Even the demise in 1992 of Central
Guaranty Trust of Halifax caused the House of Commons finance
committee to call witnesses and dig for truth.

Northland, founded in 1976, had grown to $700 million in assets
by May 1983. To that point, the bank had never ventured east of
Winnipeg. That year, Northland opened in Toronto and, within two
years, had doubled assets to $1.3 billion before collapsing. CCB,
founded in 1975, had reached $113 million in assets by 1977, then
mushroomed to $2 billion in five years. Confed was even more
aggressive, but no one seemed to have any institutional memory
about what had happened to such weeds when they became noxious
in the past.

Mr. Justice Willard Estey's 1986 report on CCB and Northland
contains phrases that precisely describe the situation at Confed less
than six years later. "By later 1984, it should have become clear that
this was not an enterprise on the verge of a breakthrough to prosperity. It was descending rapidly into liquidation." "There was apparently
no close liaison between the United States and Canadian regulators or
a sharing of their reports." "[T]he condition of the CCB was seriously
misjudged in the process that led to the establishment of the support
package." One of the expert witnesses said that one of the roles of the
auditors is to decide if a bank is a "going concern," in other words, if
it can meet its obligations. "One of the responsibilities of the auditor
is to satisfy himself that the going concern presumption is valid."
When the auditors accept management's views and the superintendent takes comfort, the public is left unprotected. And, finally, this:
"Northland simply ran out of money. The bank was putting into the
cash box IOUs which could not be collected, while simultaneously
taking out of the cash box what little cash remained to pay the operations costs of the bank. Eventually the paper well ran dry."

Michigan's efforts at a post-mortem have been equally lacklustre.
The lone voice to raise questions in the Michigan legislature about
David Dykhouse and the job he did has been Pat Gagliardi, Democrat,
of Drummond Island, a part of Michigan's northern peninsula. When

the Democrats controlled the legislature, Gagliardi was majority floor leader. In the 1992 election, the Republicans gained ground to tie the Democrats 55-55, so power was shared. Since 1994, when the Republicans won cleanly, Gagliardi has been minority floor leader.

On February 24, 1995, Gagliardi wrote to Michigan Attorney General Frank Kelley saying, "There appears to be overwhelming evidence of willful neglect of duty on the part of former Insurance Commissioner David Dykhouse and Director of Receiverships Jacqueline Reese regarding Confederation Life Insurance and Annuity Company of Atlanta. It appears that the Commissioner willfully ignored clear signs that Confederation Life was in serious financial trouble and willfully neglected to act, though under a clear duty to do so."

Gagliardi noted that Confed's assets in the United States mushroomed from US$3 billion to US$8 billion in just four years. Such growth was not sustainable, he charged, and should have set off alarm bells. Gagliardi also pointed out that Confed's repo obligations went from zero in 1991 to $300 million in 1992 to $661 million in 1993, activity that should also have aroused suspicion. He claims many financial ratios were outside usual standards, yet nothing was done by the regulator.

While Kelley did not pick up Gagliardi's challenge, Michael Dettmer, the United States attorney for the western Lower Peninsula and the Upper Peninsula, did agree to look into the charges but only on a confidential basis that did not allow him to report any findings.

Action by regulators in both countries leans towards secrecy and away from openness. Dykhouse retired in January 1995 and was quickly placed on retainer by the acting insurance commissioner, Patrick McQueen.* When Joseph Olson was named commissioner on May 1, he continued the cosy arrangement. "If I didn't have David to keep me informed, I'd spend half my time on Confed," said Olson. "David Dykhouse is a bargain."

In Canada, chief regulator Michael Mackenzie was singularly

---

* No relation.

unhelpful throughout his time in office as other regulators tried to carry out their own roles. He steadfastly refused to assist legislators or others investigating corporate failures in which little people lost money. Mackenzie repeatedly refused to turn OSFI material over to the Blenkarn committee, claiming that rules prevented any such disclosure.

Mackenzie took a similar stance when he was asked to testify at an Ontario Securities Commission (OSC) hearing into the collapse of Standard Trustco Ltd. (the ninth-largest trust firm in Canada), which was seized by OSFI in 1991. Mackenzie cited confidentiality rules, and, although the commission had promised a long battle to obtain his testimony, the OSC eventually backed off and didn't bother to subpoena him.

Regulators insist they have very restricted duties, which somehow preclude a public responsibility. "Our job is not to prevent failures but to influence the process or events as much as we can to minimize losses to policyholders," says OSFI's John Thompson. "You can't, as a regulator, manage a company so that these things don't happen. We were on top of the issues, and we did as much as could be expected."

"Failure is a fact of life in the United States," says OSFI superintendent John Palmer. "In Canada, we have difficulty coming to terms with it. In Canada when people lose money, there is a need to search for a villain who is always by definition not the person who loses the money. We have to mature as a country and part of that maturity is to allow failure of financial-services companies."

Regulators claim that pressure from ratings agencies capture a company's attention more than the regulators. "If a company wanted to ignore anyone, they could ignore the regulator a lot more effectively than they could ignore a rating agency," says Thompson. "They have more influence on the opinions of the investing public."

This is all rather self-deprecating stuff. In fact, OSFI has sweeping powers, including the capacity to restrict investment or lending activities. In the case of Confed, the full arsenal was hardly rolled out for inspection on the parade square, let alone used. OSFI seemed paralysed, hoping above hope that real-estate markets would somehow improve or, miraculously, corporate health would return all on its own. "As a regulator, you always wonder: Was there a road not taken?" asks Blair Tully, who, as head of the Ontario Insurance Commission, was not directly involved in the rescue but was kept informed of events.

Indeed, there was. When Saddam Hussein invaded Kuwait in 1990, a Canadian bank phoned Michael Mackenzie to say that it had received a message, accompanied by all the appropriate security codes, to transfer US$10 billion in Kuwaiti money out of an account in London, England. What should they do? Mackenzie looked into the matter and discovered that Canada had no way to block such request. He talked to American and British authorities and found that they both had authority to freeze assets. Mackenzie concluded that he should do the same, so he made up a phrase saying that to release this money would be "unsafe and unsound." The money stayed where it was. If OSFI had really wanted to protect policyholders in particular and the industry in general, regulators could have put Confed into a holding pattern and bought more time for a solution. There certainly was precedent for such action. Why shouldn't Canadian policyholders get the same tough, authoritative action as a Canadian bank?

Ratings firms have also chided regulators for their tardiness and say that Confed might well have been saved. "A. M. Best does not subscribe to the theory that regulators acted too early in the Confederation Life situation," says Thomas Upton, assistant vice-president with Best in New York. "On the contrary, we believe that a much more persuasive case can be made for the thesis that they did not act early enough."

In a sweeping report on OSFI, issued in May 1995, Auditor General Denis Desautels cited a huge flaw in the relationship between OSFI and the CDIC. "CDIC has the mandate for the stability and competitiveness of the system, but has not explained to Parliament how this is discharged. There is a need to establish clearly whose responsibility it is to detect and gauge the seriousness of problems faced by an institution, so that appropriate corrective measures can be taken. It is essential to determine which one has the principal responsibility at each stage of intervention, so that it can be held accountable."

As it stands now, OSFI and the CDIC carry out parallel examinations and risk-assessments of financial companies, but have different triggers for putting troubled companies on a watch list. That leaves unanswered questions about which agency is to blame for failures. "When problems are not identified early enough, it becomes difficult to ascribe responsibility to either OSFI or CDIC," said Desautels.

One thing is for sure, OSFI now pays more attention to what's going on in the United States trust accounts. "We're much more interested than before in where a company's capital is located," says Palmer. "You want to look more carefully at what is involved in various legals pots."

So, one lesson was learned, but why were there not more? Why, exactly, was there no instructive inquiry into the reasons for Confed's failure? The most likely explanation is that Ottawa, the regulators, and the accounting profession were embarrassed that they let the whole tragedy occur. They could have stopped the debacle, but they didn't. They could have rescued Confed, but chose not to. An inquiry would have demonstrated too much cowardice, incompetence, and a reckless disregard for a financial-services sector they were prepared to abandon. Instead, they closed ranks to protect each other from scrutiny.

As is so often the case, the members of the Establishment on whose watch failure occurred have been able to get off scot-free. The people who hurt the most are the policyholders, who could not possibly have been aware of the problems and had no say in how they were handled, despite the fact that they "owned" Confed. "The pain in these huge cases is not nearly so much financial as it is emotional," says Victor Palmieri. "But how can you measure the emotional cost, the anxieties of aging or disabled annuitants, the fears of long-term employees suddenly faced with lay-offs, and the wrenching career crisis for agents whose professional lives were built on the foundation of the company's good name? The answer is simple. You can't measure it. All the regulators and judges and people like me can do is distribute the financial loss." If this is all that regulation of an industry amounts to, what's the point?

There are lessons in all of this for everyone, not least the actuaries, those gnomes who control the black box at the heart of an insurance company, where risk/reward scenarios are sketched out for the next hundred years. The art is so mystical that many actuaries have convinced their firms that they know what they are doing when, in fact, much of it is by guess and by golly.

Canada can also learn some solutions from the United States, where a company in trouble has some choices: sale of in-force business to an industry buyer, as in the case of Fidelity Bankers; sale to a company formed by the state guaranty association (Guaranteed Security); sale to a group of foreign investors (Executive Life); and controlled run-off of the business with no injection of new capital or change of ownership (Mutual Benefit). Had the industry-run CompCorp roused itself to act, Confed might have been saved.

Some individuals with Confed policies would have fared better under the American system. Disability insurance (DI) policyholders have been particularly mistreated as that block of business got shunted through four different carriers following bankruptcy. "If you were an individual DI policyholder with Confed, you're going to wonder what the hell happened. That's a considerably different process than going into rehabilitation, then merging with somebody else," says lawyer Jill McCutcheon, who offered legal advice to Confed under contract from 1990 to 1994 and is now with Manulife.

"One halfway house is less painful than four. I've tried to mediate some claims where policyholders have gone from Confed through four other companies, and by the time you get to the table with them they're so miserable because of all the administrative difficulties during the last two years. For that individual person, it's not the same journey at all as going from Confed to one other company."

Protection and customer service is what insurance is supposed to be all about, says McCutcheon. "Lest we forget, that's what we're in the business of doing. They should at least know which 1-800 number they're supposed to call."

A version of the British system might also suit Canada. A co-insurance scheme begun in 1975 means that 90 per cent of a claim is paid quickly after a failure. A smaller band of regulators than exists in Canada monitors an industry that's three times larger. Regulators rely on financial-services executives to tell them when something's gone wrong. Most life-insurance failures have been handled through mergers or

acquisitions. The British system is far less costly. Canada has forked out
$8 billion for losses through the CDIC, Britain about $500 million.

CompCorp was all but useless in advance. "It only acts when
companies get into the shit," says Blair Tully, who handles licensing in
Ontario. "There was no shit-avoidance mechanism." The Canadian
industry has since been shamed into taking some action in the wake of
the Confed collapse. CompCorp has been strengthened by raising the
amount that the industry can be assessed annually from $200 million to
$600 million, thereby making more funds available for efforts that
could include restructuring, soft-landings, or going-concern solutions.
Unlike banks or trust companies, which are backed by the Canada
Deposit Insurance Corp., no taxpayer money is involved, but the
consumer will get docked anyway as the industry raises premiums and
fees for products and services to cover the higher assessments.

CompCorp also established an independent board in 1995, so that
now, when the superintendent of insurance decides that an insurance
company is in trouble, the regulator has somewhere to turn other
than to the battered company itself. The board cannot muscle in as
advisers, but is empowered to consider action, such as a merger or
asset sales, without starting a run. By working in secret, using industry money, CompCorp hopes the independent-board approach can
maintain public confidence in both the company and the industry by
acting more quickly to avoid corporate fatalities. "We think there's a
much greater chance of avoiding trains going over the cliff," says Alan
Morson, president of CompCorp. But first, the regulator has to see
the runaway train in time to act, a talent too little demonstrated in
the past.

Financial involvement by the committee is limited either to sale of
the troubled company's business units to one or more purchasers or
the orderly wind-down of the company. No money will be injected
simply to restore corporate health so that it can rise again to fight
another day. If a troubled company is seeking a merger partner, but
has a block of assets no one wants because future values are uncertain,
CompCorp could acquire the assets rather than see them go at fire-
sale prices if the merger can then be finalized. Second, if a troubled
company has sold various blocks of business, but is left with unwanted

items, CompCorp would buy those assets, so the company can with-draw from the scene in an orderly manner. CompCorp would serve as a long-term warehouse until markets improved. The system is, as yet, untried. If Confed is any criteria, hope is slim for effective action. The insurance industry was not prepared to save Confed, a decision that will haunt them in the years to come.

The federal government must decide whether it's going to regulate the industry and protect the public or whether it's just going to take a hands-off approach. At the moment, Ottawa is trying to have it both ways and achieves nothing. Even the exotic area of derivatives contin-ues to escape scrutiny. Rules governing this area took OSFI ages to draw up, were finally unveiled in 1995, but won't come into effect until the end of the insurance companies' 1996 fiscal years – which means that it won't be until sometime early in 1997 that companies will have to reveal their revenues (or losses) from derivatives and the risks taken to get there.

"Either the government stands back and says, 'It's all yours, baby,' or – if they're going to have this system of regulators and accountants – they better make it work," says Stanley Stewart, a former officer at CCB who is now a Toronto consultant advising corporate clients on strat-egy and governance. "If something happens, somebody has to carry the can."

The costs of liquidating Confed will be high. Dozens of litigators and lawyers are at the trough; the highest hourly rates for a Canadian lawyer or accountant involved is $400. In the United States, the top of the range is US$600. The Canadian insurance industry is paying those fees, and estimates that the total will reach $75 million in Canada before liquidation is completed – and that's without the rehabilitator in the United States going to court. "A huge war between us and the United States could blow through that number very quickly," says Bob Sanderson, the Peat Marwick president in charge of the liquidation.

It won't take much of a war. About $55 million will be billed in Canada by the end of 1996. In the United States, the running total for the same period will be $70 million. In Canada, the industry pays. In the United States, the money comes from the *corpus* of the late

company. Avarice is commonplace. "I have been astounded at the
pettiness, the level of acrimony, the backbiting," says Susan Rowland,
who acts for former Confed employees. "These big firms have a lot
of people to keep employed." To be sure, Rowland's Toronto firm,
Koskie Minsky, has done all right, too. By the time everything is
over, she expects to bill about $500,000.

Typical of the wretched excess was an April 27, 1995, meeting in
the offices of the Wall Street law firm of Cadwalader, Wickersham &
Taft. It was billed as an initial information exchange between American and Canadian interests. Representatives were invited from
CompCorp and Peat Marwick on the Canadian side, the rehabilitators and National Organization of Life and Health Insurance Guaranty Associations (NOLHGA) for the Americans. Three dozen lawyers,
auditors, and regulators showed up and sat shoulder to shoulder all day
around a boardroom table. Even at a modest average billing rate of
$300 per hour, the eight-hour meeting would have generated $85,000
in fees.

Richter & Associates Inc., trustees in bankruptcy, was retained in
February 1995 to do forensic work for a creditors' committee. As
many as thirteen members of the firm (at rates as high as $400 an hour)
worked on the project over a seven-month period from April to
October; Richter billed $922,000. In the United States, Deloitte &
Touche was retained by the rehabilitator in 1995 to assist Lehman
Brothers Inc. in preparing to securitize eight hundred mortgages and
fifty-three properties that had been in the Confed portfolio and were
worth about US$3.2 billion; Deloitte billed about US$3.5 million and
charged US$500,000 in expenses for six months' work.

Mitch Sonkin, the insolvency specialist who heads the rehabilitator's legal team at Cadwalader, is unrepentant about the costs
involved. He charges US$475 an hour for his services. In the first year
of liquidation, his firm billed US$5 million in fees. "Confed was one
of the larger financial institutions in the world, and the thought that
these kinds of things can happen sends shivers up my spine," he says.
"Life insurance has a remarkable place in our society. It's a fundamental part of most people's financial planning, not only for this present
life but for survivors," says Sonkin.

"People go to sleep at night somewhat comforted by the fact that if anything happens, my family will be taken care of because I've taken some of my hard-earned dollars and I've bought life insurance," he says. "To wake up in the morning one day and find out that company is insolvent and I may not get everything I want or my pension fund is tied up – how can this happen? They've saved and they've trusted. Our job is to seek redress and seek recovery. The big-business aspects and high-cost lawyers frequently mask the real victims and what it really means to the system and make you forget how important life insurance is."

Beyond the fees they earn, there is another, more primal appeal. There are only about three hundred lawyers who can call themselves Bay Street lawyers (a term of status for them, a description of derision in the rest of society) at the six top firms. For them, being involved in Confed also means that your peers know that you are offering counsel in the case of cases, the US$2 billion Michigan suit, and that someone will phone to ask for advice and will not only need it right then but will pay to hear you speak. For lawyers and litigators, there may be no other gravy train like this during their lifetime. And such work *can* last a lifetime. There are two audit partners at Ernst & Young still engaged in the matter of Bernie Cornfeld's Investors Overseas Services, the mutual-funds empire that collapsed twenty-five years ago.

The insurance industry has been scrambling to restore confidence. Some companies have formed their own protection plan to quell consumer concerns in the wake of Confed's collapse. A new product, called Shared Risk, provides insurance coverage beyond the $200,000 CompCorp ceiling. The firms involved – Assumption Mutual Life Insurance Co. of Canada, of Moncton, New Brunswick, ITT Hartford Life Insurance Company of Canada, based in Burlington, Ontario, and Mutual Life Assurance Co. of St-Hyacinthe, Quebec – have combined to offer the policy, which in turn is reinsured by RGA Life Reinsurance Co. of Canada, of Montreal. The partnering, in fact, is little different than what's been available for years to corporations where the risk is too large for one carrier to handle. Still, why shouldn't individuals have access to certainty, too?

And what about fraud? Every auditor and forensic accountant who has looked at Confed's books claims to have found no fraud, no former officer with a stash in the Caymans. Yet the opportunities were there for graft and kickbacks. It's hard to believe there was no criminal activity.

For instance, since, by law, sufficient money was to remain in the Michigan trust fund to protect U.S. policyholders, why shouldn't those involved stand trial? How is what they did different from the finagling that went on to prop up the empire of newspaper magnate Robert Maxwell, who stepped (or slipped) from his yacht at sea.

His son Kevin Maxwell was charged with conspiring to defraud the firm's pension-fund assets, worth £122 million, in order to get a bank loan for another entity under the corporate umbrella. Maxwell (who was later acquitted) defended the actions taken by him and his father by saying that shuffling assets around would stop illiquidity problems elsewhere in the empire. Everything belonged to the company; what difference did it make whether it was moved from one pot to another? "The whole group suffered from illiquidity throughout the period," young Maxwell told the court. "However, I believed at all times that the assets of the group exceeded its liabilities and I believed all its obligations could be met in due course."

Sound familiar? U.S. policyholders don't have the funds available to them that the law says they should. Does not a trust fund have the same stature as a pension plan, money meant to be there for all eternity? To date, no criminal charges have been laid. No fraud investigation has even been begun.

Someone needs to keep an eye on what's happening, no matter how difficult that is. The forensic investigation of CTSL, for example, took months, because it involved sifting through more than six hundred boxes containing an estimated one million pieces of paper. Yes, white-collar crime is difficult to control, but the answer cannot be to give up. Business needs neighbourhood-watch programs and more cops in the streets, just like big cities. Accounting firms could become the first line of defence. At the moment, they check corporate processes, but they too often accept at face value the word of those firms that hire them.

"Auditors have been slow to accept really rigorous accounting," says Michael Mackenzie, himself a former auditor. "This is getting better – but only when we write new rules. While I believe audit performance has generally improved in recent years, I have to tell you, there is, in the regulatory and government circles in which I work, a high degree of scepticism about the capacity and independence of auditors."

There are other participants who need to be more watchful and accept responsibility when stupid strategies are proposed or pursued. Directors should have to meet a certain level of qualification. In the case of mutual companies, for example, where there are particular mysteries, directors may need to be educated.

Regulators should have the power to remove directors and officers they judge to be falling short. OSFI audit staff needs to be beefed up and inspections done annually, not every other year.

Insurance firms can now wait until March to file the previous year's financial results. That process should be accelerated. Key comparative ratios such as the minimum continuing capital and surplus requirements (MCCSR) should be made public, so the public can compare the various insurance companies and judge for themselves.

In fact, all information about liquidity and solvency should be made public. In New Zealand, a country often held up as a role model for Canada because of the way it successfully dealt with national debt, the governor of the central bank can be fired for missing inflation targets. There is no longer any government oversight of financial institutions. Banks must make detailed quarterly statements about their financial health and post a two-page summary in each branch, so that depositors can make their own judgements. The responsibility lies with the directors; if they are negligent, they can be sued.

In the wake of the Confed failure, Canada has two choices: either give regulators tough, interventionist powers, so they can act like real cops, or have them back off entirely. At the moment, there is the widespread belief that regulators can and will act, when the reality is that they don't. As a second step, deposit insurance should be abandoned, because it offers a crutch for weak firms and renders all depositors indifferent to the financial health of the institution with which they're dealing. Among other reforms, there should be more public disclosure of essential bottom-line information in a form that would help everyone from consumers to rating agencies make considered investment decisions. A complete list of twenty public-policy recommendations, flowing from the research on this book, is included in Appendix Four.

The proposals will take time to introduce in Canada. People would need to be weaned from the old way before they accepted the new. But it is clear there can no longer be a combination of depositor support from government for some financial institutions and a market solution for the others.

As an interim measure, it should be mandatory for insurance companies to have directors' and officers' (D&O) liability coverage. If an underwriter refuses coverage, that would send a signal to the rest of the world. "What amazes me is how quickly these disasters are forgotten and the main culprits disappear from public view," says Mike Hogan, a D&O expert for more than thirty years.

Meanwhile, one way individuals can protect themselves is by spreading business around. Coverage of $1 million should be divided among five companies, so no one firm has more than $200,000, the limit of CompCorp's guaranteed protection. "You have to be ruthless. The life companies are ruthless with us if we fail to pay a premium," says Geoffrey Jarvis, an agent who represents thirty companies. "There's no reason to support a company on emotional grounds."

In the matter of the murder of Confederation Life, there was no one culprit. It was as if a wealthy dowager in an Agatha Christie thriller died after being given small amounts of arsenic over a long period of time by family, friends, physicians, and police – the very people who should have been dedicated to her care and protection. The first round of poison was supplied by a management that swung between misguided and mediocre. It included Pat Burns, who wanted to prove his worth to the world, but didn't have the "royal jelly." There was also his sidekick, Bill Douglas, who is widely regarded by his peers as the architect of the debacle.

But Burns and Douglas had accomplices at the office. "The reality is that the blame can be shared by the entire senior management group," says John McNeil of Sun Life. "There are certain things in this company I cannot do. The chief investment officer would not put up with it; the chief actuary would not put up with it. He'd just say, 'I'm sorry, I can't go along with that.' If I insisted, I think it would go in front of the board and the board would decide. The chief actuary and the chief investment officer and a variety of other people have a responsibility. Every time Pat [Burns] said, 'Jump,' they said, 'How high?'"

As for the Confed directors, those great lights of the business community thought they'd signed on to a sinecure, a ticket on the cruise ship *Establishment Prince*. They approved every step that management took, stupid and otherwise. "It's always that way. The same directors, they could exchange chairs, and the same CEO could exchange," says Victor Palmieri. "They always have this growth mania, and they're always selling snake oil, and the directors are drinking it, and they sit around having lunch and the company gets imbedded deeper and deeper in risk. I've always said that a child could have told them that the strategy *had* to result in disaster. The problem is that there is never a child in the boardroom."

And what of the auditors at Ernst & Young? Is there really any point in counting the beans without deciding which is safe to eat and which is not? There's no question, too, that regulators in both Canada and the United States failed badly. Michael Mackenzie and David Dykhouse spotted the trouble too late and achieved too little. They claimed they had no real powers to wield, yet didn't even wave what swords they had.

As for the Ottawa politicians and their faithful lackeys, the bureaucrats, never has so little been done by so many in the sorry service of their country. They offered no ideas, no courage, no leadership. "Early intervention done behind the scenes is a vitally important tool to have available to restructure situations," says Bob Sanderson of Peat Marwick. "Economics doesn't enter into it. It's faith. The whole financial system is based on people's belief that, when they want their money, it will be there."

Paul Cantor, who could have played the physician's role, arrived in time to act, but his lack of knowledge about the dowager's condition and how she got into that state contributed to her death. Classic corporate turnaround techniques might have worked, such as sell-offs of entire divisions and downsizing of complete departments, but his banking experience had taught him none of that, so he didn't know how to proceed. By the time negotiations with Great-West Life were launched, the patient was probably dead. The doctor survived. They usually do.

Then there were those titans of the Canadian insurance industry who were present at the deathbed for the last-ditch talks. Fortunate were they that their own firms hadn't suffered the same deterioration as Confed. They were free-marketers all – at least until trouble arrived. At that point, they suddenly became cripples who cried out for the crutch of government support. If the future of the insurance industry depends upon handwringers of such limited vision, prospects are very dim indeed.

The real loser is the financial system itself, a system that encourages people to purchase insurance policies based on blind faith and impossible promises. Consumers had been convinced by fast-talking agents that what they were buying was long-term security for themselves and their loved ones.

In the long run, doing nothing was everyone's worst possible choice. Their cowardice and lack of imagination resonates still. For the price of Confed, the life-insurance industry could have retained its reputation. Today, it might have been business as usual, for all concerned. Instead, the industry CEOs have ceded their position in the financial firmament, such as it was. Politicians seeking strong financial-services players will eventually allow the powerful banks into the insurance business and those companies now enjoying the last gasp of protectionism will fade from view. As for the public, they will never again completely trust what their life-insurance agent promises across the kitchen table.

EPILOGUE

Pat Burns lives in Toronto with his wife, June. They winter on St. Simons Island, Georgia, and stay in Toronto during the summer. He is a broken man.

Confed's head office final folly, One Mount Pleasant Place, was purchased in 1996 by Rogers Cantel Inc. for $33.5 million, about one-third of its construction cost only four years earlier. Also thrown in was Confed's collection of Canadian art.

John Heard, the former number two, who retired in 1992 after forty-five years, was forced to sell his house once his pension was cut. He and his wife, Barbara, moved into a two-bedroom condo in Markham, Ontario. A needlepoint cushion on a bench in the Heards' front hall reads, "Screw the golden years."

After thirty-five years as a stellar member of more than forty corporate boards, Adam Zimmerman has decided there is no point at all in having directors, as the role is now constituted. Instead, he would create something new: corporate advisers who are not liable for the losses if a business goes broke. Just like eunuchs in a harem.

Of all the players in the troupe, only Bill Douglas accumulated serious money. After Confed went bankrupt, he took a year off at his place on the aptly named Skidaway Island in Savannah, Georgia. Despite all that time to golf, his game did not improve. He holds 450,000 shares of Newcourt, the leasing company, free and clear. In 1996, they were worth more than $14 million.

Just in case policyholders were worried about the financial health of other life-insurance companies, at least one of them has sought to reassure them that all is well. Canada Life created an indoor rain forest in its Toronto headquarters. The 1,600-square-foot room, officially opened in October 1994, contains 350 plants, as well as 100 frogs, salamanders, snails, clams, mussels, and worms, not to mention several hundred insects. The project cost $500,000.

Former Confed Trust officers have gone on to lesser things. Barry Walsh lives in Delta, British Columbia, where he helps out a friend who runs a Mailboxes Etc. franchise. Chuck McIlravey is a consultant in Toronto assisting life-insurance companies to work out their real-estate problems. Shelly Fenton survived very nicely and is still in the development business. He lives in Forest Hill, just a few doors from George Eaton, president of Eaton's of Canada.

Two years after the 1994 seizure, the flagship Confederation Trust branch at Yonge and Wellington streets in downtown Toronto remained empty. The signage is long gone, but idle service counters are still visible through the 175 feet of windows, as if it were some Museum of Firms Gone Blooey.

Confed lines of business sold to Maritime Life, Manulife, Great-West Life, and other firms did not necessarily translate into continuing jobs for the former Confed workers who were included in the original transaction. An estimated 70 per cent of Confed's employees discovered that their jobs at the various new employers were short-lived. Thank you, saviour.

Michael Mackenzie is retired, lives in Cobourg, Ontario, and does some lecturing at York University. In 1994, he gave a speech in which he noted that all policyholders receive an annual statement from their life-insurance company and "they should read it pretty carefully." Thank you, regulator.

After John Palmer took on the job as superintendent of insurance in September 1994, his annual compensation plummeted from the private-sector heights of $500,000 to a still-healthy public-sector $200,000. He sold his Rosedale home – where he lived next door to Jack Rhind – for $1.3 million and moved half-a-mile away, paying $777,500 for his new residence. The purchaser was Larry Murphy, the thirty-four-year-old defenceman, who signed a US$7.1-million three-year contract in July 1995 with the Toronto Maple Leafs. His coach was Pat Burns. No, not that Pat Burns. In March 1996, Coach Burns was fired, too.

Suzanne Labarge returned to the Royal Bank in April 1995, from whence she'd sprung in 1984. They named her an executive vice-president, corporate treasury, and put her in charge of derivatives.

Michigan commissioner David Dykhouse stepped down in January 1995, before his term was up, claiming he'd achieved all he set out to do once the National Association of Insurance Commissioners had accredited Michigan in December 1994 as having the appropriate laws, regulations, and financing to regulate insurers. Not a bad honour, considering the botch Michigan made of Confed. Out of harness, Dykhouse was immediately retained by his former employer as an adviser on Confed. In his first six months, Dykhouse billed US$142,800, about twice his annual salary as commissioner.

Paul Cantor helped the liquidator until March 1995, then became chairman and CEO of National Trust at an annual salary of $495,000, plus a 60-per-cent performance bonus. He describes his new company, with its $15.5 billion in assets and 3,700 employees, as "fiscally sound but strategically challenged." Cantor brought along his old cohort-in-arms from Confed, Michael White, as president and chief operating officer. In Cantor's first year there, profit fell 44 per cent, and he began to worry that he'd left the *Titanic* for the *Lusitania*. As for his time at Confed, Cantor says, "I'd rather be remembered for my Harley than my table dance."

Orest Dackow became a pariah. When Confed went under, an unnamed veteran industry-watcher was quoted as saying, "If Orest Dackow was in the middle of the desert and wanted a glass of water, and other chief executives passed him with a tanker truck, he wouldn't get it." The comment resonated so far and for so long that more than a year later, when Dackow spoke to the Actuaries Club of Toronto, he said, "I no longer wonder whether your local financial press was correct when it stated that Toronto insurance executives would not give me a drink of water even if I were lost in the middle of a desert. Like any conservative actuary, I now, when visiting that far eastern desert called Toronto, bring my own water."

Litigators and liquidators have their meters running. In three countries.

Chronology

1871: Confederation Life Association established by John Kay Macdonald.

1891: New headquarters opens at Yonge and Richmond streets in Toronto.

1902: International expansion begins to two dozen countries.

1921: Confed is the first Canadian company to issue a life-insurance policy without requiring a medical.

1927: First group life and health plan issued.

1931: Confed celebrates silver jubilee; assets hit $81 million.

1947: J. K. Macdonald, "the young J. K.," appointed president, the last of his line to head Confed.

1955: Move to new headquarters at 321 Bloor Street East, Toronto.

1968: Confed becomes a mutual company, owned by its policyholders.

1976: J. Craig Davidson replaced as chief executive officer by Jack Rhind.

1980: Pat Burns is appointed executive vice-president and begins his final ascent to the top; assets are $2.7 billion.

1982: United States head office opens in Atlanta; Confederation Real Estate Fund launched to take equity positions in property.

1985: Burns appointed CEO; go-for-growth strategy begins.

1987: Confederation Trust launched; new head-office building opens in Atlanta.

1988: New head-office building opens in Stevenage, England.

1989: May – Confed announces its largest real-estate project ever, a 50-percent interest in The Portals, in Washington, D.C. Plans called for the expenditure of $650 million on 2 million square feet of office space, 125,000 square feet of retail, and the 568-suite luxury Fairmont Hotel.

October – With almost 74 per cent of Confed's assets invested in real estate, insurance superintendent Michael Mackenzie issues his first warning that Confed is sailing perilously close to the edge of the world.

December – Pat Burns turns the sod to begin building the final folly, One Mount Pleasant Place, in Toronto.

1990: Board continues to approve Burns's quick-growth strategy by appointing him chairman as well as president and CEO; Burns finishes one-year term as chairman of the industry trade association and becomes founding chairman of CompCorp, the newly formed industry support group for policyholders of failed companies.

1991: July – Ontario regulator Brian Cass launches examination of Confederation Trust.

October – Mackenzie delivers the Confed board its second wake-up call, declaring that poor real estate and insufficient financial controls are weakening financial strength.

1992: March – Shoppers Trust Co. seized by regulators.

May – Confed board decides to accelerate Burns's retirement.

November 20 – Paul Cantor starts as president and CEO at annual salary of $500,000.

December 31 – The Toronto–Dominion Bank acquires most of the assets and deposit liabilities of Central Guaranty Trust Co. and Central Guaranty Mortgage Corp.

1993: March – Adam Zimmerman, board member since 1990, replaces Burns as chairman.

April 28 – Farewell party for Burns.

Fall – Of eighteen firms approached, only five show a serious interest in a strategic alliance with Confed.

November 10 – The Dominion Trust Co. goes under.

December 3 – Prenor Trust Co. is also seized.

December 15 – Confed agrees to exclusive negotiations with Great-West Lifeco Inc.

1994: February 8 – Monarch Trust Co. placed in liquidation.

March – Dackow and Cantor take draft package involving capital injection, downsizing, asset sales, and expense reductions to ratings agencies.

April 14 – Standard & Poor's drops its rating regardless.

April 28 – Great-West and Confed, with help from Department of Finance and OSFI, sign letter of intent for a strategic alliance to inject $225 million in capital.

mid-June – Tom Di Giacomo chairs a group of five Canadian insurance CEOs who agree to help Confed take on its $1-billion corporate-owned and bank-owned life insurance in the United States.

June 22 – Cantor spouts brave words at annual policyholder meeting.

July 21 – Great-West concludes deal too big for one firm, suggests industry coalition.

July 23 – Great-West and Confed CEOs meet with Di Giacomo and five insurance-industry CEOs to convince them to pump new capital into Confed.

July 24 – Rescue group expands to include OSFI's Suzanne Labarge and John Thompson, plus David Dodge, Sheryl Kennedy, and Nick Le Pan from the Department of Finance to see how Ottawa can help; daily meetings ensue.

July 26 – Under discussion are ways to structure the coalition, possible tax breaks on a preferred share issue, and a Crown corporation, dubbed CDIC-II, that would replace CompCorp, the industry-run protection scheme for policyholders.

July 27 – Michigan insurance commissioner David Dykhouse, who regulates Canadian companies operating in the United States, visits Toronto to be briefed.

July 29 – Dykhouse phones Confed CEO Paul Cantor to say he'll try to round up enough American insurers to contribute $150 million, leaving $450 million for Canadian companies.

Aug. 1 – Canadian coalition meets in a boardroom at Toronto law firm Tory Tory DesLauriers & Binnington; while there are many problems yet to overcome, there is optimism.

August 4 – Confed confirms it is working with a consortium of companies to raise $600 million in capital. Rating agencies downgrade Confed.

August 5 – Eight American insurance firms meet in New York to consider helping out by contributing $150 million.

August 8, 9 – The American companies are briefed in Toronto; the information is bleak, and they give no guarantees they will participate.

August 9 – Bob Astley of Mutual Life pulls out; the consortium collapses.

August 10 – Labarge informs Cantor she will recommend that the government invoke the Winding-Up Act.

August 11 – Secretary of State Doug Peters orders OSFI to take control of Confederation Life Insurance Co. and Confederation Trust. Labarge tells hastily convened board meeting that time's up; Peat Marwick Inc. is appointed agent of OSFI, and an application is made to the attorney general of Canada to wind-up the companies. Liquidators arrive at 10:40 P.M.; Confed is out of business. CompCorp announces that it will protect Canadian policyholders up to its published limits.

August 12 – Six Confed subsidiaries, including Confederation Life Realty Services and Confederation Funds Management, are granted court protection under the Companies' Creditors Arrangement Act. Michigan and Georgia regulators take control of Confederation Life's American operations.

August 17 – Peat Marwick announces an agreement to sell Confederation United Kingdom Holdings Ltd. to Sun Life Assurance Co. of Canada for $430 million in a deal to close September 30. Confed United Kingdom employs 1,600, has 40 branches, $1.9 billion in assets, and $9.7 billion in assets under management. Profit in 1993 was $52.4 million on revenues of $280 million.

August 24 – Great-West Life & Annuity Insurance Co., the American subsidiary of Great-West Assurance, receives regulatory and legal approval to acquire most of Confed's group business in the United States. The transaction involves $480 million worth of life and health revenue and means Great-West's United States group life and health revenue will be $3.5 billion in 1994.

August 29 – Manulife Financial agrees to buy Confed's Canadian group life and health business in deal to close by the end of September. The business employs 867 people, includes 800 clients insuring 1.5 million Canadians with annual premiums in force of $1 billion.

September 1 – John Palmer assumes duties as new OSFI superintendent.

September 22 – Senior managers of Confed Investment Counselling Ltd. agree to buy the company that oversees $1 billion in assets for pension clients.

October – Deposit base of Confederation Trust moves to National Bank of Canada; Confed Trust's $450-million estate, trust, and agency business sold to North American Trust Co.

November 28 – Confederation Funds Management (Canada) Ltd.,

managers of two mutual funds (Confed Growth Fund and Confed Mortgage Fund, with total net-asset value of $9.6 million), put up for sale. Group-mortgage business, 3,000 residential mortgage loans with a principal balance of $308 million, put up for sale.

November 30 – Canada Life Assurance Co. agrees to buy CL Capital Management Inc., the United States group-annuity contracts.

December 16 – Toronto–Dominion Bank buys the residential-mortgage portfolio from Confed Trust of 2,000 mortgages, worth $205 million. (The bank also buys Confed Trust's $22-million portfolio of consumer loans and personal lines of credit, paying the principal amount, plus a premium of $225,000.)

1995: February 3 – Third-party mortgage-benefit business sold to FirstLine Trust Co., a subsidiary of Manulife Financial.

February 9 – Binding letter of intent signed by Maritime Life Assurance Co. to acquire Confed's individual life and health business, consisting of 170,000 life policies and 12,000 health and disability policies.

May 9 – Confed's individual and group-pension and annuity business put up for sale. Business includes 16,000 individual deferred annuities, accounting for $450 million in liabilities, 29,000 individual and group immediate annuities accounting for $117 million in annual payments, and 900 group-pension contracts accounting for $925 million in liabilities.

May 10 – Third-party administration of Confed's mortgage, commercial loan, and securities portfolios put up for sale. Mortgage portfolio comprises 2,100 mortgages with an outstanding principal of $1.6 billion; commercial-loan portfolio includes 70 loans, leases, and other securities with $1 billion in principal, bond portfolio is comprised of publicly traded bonds and Treasury bills with a book value of $700 million.

June 6 – CompCorp increases its borrowing powers from member companies from $200 million to $600 million.

June 28 – Michigan insurance commissioner D. Joseph Olson, rehabilitator of the American branch of Confed, sues Harris Trust and Savings Bank of Chicago, Ernst & Young, and twenty-seven former directors and officers of Confed. The suit charges breach of trust, negligence, common-law fraud, breach of fiduciary duty, professional malpractice, and breach of contract.

July 28 – Royal Bank of Canada signs a deal to assume administration of Confed's portfolio of 2,000 commercial and residential mortgages, with outstanding principal of $1.5 billion.

August – Policies worth $220 million are sold to New York Life Insurance Co.

August 25 – Citicorp International Insurance Co. takes over 170 life policies from Confed's branch in Bermuda, with annual premium income of $3.2 million.

September – One Mount Pleasant Place, luxurious home to Confed's head office and Canadian operations, goes up for sale.

September 4 – American rehabilitator announces the proposed sale of Confed's bank-owned life insurance business (BOLI) to New York Life Insurance and Annuity Corp.

September 7 – Manufacturers Life Insurance Co. and North American Life Assurance Co. merge to create the largest life insurer in Canada, with $40.2 billion in assets. The deal is the first such merger between two mutual companies.

September 13 – Penfund Management Ltd. takes over the administration (although Confed retains the ownership) of $1.1 billion in private pension assets consisting of 150 commercial loans and private equity deals.

September 26 – DuPont Canada Inc. sues investment dealer Wood Gundy Inc. and rating agency Dominion Bond Rating Service to recover $10 million it lost on commercial paper issued by Confed.

October 2 – Aetna Life Insurance and Annuity Co., of Hartford, Connecticut, agrees to buy individual life (5,000 policies, with a face amount of US$2.3 billion), variable annuity (7,000 contracts with US$275 million of assets), and guaranteed-investment business (liabilities of US$70 million) of Confederation Life Insurance and Annuity Co., of Atlanta.

October 10 – Empire Life Insurance Co., of Kingston, Ontario, takes over administration of $400 million in liabilities, which include 15,000 individual deferred annuities and 3,000 registered retirement income funds.

October 17 – Pacific Mutual Life Insurance Co., of Newport Beach,

California, awarded the US$1.4-billion corporate-owned life insurance (COLI) business.

October 18 – Enterprise Property Group, of Toronto, acquires portfolio of 2.5 million square feet of real estate run by Confed Realty Services Ltd. Deal includes such properties as Toronto's Hazelton Lanes, Eaton Centre in Edmonton, and the Tower office complex in Calgary.

October 19 – Crown Life Insurance Co., of Regina, agrees to administer 28,000 individual annuities, with annual payments totalling $92 million, backed by assets of $600 million.

October 26 – Institutional bondholders and other creditors reject deal proposed by Deloitte & Touche Inc. that would have paid out forty-eight cents for every dollar owed to creditors of Confederation Treasury Services Ltd. Bankruptcy proceedings ensue.

1996: February 20 – Canadian rehabilitator agrees in principle to pay $225 million to American rehabilitator in order to balance the pots in the two countries and reduce chance of more lawsuits; American rehabilitator retains the right to proceed with action already launched against officers and directors.

April 17 – Rogers Cantel buys One Mount Pleasant Place for $33.5 million.

April 30 – Bell Canada reaches a settlement with 1,800 pensioned employees whose access to money in a voluntary company plan managed by Confed had been frozen since the seizure. An activist pensioners' group convinces Bell to pay $21 million so pensioners can recoup 100 per cent of the plan's value.

June 11 – Deal signed that sees Canadian liquidator pay American liquidator $225 million. Court approval required.

Confederation Group of Companies

(at July 23, 1992)

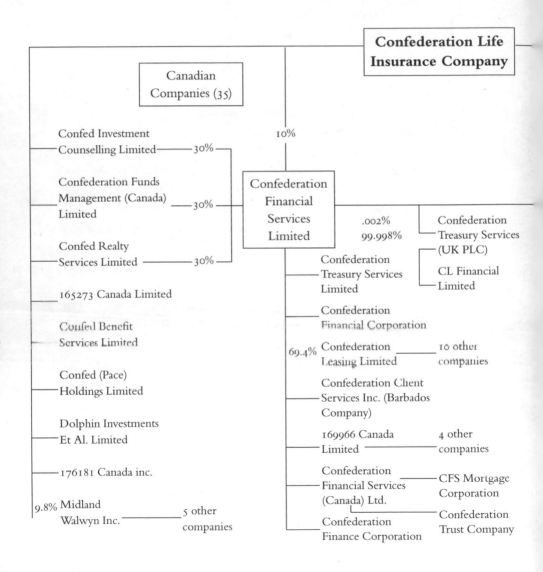

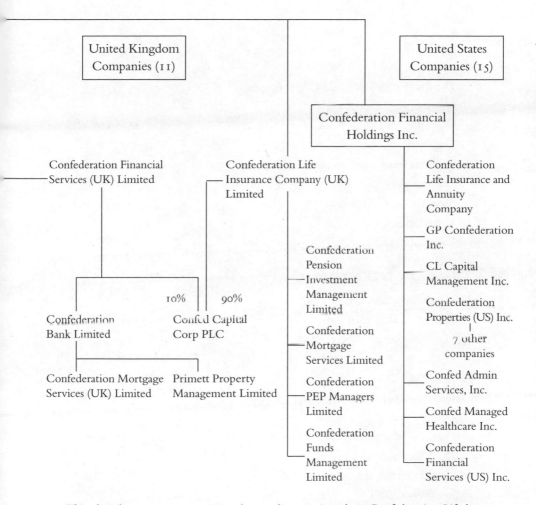

| United Kingdom Companies (11) | | United States Companies (15) |

Confederation Financial Holdings Inc.

Confederation Financial Services (UK) Limited

Confederation Life Insurance Company (UK) Limited

Confederation Life Insurance and Annuity Company

GP Confederation Inc.

Confederation Pension Investment Management Limited

CL Capital Management Inc.

10%   90%

Confederation Bank Limited

Confed Capital Corp PLC

Confederation Properties (US) Inc.

7 other companies

Confederation Mortgage Services Limited

Confederation Mortgage Services (UK) Limited

Primett Property Management Limited

Confederation PEP Managers Limited

Confed Admin Services, Inc.

Confederation Funds Management Limited

Confed Managed Healthcare Inc.

Confederation Financial Services (US) Inc.

This chart lists common or voting shares of companies where Confederation Life has direct or indirect ownership.

Unless stated otherwise and except in the case of certain subsidiaries of Confederation Leasing Limited, ownership is 100 per cent. Confederation Leasing has four wholly-owned subsidiaries and indirectly holds a majority of voting rights in six other companies.

North America's Twenty-five
Largest Life-Insurance Companies

(in US$ at December 31, 1994)

1.	The Prudential Insurance Co. of America, Newark, N.J.	$167,339,273
2.	Metropolitan Life Insurance Co. New York, N.Y.	$131,176,953
3.	Teachers Insurance and Annuity Association New York, N.Y.	$73,347,834
4.	New York Life Insurance Co. New York, N.Y.	$55,343,092
5.	Connecticut General Life Insurance Co. Bloomfield, Conn.	$50,911,548
6.	Northwestern Mutual Milwaukee, Wis.	$48,110,606
7.	Aetna Life Insurance Co. Hartford, Conn.	$47,357,221
8.	Equitable Life Insurance Society New York, N.Y.	$46,879,308
9.	John Hancock Mutual Life Insurance Co. Boston, Mass.	$46,851,728
10.	Principal Mutual Life Insurance Co. Des Moines, Iowa	$44,116,561
11.	Lincoln National Life Insurance Co. Fort Wayne, Ind.	$37,381,320
12.	Manulife Financial* Toronto, Ont.	$37,130,678

13. Hartford Life Insurance Co. $36,835,524
    Simsbury, Conn.

14. Massachusetts Mutual Life Insurance Co. $35,174,150
    Springfield, Mass.

15. The Travelers Insurance Co. $31,519,454
    Hartford, Conn.

16. Sun Life Assurance Co. of Canada $30,156,775
    Toronto, Ont.

17. IDS Life Insurance Co. $29,916,858
    Minneapolis, Minn.

18. Nationwide Life Insurance Co. $27,516,582
    Columbus, Ohio

19. Allstate Life Insurance Co. $22,951,693
    Northbrook, Ill.

20. Variable Annuity Life Insurance Co. $22,091,569
    Houston, Tex.

21. The Great-West Life Assurance Co. $20,377,825
    Winnipeg, Man.

22. Aetna Life Insurance and Annuity Co. $19,482,289
    Hartford, Conn.

23. Jackson National Life Insurance Co. $19,307,506
    Lansing, Mich.

24. State Farm Life Insurance Co. $18,704,705
    Bloomington, Ill.

25. The Mutual Life Group† $16,580,250
    Waterloo, Ont.

---

* Manulife Financial ranking includes North American Life Assurance Co. acquired in 1995.
† Mutual Group ranking includes individual Canadian business of Prudential Assurance Group of England, acquired in 1995.

Recommendations

OSFI should:

1. Act more like a cop and less like a coach.

2. Conduct more on-site inspections; have coordination with American regulators.

3. Make information public (e.g., MCCSR and audits) so policyholders can decide about financial health and solvency.

4. Establish a meaningful rating of financial strength and claims-paying ability based on international standards; make it public.

5. Have the power to replace incompetent management and directors.

Companies should:

6. Provide continuous reporting, so problems can be spotted as they develop, not two years later.

7. Make full provision for losses in the six-month periods when they occur.

8. Follow investment and portfolio guidelines to prevent over-concentration of assets, e.g. no more than 30 per cent of any portfolio should be invested in stocks, real estate, bonds, or any other single category.

9. Have sufficient readily liquifiable assets on hand to cover liabilities.

10. Invest no more than 1 per cent of assets with any one corporate entity including total assets in all affiliates, subsidiaries, or other entities.

Boards should:

11. Divide role of chairman and CEO between external and internal individuals.

12. Be constituted with a majority of independent, outside directors who chair all board committees. Annual retainers and per-meeting stipends should be in

accordance with time spent and responsibilities taken. Company employees and officers should comprise no more than 20 per cent of a board.

13. Ensure that directors are on no more than six different boards; any more means that they cannot spend sufficient preparation time in advance of board or committee meetings. Give directors job descriptions and put them through orientation courses about the company, the industry, and their responsibilities.

14. Make corporate funds available so that outside directors can hire their own staff, consultants, auditors.

15. Regularly measure their own effectiveness, including such aspects of their role as preparation for meetings, conduct of the meetings themselves, role and make-up of the board, and the contribution of individual members. No one operating below standard should be permitted to continue.

16. Approve any and all loans, share options or other deals affecting compensation of officers, including subsidiary companies.

Auditors should:

17. Publicly report fraud and other practices detrimental to shareholders, employees, customers.

18. Improve standards and practices, with particular focus on inter-company activities.

19. Warrant the balance sheet, not just procedures, and attest to the adequacy of internal and financial controls.

General:

20. Eliminate deposit insurance through CDIC and policyholder support through CompCorp coverage over a five-year period.

ENDNOTES

Author's Note About Sources

Retrospective journalism has its advantages. With the passage of time can come perspective and clarity. Meaning and shape, impossible during daily reporting, becomes visible. There's also a disadvantage to such middle-distance journalism, particularly with an event of such catastrophic proportions as the 1994 collapse of Confederation Life Insurance Co. Everyone involved claims to have acted in the best interests of the company; each blames someone or something else for the debacle. Perhaps it was the economy, or the system, or events beyond anyone's control.

In such circumstances, participants try to put themselves and their roles in the best possible light. That can amount to full-blown revisionist history, or it can simply be the result of human nature where recollections cannot always be reconciled with the facts. Whatever the explanation, I was continually confronted with people who honestly believed that their memory was accurate when what they were saying was patently not true.

With every interview, I always asked myself, "Why am I being told this?" That rigor meant not only trying to understand motives but also placing new information into the context of what else I already knew. Because there were so many reasons for people to mislead, key elements of the story required corroboration and documentation.

Such proof was not easy to come by. Court proceedings are at the early stages, so filings are minimal. Still, there already exists the equivalent of twenty boxes and thirty binders that are available for public examination. Moreover, the Confederation Group was regulated by officials in Ottawa, Toronto, and Lansing, Michigan. Access under Freedom of Information legislation proved to be limited in all three jurisdictions. In Michigan, files were simply declared to be part of the office of the governor and therefore not available. A request to Ottawa produced hundreds of pages, most of them blank. Officials cited various sections of the Act that prevented open disclosure. Ontario dithered for months, claiming there were no records, then finally admitted having fourteen running feet of files. Access, however, was another matter. Appeals to these decisions remain mired in the bureaucratic system.

The research process was further complicated by the fact that more than two dozen directors and officers of Confederation Life have been named in lawsuits with a potential claim of nearly US$2 billion. In addition, a number of class-action suits have been filed. Those proceedings could take years in the courts, so all the defendants are living under lawyer's instructions not to talk to the media about these matters in case what they say ends up being used against them. This book drew particular attention, and counsel repeatedly told defendants not to speak to me.

Fortunately, not everyone heeded the warning. I talked to many of the named directors and officers, some on the record, and some on a not-for-attribution basis. Other Confed executives and employees who are not named in the lawsuits are also worried about becoming entangled; they formed a second frightened cadre. Again, there were many who offered help both off and on the record. As a result, there are a few quotations and some information in the book without cited sources. In every case, however, those pieces of the puzzle came only from people with direct, firsthand knowledge of events.

Footnotes below give specific references if a quote or other information has appeared elsewhere; all other comments in quotations come from my interviews, 125 of them over a two-year period.

Chapter 1

p. 3 "financial-services flops" *Fortune*, July 8, 1996, p. 131.

p. 6 "Selecting the name" Early history is drawn from *Confederation Life Insurance Company, 1871-1971*, published by the company.

p. 12 "In 1942, a staff house" When Confed moved to Bloor Street in 1955, the staff house became the Engineers' Club. Condominiums now occupy the site.

Chapter 2

p. 18 "A major lesson" *Perspectives*, Number one, 1993. *Perspectives* was the name used, beginning in 1990, for the regular employee publication, which had been called *Courier* since 1967. Before that, the house organ was entitled *Clan*.

p. 18 "It was in this role" Ibid.

p. 19 "I think it gives" *Financial Post*, August 1, 1970, article by David Bentley. A handwritten note on the copy of the story filed in the *FP* library reads, "doesn't ride it now – May '73."

p. 20 "The principles which" *Financial Post*, February 19, 1972.

p. 20 "We touch on the lives" *Impact*, the hundredth-anniversary publication of the CLHIA, Jonathyn Forbes and Bruce Allen Powe, 1994.

p. 25 "no Conrad Black" Black was appointed to the Confed board in 1977 when he was chairman of Sterling Newspapers Ltd., a year before he bought Argus Corp. and began his acquisitive career at age thirty-three.

p. 27 "We've got them" *Toronto Life*, November 1983, article by the author.

p. 31 "After all" Burns's views of himself and the planning come from an article he wrote in *Business Quarterly*, August 1989.

Chapter 3

p. 41 "We were wrestling" Swan-song address by William Bradford as the outgoing chairman of Life Office Managers Association (LOMA), September 19, 1995. Despite a seven-year-long effort to cut staff, pare costs, and find profitable new niches, North American Life didn't make it. In 1995, Manulife acquired the company and the North American name disappeared, along with most of the employees.

p. 41 "If you went out" *Impact*, the hundredth-anniversary publication of the CLHIA, Jonathyn Forbes and Bruce Allen Powe, 1994.

p. 43 "The additional freedom" *Financial Post*, May 18, 1987, article by Bernard Simon.

p. 48 "over-leveraging" *Financial Post*, September 28, 1990, interview with Diane Francis.

Chapter 4

p. 61   "An auditor with" *Report of the Inquiry into the Collapse of the CCB and Northland Bank*, Willard Z. Estey, Canadian Government Publishing Centre, Ottawa, 1986, p. 28.

p. 61   "were two small banks" Ibid., p. 27.

p. 62   "Everyone fumbled" *Toronto Star*, January 29, 1987, article by Diane Francis.

p. 63   "Kennett left it" Estey, op. cit., p. 245.

p. 63   "There is nothing" Ibid., p. 247.

p. 63   "assistance was illusory" Ibid., p. 246.

p. 63   "I should have said" *Toronto Star*, January 29, 1987, article by Diane Francis.

p. 63   "It may sound corny" *Maclean's*, March 16, 1987, article by Madelaine Drohan.

p. 64   "While one can glean" *Financial Post*, February 2, 1987, article by Sonita Horvitch.

p. 67   "We did a risk-based" Senate hearings, September 29, 1994.

p. 69   "adopted the goal" *Perspectives*, Number three, 1990.

p. 69   "Moving towards the goal" Ibid.

p. 69   "We simply are not" Canadian Club speech, Toronto, January 22, 1990.

p. 72   "It was just to keep" Senate hearings, September 29, 1994.

p. 72   "I call the consumer-protection plan" Burns's speech to the CLHIA annual meeting, Ottawa, May 28, 1990.

p 77   "Central Guaranty will be" Story related by Kolber, Senate hearings, April 28, 1994.

Chapter 5

p. 83   "preferred access" Newcourt prospectus, February 11, 1994, p. 21.

p. 83   "to leave control over" Ibid.

p. 87   "As far back as 1988" Senate hearings, September 28, 1994.

p. 96   "They had a reverse" *Globe and Mail*, August 29, 1994, article by John Saunders.

p. 97   "Canadians have never understood" Margaret Cannon, "Surreal Estate," *ROB Magazine*, (June 1993), p. 62.

p. 100 "Once, Ray Wolfe" Wolfe, appointed to the Confed board in 1969, died in January 1990.

Chapter 6

p. 103 "derivatives with a notional value" Derivatives are as much misunderstood as they are feared. They are financial contracts, where values come from some form of underlying asset – stocks, bonds, currencies, or commodities. A typical derivative is a swap, a deal, or agreement between two people who each agree to interest payments owed by the other. A currency swap means that two parties agree now to exchange set amounts of currency at a specific future date. Using such tools, companies can take the guesswork out of fluctuations in currency markets. You do a deal now that won't be concluded for months but you are setting values today. CTSL would put two parties together, one of whom had $100 million in Canadian payable in six months, the other with a US$100-million liability due at the same time. The two companies would "swap" the amounts, and the difference in value, say $2.5 million, would be the amount on CTSL's books. The notional value was the face amount owing, so, foolish as CTSL and Confed were, the $10.1 billion in notional value wasn't all for Confed's account. Operated properly, a derivatives program is balanced, and the money is made in fees for putting parties together and managing the deal.

p. 104 "Michigan on its state" Foreign companies are required to choose one jurisdiction as the state of entry for regulatory purposes. For three decades, Michigan has been favoured by Canadian companies. Michigan was geographically convenient, there were trade links and tradition involved, and it also demanded a lower threshold of compliance than New York State, which has the toughest criteria. Most major Canadian companies use Michigan, including: Canada Life, Crown Life, Great-West Life, London Life, Manufacturers Life, Mutual Life, and Sun Life.

p. 115 "We observe a general unwillingness" Empire Club speech, Toronto, January 21, 1993.

p. 117 "down and down" Indeed, Crown's troubles continued. In 1995, the province pitched in with another $150-million loan guarantee, even though it had yet to receive either principal or interest payments on the first loan.

Chapter 7

p. 118 "Boards may not want" Senate hearings, September 29, 1994.

p. 120 "The eighties were a" Speech to a conference, "The Battle for the Canadian Insurance Industry," Toronto, May 10, 1995.

p. 122 "We feel quite strongly" *Financial Post*, January 8, 1992, article by Chethan Lakshman.

p. 123 "The unexpected work" Letter from Sheryl Teed to Borden Rosiak, May 13, 1992.

p. 124 "by retaining outside" Board minutes.

p. 124 "two regulators, various Coopers" Ibid.

p. 124 "David McCamus" McCamus, appointed to the board in 1986, resigned effective February 21, 1992, because he was also on the board of Trilon and worried that being a director of two financial-services companies would put him in a conflict-of-interest position.

p. 128 "I did approve" *Toronto Star*, November 13, 1994, article by James Daw and Jonathan Ferguson.

p. 137 "Until a recovery comes" *Maclean's*, August 22, 1992, article by John Daly.

Chapter 8

p. 140 "Financial strength" Lombardi and Nowacki quotes from a panel discussion at the Society of Actuaries spring meeting, Vancouver, June 28, 1995.

p. 141 "I would not say difficulty" *Financial Post*, September 8, 1992, article by Chethan Lakshman.

p. 142 "either CEO or out" *Canadian Business*, July 1992, p. 38.

p. 144 "I realized" *Canadian Business*, November 1988, p. 179.

p. 147 "I'd been thinking" *Financial Post*, September 2, 1993, article by Robert English.

Chapter 9

p. 152 "OSFI's concerns seem" Board minutes.

p. 153 "People only refer" *Perspectives*, Number three, November 1992.

p. 155 "The sumptuous buffet" *Canadian Insurance*, September 1994, article by Geoffrey Jarvis.

p. 155 "Troubled and non-performing" 1993 audit engagement overview from Ernst & Young.

p. 157 "Grand Canyon" Confed was coming under pressure elsewhere. In a July 1993 cover story by *Consumer Reports* on term insurance, Confed was cited as among those companies that refused to cooperate with a Consumers Union (CU) survey. CU went ahead and obtained information anyway, and, among two hundred firms surveyed, Confed ranked with the five worst on term policies that were annually renewable to age one hundred. Of course, CU was not measuring financial strength, just premium prices.

p. 159 "Survival is the issue" *Perspectives*, Number three, 1992.

p. 172 "We were looking" DeGrow and Hills quotes from *Detroit Free Press*, March 1, 1994.

p. 173 "Michigan raised the notes" White affidavit, dated September 6, 1995, and filed with the circuit court of Ingham County, Michigan.

p. 173 "didn't know about the notes" Cantor affidavit, dated September 6, 1995, and filed with the circuit court of Ingham County, Michigan.

p. 174 "International institutions" Senate hearings, October 5, 1994.

p. 177 "more than twice as high" *National Underwriter*, February 27, 1995, p. 1.

Chapter 10

p. 180 "foreboding and loneliness" National Club speech, Toronto, May 17, 1994.

p. 182 "Some grew and strengthened" Ibid.

p. 187 "Most of us went" Senate hearings, October 6, 1994.

p. 190 "Almost by definition" Paper prepared by Palmieri for the Stanford Law School Business Leaders' Conference, "Tools for Executive Survival," June 1993.

p. 199 "two meetings in the spring" Alexander affidavit, dated September 5, 1995, and filed with the circuit court of Ingham County, Michigan.

p. 201 "That's why you can" National Club speech, Toronto, May 17, 1994.

p. 202 "In analysing a company's" Dackow's speech to the Actuaries Club of Toronto, September 14, 1995.

Chapter 11

p. 215 "It's in the best economic" *National Underwriter*, August 15, 1994, article by Colleen Mulcahy.

p. 215 "What they did was" Senate hearings, September 27, 1994.

p. 215 "When dealing in the retail" Cantor's comments to journalists, August 8, 1994.

Chapter 12

p. 227 "We had assurances" Puccia and Wideman quotes from *Investment Dealer's Digest*, August 22, 1994, article by Jack Willoughby.

p. 230 "In the United States, policyholders" The benefits are usually US$300,000 for death benefits, US$100,000 for cash-surrender value of life insurance, US$100,000 for health-insurance claims, and US$100,000 for an annuity. The overall cap for an individual is US$300,000. State guaranty associations collect the money from the industry and pay policyholders.

p. 231 "We were willing" Senate hearings, September 27, 1994.

p. 234 "Twenty-seven former directors and officers" Officers and directors named (directors titles included; where city is not listed, Toronto): George Albino, former chairman and CEO, Rio Algom Ltd., Paget, Bermuda; William Alexander; John Allan, former chairman and CEO, Stelco Inc.; William Benton; Conrad Black, chairman and CEO of Hollinger Inc.; Bennett Brown, former chairman, NationsBank Corp., Atlanta; Pat Burns; Paul Cantor; William Douglas; Mark Edwards; Kenneth Field, president, Invescorp Ltd.; Nan-B. de Gaspé Beaubien, vice-chair, Telemedia Corp., Montreal; Irving Gerstein, president, Glenoak Capital; Anthony Griffiths, consultant, Fairfax Financial Holdings Ltd.; Sir Anthony S. Jolliffe, chairman, Management for

Industry Ltd., London, England; Thomas Ladner, partner, Ladner Downs, Vancouver; George Mara, vice-chairman, Jannock Ltd.; Robert Martin, former president and CEO, Consumers Gas Co. Ltd.; David McCamus, former chairman, Xerox Canada Inc.; Daryl McLean, partner, McCarthy Tétrault; André Monast, senior partner, Desjardins Ducharme Stein & Monast, Quebec City; Michael Regester; Jack Rhind; Michael Rosenfelder; Borden Rosiak; Michael White; and Adam Zimmerman, chairman of the board. Most of the following year was spent in court pleadings on the issue whether Michigan had jurisdiction in the matter. Claims against Black and Ladner were voluntarily dismissed by the plaintiff.

p. 236 "Although I was required" Burns affidavit, dated September 5, 1995, and filed with the circuit court of Ingham County, Michigan.

Chapter 13

p. 247 "There seems to be reservation" *Current Topics*, a CLHIA publication, Fall 1983, p. 7.

p. 247 "They are not quite in the same" *Globe and Mail*, December 8, 1995.

p. 249 "The system of distribution" Palmer's speech to the CLHIA annual meeting, June 1995.

p. 249 "The board only knows" *Toronto Star*, August 21, 1994.

p. 252 "cost to the CDIC" New rules in 1993 mean that the CDIC can now cut off deposit insurance for a particular firm that's not up to snuff and hold directors and officers responsible for losses.

p. 253 "Even for companies" LOMA speech, September 19, 1995

p. 253 "The Canadian life-insurance industry" Senate hearings, September 27, 1994.

p. 256 "By later 1984" *Report of the Inquiry into the Collapse of the CCB and Northland Bank*, Willard Z. Estey, Canadian Government Publishing Centre, Ottawa, 1986, p. 100.

p. 256 "There was apparently no" Ibid., p. 105.

p. 256 "The condition of the CCB" Ibid., p. 124.

p. 256 "One of the responsibilities" Ibid., p. 138.

p. 256 "Northland simply ran" Ibid., p. 261.

p. 257 "If I didn't have David" Gongwer News Service report no. 178, September 15, 1995.

p. 258 "As a regulator" The Ontario Insurance Commission has oversight of five life-insurance companies: AFLAC Life Insurance Co. of Canada, Canadian Trinity Life Insurance Co., Gerling Global Life Insurance Co., Security Life Insurance Co., and Union du Canada Assurance Vie.

p. 259 "A. M. Best does not subscribe" Senate hearings, September 27, 1994.

p. 260 "The pain in these huge" Speech to Association of American Life Underwriters, March 1995.

p. 261 "has some choices" *Insurance Executive Report,* Winter 1993/4 issue, p. 4.

p. 262 "independent board" Original board members were: Stanley Beck, former chairman of the Ontario Securities Commission; André Dionne, former general manager of La Mutuelle Vie des Function-naires du Québec; Graham Donald, one-time deputy chairman of accounting firm Thorne Ernst & Whinney; Gaëtan Drolet, who taught law at Laval University; Alastair Fernie, former president of the Canadian operations of Standard Life Assurance Co.; Ronald McKinlay, retired chairman of the Canada Deposit Insurance Corp.; Emile Reinhardt, former vice-president of Industrial-Alliance Life Insurance Co.; Fred Richardson, former CEO of Crown Life Insurance Co.; and Alan Morson, president of CompCorp.

p. 264 "Richter billed" The real workhorse on the project was Robert Kofman, whose hourly rate was $200. In April, he billed for 168.5 hours of work, in May, 292 hours, for a total amount payable of $92,100. June's docket is missing, but, in July, Kofman was still maintaining a similar pace – 156 hours that month, for $31,200. In August, the final push saw him do 202 hours for $40,400. Assuming an unharried – for him – June of 150 hours ($30,000), Kofman's total billings for the five months were $193,700 for 968.5 hours. If he took Sundays off, that's almost 7.5 hours a day, every day, six days a week. A few final items in September and October required 69 hours, putting total billings by Kofman over seven months in excess of $200,000.

p. 266 "The whole group suffered" *Financial Times,* October 17, 1995.

p. 267 "Auditors have been" Empire Club speech, Toronto, January 21, 1993.

Epilogue

p. 273   "If Orest Dackow was" *Globe and Mail,* August 16, 1994, article by John Partridge.

p. 273   "I no longer wonder" Speech to the Actuaries Club of Toronto, September 14, 1995.

GLOSSARY

ACLI: American Council of Life Insurers, the United States trade association.

ACLIC: Association of Confederation Life Insurance Contractholders, a not-for-profit organization whose membership includes trustee owners, plan sponsors, investment advisers, and others who purchased or have an interest in approximately US$2 billion of group annuity contracts issued by Confed.

ACLIP: Association of Confederation Life Insurance Policyholders.

actuary: someone who is a fellow of the Canadian Institute of Actuaries and is professionally trained and qualified in the mathematics and technicalities of insurance; calculates premiums, reserves, and other mysterious items.

annuity: a contract providing payments at regular intervals for a designated length of time, at, for example, retirement; usually purchased using a lump-sum cash payment.

cash surrender value: the amount payable from a life-insurance policy if a policyholder decides to stop paying premiums and cancel the policy voluntarily; the funds are usually a small fraction of the total premiums actually paid.

CDIC: Canada Deposit Insurance Corporation, a Crown corporation providing government-backed protection for depositors of up to $60,000 in 131 banks and trust companies.

CLHIA: Canadian Life and Health Insurance Association, a trade association representing about ninety insurance companies and accounting for more than 90 per cent of the life and health insurance in force in Canada.

CompCorp: Canadian Life and Health Insurance Compensation Corporation, a non-profit consumer-protection plan operated and funded by the insurance industry offering some coverage to Canadian policyholders in case of insurance-company failure; coverage is per policyholder, per company, and includes group as well as individual; the amounts are $60,000 for RRSPs and RRIFs combined, $60,000 for non-registered accumulation products (GIC-type products) and the cash values in life-insurance products, $60,000 for cash withdrawals from policies and payments related to health benefits, $200,000 per person for life-insurance claims (death benefits), and $2,000 per month per person for life annuities and disability income policies.

CTSL: Confederation Treasury Services Ltd.

commercial mortgage: a mortgage secured by an income-producing property like an office building, factory, or other industrial property; can also be a development loan on a multiple-unit residential property until the sale is completed.

derivatives: financial contracts with values "derived" from the value of an underlying asset or index; types of instruments include options, futures, swaps, and forward contracts.

four pillars: a term formerly used to describe the four different financial-services sectors: banking, insurance, securities, and trust services; the four pillars now have become one pillar and three posts.

GIC: guaranteed investment certificate, an interest-bearing investment issued by a financial institution for fixed terms, usually up to five years, guaranteed as long as the issuing company stays healthy; interest rates are usually higher than deposit accounts.

group life and health insurance: policies, usually paid for by a combination of company and employee money, providing life, medical, dental, and other coverage for employees; usually up for renewal annually; no cash value.

LIMRA: Life Insurance Marketing and Research Association.

MCCSR: minimum continuing capital and surplus requirements, a ratio monitored by OSFI that shows an individual company's financial health.

mutual insurance company: an insurance company with no shareholders; management is supposed to be directed by a board elected by those individuals who hold participating policies.

NAIC: National Association of Insurance Commissioners, an American organization that sets regulatory standards followed by state watchdogs.

NOLHGA: National Organization of Life and Health Insurance Guaranty Associations, an American organization through which state guaranty funds pay policyholders for shortfalls when a company's liabilities are greater than assets.

OSFI: the Office of the Superintendent of Financial Institutions, regulates federally incorporated banks, insurance companies, and trust companies.

participating insurance: dividends are paid to policyholders that reflect financial results; wise, conservative companies base premiums paid by individuals on lower earnings and higher expenses than they really expect will occur in the future.

policy: the document issued by an insurance company to an individual, setting out the terms and conditions of the contract.

premium: payment by the policyholder, usually monthly, to keep a life-insurance policy in force.

reinsurance: insurance for the insurance companies; one or more insurance firms share the transferred risk of the primary insurer.

reserves (a.k.a. actuarial liabilities or policy reserves): funds held by a life-insurance company for the fulfilment of its various obligations due to policies; estimates by actuaries of amounts that, combined with future premium payments and investment income, will be enough to cover all benefits, dividends, and expenses; shown on the liability side of the insurance-company balance sheet.

retrocession: insurance for the reinsurer; a portion of a reinsurer's risk is shared with someone else.

segregated fund: assets which are kept separate from a life-insurance company's general funds and run like a mutual fund; used mainly for the investment of pension-plan contributions or products linking insurance and savings.

stock-insurance company: an insurance company that has share capital; management is supposed to be directed by a board that's elected both by the shareholders and the participating policy holders; shareholders share in profits.

surplus: the excess of assets over liabilities and other obligations.

underwriting: the process of assessing the risk when an individual applies for coverage.

structured settlement: an annuity yielding regular payments for a set period, purchased to cover a liability resulting from the settlement of a judgement or court order.

Treasury bills (T-bills): short-term government obligations, paying interest to the bearer.

unit-linked policies: insurance contract where the savings portion of the premium earns income based on the performance of investments; commonplace in the United Kingdom.

universal life insurance: premiums, dividends, and cash value can swing wildly based on interest and investment income.

INDEX